Indian Education

Indian Education:

Quo Vadis?

Prof. P. M. Kamath

GenNext Publication

VPM's Centre for International Studies (Regd.)

KNOWLEDGE IS POWER

First Published, 2018

Published by

GenNext Publication
5, Ansari Road
Daryaganj, New Delhi-110002
Phone: 9811692060
E-mail: gennextpublication@hotmail.com

Printed at: G. Print Process, Delhi.

Cataloging in Publication Data—DK
Courtesy: D.K. Agencies (P) Ltd. <docinfo@dkagencies.com>

Kamath, P. M., author.
Indian education quo vadis / Prof. P.M. Kamath.
pages cm
ISBN 9789380223209 (HB)

1. Education—India. 2. Education and state--India. I. Title.

LCC LA1151.K36 2017 | DDC 370.954 23

Contents

Preface 9
Introduction 13

1. Democracy and the Standard of Education 41
2. Why Do Our Universities Lack Research Output? 47
3. Teachers or Qualified Clerks? 53
4. Unaided Schools Get Raw Deal 59
5. Saving Education from Bureaucracy 61
6. Decentralise Education 65
7. Are Aryans Original Inhabitants of India? 69
8. Another Indian History 73
9. Corrupt Campuses 77
10. Funding Progress 81
11. Towards Breaking the Language Barrier 85
12. Language Muddle 89
13. In Defence of 91
14. No Defence 95
15. Harsh Realities 99
16. Free For All 101
17. Down with Groupism 105
18. Black or White? 109

19. Global Varsities must be Started 113
20. Lost Cause 117
21. Forgotten Ideal 121
22. Spitter Spatter 125
23. Paying Proposition 129
24. Primary Need 133
25. Easy-to-Get-Ph. Ds 137
26. An Active Interaction 141
27. Delink PhDs from Jobs 143
28. The KG Rushhh 147
29. Why the Neighbourhood Policy won't Work? 151
30. New Pre-Primary Admission Policy is Unworkable 153
31. Examiners should be Men of Highest Integrity 157
32. For Better Education 161
33. Class Action 165
34. Whose Failure is it? 169
35. Graceless Gesture 173
36. Government's prescription of PTA's approval for a fee hike irrational 177
37. Internalise Post Graduate Examination System 181
38. Fooling the Public 187
39. Teachers as Contract Labourers 191
40. Footpath Lawyers 195
41. Modern Day Tughluqs 199
42. Unaided English Schools Face Closure 203
43. What Crime have they Committed? 207
44. School V/s Classes 211

45. Breathing Fresh Air into the System of School Education 215
46. Is Collection of Donations Justified? 219
47. Curbing School Donations under Rules 223
48. Priya Tendulkar as a Prosecutor and Judge! 227
49. Mess of Fees: Govt. must not Meddle with Unaided Schools 231
50. New Fee Structure Discriminatory in Nature 235
51. Opening up of Indian Education to Foreign Universities 239
52. Primary Certificate Examination Scheme can only bring ruin 243
53. How to Achieve the Purpose without Board Examination? .. 247
54. American Studies Losing Importance in Mumbai University 251
55. Case for Rotation of Department Headship in Mumbai University 255
56. Inter University Centre for Astronomy and Astrophysics 259
57. Let Every School Decide which History Textbook to Follow 263
58. Is Money Meant for Education Rightly Spent? 267
59. Mumbai University Restoring the Lost Glory 271
60. The World is Our Lecture Room 279
61. Keep the Channels Open 283
62. Schools: The Way Forward 287
63. Need to Strengthen Research in Universities 291
64. Government should not Harass Private School Managements 297
65. Bidding for an M.Phil 301
66. The Plight of Schools Told to Close Down 305

67. Admission Chaos: Govt must allow more School, College Divisions ... 309

68. Let's Say Bus to This Nasty Problem ... 313

69. Avoid tragedies: Provide School bussing for Kids ... 315

70. BMC Needs to Learn a Thing or Two ... 319

71. Some Pitfalls in Implementation of Right to Education ... 323

72. Eradicate Fundamental Causes Behind Rising Fees ... 327

73. Populism in Education Augurs ill for Quality ... 331

74. Can We Chop off a Hand for Making a Mistake? ... 335

75. Regional Media Schools in Mumbai as well as in the Nation do not have Good Time ... 339

76. Service in Education is my Payback to Society ... 343

77. Globalisation and International Schools ... 347

78. A Report Card of the Modi Government ... 351

79. Is there a Fundamental Right to Pass? ... 357

Index ... 361

Preface

Indian Education: Quo Vadis consists of 79 articles written over the period years between 1962 and 2016. During this period, I have taught for two years (1962-1964) in a High School during day as well as in a night school; for eight years (1964-1972) in the undergraduate Colleges, and for 25 years at the Bombay University Post-Graduate (P G) Department of Civics & Politics (1972-1997). But during the entire period, I was actively associated with an educational trust and continued to administer, develop and expand the activities of this educational trust: Vidya Prasarak Mandal (Regd), to develop an in-depth understanding of prevailing education system and incessant changes through which it was passing from the KG (Pre-primary) to the P G level in this country. It is very rare for anyone to be so lucky as to get an opportunity to acquire such widest experience in the field of education. I owe my sense of gratitude to the trust as it permitted me to work with it and relentlessly pursue my goals in purely an honorary capacity!

Hence, *Indian Education: Quo Vadis,* title is carefully chosen to reflect author's own feelings of uncertainty as to what is the direction education is taking at the time of writing that is being provided to Indians. A careful reading of articles indicate that since Mrs Gandhi placed education in concurrent list that was originally in state jurisdiction, Education Ministers at the federal and state levels, irrespective of their party complexion, have tried to change teaching techniques, content of lessons taught, assessment system, grading philosophy and promotion of education according to their whims and fancies. Often these modifications and changes have finally landed on the table of the Chief Justice of the Supreme Court of India. It is very easy for intellectually gifted persons managing educational trusts, working in ever growing number of do-good-lobbies and parents and management associations and bureaucrats manning it to twist and bend every educational issue into a legal and constitutional issue today in India as it happens in the United States.

These articles show a remarkable insight into many issues concerned with various aspects of the field of education: issues relating to child psychology, content of class room teaching, examination patterns, prevailing corruption, medium of instruction, teachers' welfare and administrative dilemmas. I used to say: Where you stand depends on where you sit. Being myself a teacher first and the foremost, I have supported every cause relating to teachers' welfare. But as an administrator, I have never hesitated to stand firm on general issues deeply affecting child's education.

I wish to thank all members of the wonderful educational institutions managed by the trust, where many of us worked together at difficult times. More particularly, my grateful thanks are due to all teachers and heads in the field of education. I had favoured kindergarten facility to be treated essentially as a crèche without an over-emphasis on formal education, with raising of admission age to formal education in Primary classes only after completion of seven years; right to education to be made fundamental right in 1994, 15 years before it was added in the constitution as such; favoured compulsory, introduction of defence studies in Schools and regularisation of Ph. D enrolment and scores of other suggestions like introduction of bussing facility to take students to their chosen Schools, growing international interactions in the field of education, and several others. It makes me proud when I look back on my own writings of providing me a wide space of knowledge in the field of education from KG to PG. I had acquired an uncommon expertise over the entire spectrum of education. My thanks must go to a large number of teachers I enjoyed to encounter from base of the pyramid to its top. In social work I had an opportunity to interact with many ministers who come and go almost from Madhukarao Chowdhary in the 1960's to Vinod Tawde since 2014 in pursuit of my passion for education.

My wife Sushama who helped me to type in the days of typewriter and later on computers many of my articles. Nikhil Laxman and Sai Suresh for inviting me to contribute to Mid-day and Ayaz Memon who succeeded them as the editor of Mid-day who continued to invite me to write. Having read or seen my articles in the Mid-Day, many other newspaper editors in the field of Journalism, often invited me to contribute articles on a variety of issues.

In VPM my grateful thanks are due to Ms Anita Gujran, Mrs Savitri Rao who helped me in putting these articles together. My thanks are also due to Shri Amit Garg of Gyan Publications. However, if there are any lacunae in the book, I alone is to be held responsible.

Date: 21.09.2017 **P. M. Kamath**

Introduction

Late Prof. Vithalrao Anantrao Kulkarni, retired as Professor and Head of Kannada Department of K. J. Somaiya College of Arts, Science & Commerce. Before joining the College as Kannada teacher, he was a teacher of Physical Education (PE) in National Kannada Education Society's (NKES) High School, which is now located at Wadala but was in the 1950s located in Military Barracks at King's Circle Railway Station. I was a student of that school and he had taught me PE. After my passing out S.S.C (XI Std) in 1957, I became very active in reviving the Ex-students Association of NKES. I had involved Mr. V. A. Kulkarni in a Drama that we presented to raise funds for NKES. It is that involvement made him to invite me along with two other senior colleagues of mine in the Ex-students' Association like Sudama V. Shastri, who later retired as a Professor, Head of Department of English, Shivaji University, Kolhapur and Gurunath D. Joshi, who later retired as a Professor of Kannada and Principal, Junjunwala College, Ghatkopar to a place called, Mulund to join Vidya Prasarak Mandal (VPM), an educational trust and render honorary work to develop "a Kannada High School" along with our common teacher, Late Shri Damodar R. Gudi in March 1962.

In VPM, Managing Committee, I was included as a Committee Member and Shri Gudi was inducted as the Hon. Secretary. It is in the VPM that I received my early exposure to the mind-boggling problems of education in India, despite the fact that academically, I was then pursuing my M.A. in Politics. Though Kannada High School started working in June 1962, since fund raising was my forte, I suggested a formal inauguration of the School. In August 1962 Pejawar Mutt Swami H. H. Shri Vishweshwar Theertha Swami, inaugurated the school in Seth Moti Pachan Rashtriya (SMPR) School - a Gujarati High School at a small inaugural function. A souvenir was released.

This Souvenir carried in it my article: "*Democracy and the standard of education*". It was probably the first article in English written by me then! It argues that the concept of 'standard', in education is relative – mainly to time and kind of society in which it is used. Though education was vigorously pursued in ancient India, it was limited to a few because of general respect for *Varnashrama System*. However, political democracy demands a democratisation of society and equality, liberty and justice are important pillars of it. Naturally mass education, gives an impression of falling standard, but if it has fallen, it has not fallen from great height! As democracy, is the best form of government, mass education alone could create intelligent voters to sustain it. Among others it recommends giving Primary School better qualified teachers to make foundation of education solid.

"Why do our Universities lack Research Output?"*(Free Press Journal (FPJ) 9 September 1985)* discusses at length with illustrations, three problems that contribute to absence of research outputs: 1) Absence of congenial atmosphere to encourage research, 2) Lack of physical facilities and 3) Lack of financial resources. Lord Macaulay had advised the English Education to create an army of loyal bureaucrats, who will reject everything Indian to promote and stabilise British rule in India.

"Teachers or qualified clerks" *(Indian Express, 21 Dec.1988)* saw entry of trade unionism among the teachers in the institutions of higher education because of adamancy of government. In the face of teachers' strike, Vasantdada Patil, the then Chief Minister (CM) of Maharashtra (1983 to1985) had said that let the strike continue or the educational institutions be closed, it won't matter, as he had studied only upto IV std; yet became the CM of Maharashtra! Educating children became a "load" for the government expenditure on higher education and a "burden" for the teachers! The article raises the questions: How can the teachers be expected to teach for 20 hrs in a week and also ask them to conduct individual research and maintain quality of education?

Turning to school education in "Unaided schools get raw deal" *(FPJ, 9 August 1990)* argues that as providing education to children in the State is the primary responsibility of the State, and Federal

Governments, the concept of "Unaided School" is fundamentally discriminatory. If the government is ideologically against the idea of education through English Medium, how can in the same area, one English Medium School get's aid and another just because it is started in or after 1984, makes parents to pay 8 to 10 times more fees than a student in aided Schools? Today this question has become more acute as government has made education in aided schools free, while unaided schools have to totally depend on parents to continue to provide quality education!

Next article "Saving education from bureaucracy" *(The Observer of Business and Politics, 12 May 1992*) in the background of liberalisation of Indian Economy by the P. V. Narasimha Rao government says: If liberal economy can flourish without much of state control, more control means ruining the economy; similar approach be followed in the field of education. On the other hand, since politicians/bureaucrats have lost a few powers over economy, have aimed to increase their strangle-hold over the field of education. Direct payment of salaries to teachers, government publishing text books, control over staff appointments and control over fee structure in un-aided schools are some areas, which are discussed in detail. Misfortune of the nation is: from Jawaharlal Nehru to Rajiv Gandhi, V. P. Singh and all PMs' since then have made tall promises to increase budgetary allocation for education from less than three percent to six percent of GDP; but have done really nothing though they say it is a "National Investment!"

Unfortunately, education in India is one important area which today suffers from initiative-curbing and quality paralysing burden of the government control. The unqualified Babus control educational administration and always think that a small quantum of aid extended to private educational trusts as loaves of bread thrown at a beggar! While ordinary citizens extending financial support for education never seek a slice of bread loaves, big fat –Babus bully to get back a sizeable chunk of the bread!

Then a wonderful thing happened in my life: I was invited by the *Mid-Day* - a daily published in Mumbai, to write a weekly column on education. Since my teaching and guiding (MA by

Research, M Phil and Ph. D) responsibilities were then growing disproportionately, I agreed to contribute articles twice a month. My first article *(Mid-Day, 13 August 1992)* was on "Decentralise Education". It highlights rampant corruption in all aspects of educational administration. Apart from admission to reputed Schools, Junior Colleges and Colleges etc., government babus make individual staff members to bribe them to clear their appointments. In case the management refuses to satisfy their greed, individual teachers are made to satisfy their greed! This article suggested creation of Education Commission at different levels like District and State to exercise minimal controls necessary on the educational institutions under the 'eagle's eye' supervision on the working of school committees and PTAs.

"Are Aryans original Inhabitants of India? (*FPJ, 4 January 1993*) argues that the idea was planted that Aryans as invaders by the Western writers to justify their rule over India to show that Indians have always been ruled by aliens! Similarly with documentary evidence, it is pointed out that Aryans and Dravidians as belonging to different races too was again created by the British. Hence, even after 70 years of independence, it is necessary for Indians to remember what Swami Vivekananda had said: "Everything that comes from India take it as true until you find cogent reasons for disbelieving it".

Similarly "Another Indian History" (*The Weekend Observer, 17 July 1993)* continues to discuss the Western mischief in misinterpreting Ancient-Indian history, deliberately. These erroneous interpretations were also freely used by Indian historians in their writings. However, efforts made by the then UP Government were considered by critics as promotion of "Hindutva"!

"Corrupt Campuses*"(Mid–Day, 9 February 1994)* discusses growing trend of corrupt practices in University Campuses, like getting marks enhanced, fake passing certificates, ghost writers to complete Ph. D's etc. This kind of corruption is entering universities in Maharashtra from North Indian Universities. There are reports of cases of huge premium paid to get an academic job. But the article argues that "teachers' unions" all over the nation should raise their voices against such corruption while fighting for better emoluments. Despite existing corruption, teachers are held with greater credibility in the society than persons in many other professions.

"Funding Progress" *(Mid–Day, 23 February1994)* Political leaders make pious promises to increase the allocation for education since as per their slogans it is a 'National Investment' That trend is reflected in P. V. Narasimha Rao's announcement in Jan. 1994 that allocation for education will be raised from 3.8 percent of the Gross National Product (GNP) to 6 percent in Ninth Five Year Plan that was to begin in 1997 (He retired as PM in 1996). On the contrary, though there is an expansion of educational facilities in the country, government allocation has declined. That is clear from the fact that in reality schools were denied matching contribution to Development Fund initially made compulsory for the Educational Trusts. The government administrators unimaginatively try only to reduce expenditure by sacrificing quality.

"Towards Breaking the Language Barrier" (*Mid–Day, 9 March 1994*) makes a suggestion to the government: "Instead of imposing a uniform language education pattern, it must give parents and schools the leeway to go in for their own formula while promoting National and Regional languages. This will ensure that students do not lose their natural roots while learning languages in schools.

The suggestion was carried further in "Language muddle" (*Mid-Day, 30 March 1994*). The sensible policy is to permit the schools of Linguistic Minorities like Gujarati, Sindhi, Hindi, Kannada Malayalam and Tamil to have a place to teach their mother tongue to children belonging to these groups in English Medium Schools without limiting the facility. It points out that currently the Urdu medium schools have this facility, since there is a combination of religion with language! Article recommends consultation with such schools in addition to political consultation with MLAs and MPs etc. before determining the education policy.

Going beyond the language policy, the next piece "In Defence of" (*Mid-Day, 4 May 1994)* recommends introduction of Defence Studies in the syllabus of IX and X Stds. Such a course will not only inculcate much needed discipline in the society, but will also instil a sense of commitment to Nation–in the sense of sacrifice of self interest to national interest.

Next article, "No Defence" (*Mid-Day, 25 May 1994*) makes a strong case for introducing Defence Studies at undergraduate and graduate students in Colleges and universities as well.

"Harsh realities" (*Mid-Day, 8 June 1994*) makes a strong point that after HSC (XII) standard, parents and students need not run to professional Colleges. While aiming to be a topper in the examinations every year, not all can be toppers. But in today's India there are several avenues open for a youngster to make a name and gain fame. We need to respect all fields of study available without making some of them as reserved for mediocre in the society. "In every course you can shine" that is the message.

Today India has an Act of 2009 that promises Right to Education (RTE) as a fundamental right to every child between the age group of 6 to 14 (Class 1 to VIII) free and compulsory education. But 15 years before the RTE as in "Free for all" *(Mid-Day, 29 June 1994*) I had made a strong case for the government to provide free and compulsory education to all as mandated by the constitution. The article argues that Right to Education to be made available "Irrespective of caste, creed, religion, sex or medium of instruction by setting up primary schools and aiding them as a national priority".

I had always stressed the aim of achieving national integration through education. If that is acceptable to states, they need to work to promote easy inter-state movement by students and teachers. With the examples of several obstacles faced by such inter-state movement of students and teachers, the article "Down with groupism" (*Mid-Day, 13 July 1994)* argues in favour of all India recruitment and national educational pension fund etc.

With Narasimha Rao, Government introducing LPG – Liberalisation, Privatisation and Globalisation in the economy of the country, "Black or White" (*Mid-Day, 27 July 1994)* makes a case to make educational institutions, congenial to market education abroad. In that context our universities need to be sensitive to the culture of foreign students in universities. There were cases of racial discrimination towards Black African students in Universities. Such incidents will not help to create foreign students as spokesmen for India when they go back to their respective countries. A suggestion is also made to appoint a Foreign Students' Adviser in every University.

Having made earlier a suggestion for every university to have a foreign student advisor, the next step is for establishing in every State an International University. Thus, Maharashtra state can have one in Mumbai and another in Navi Mumbai; so argues "Global Varsities must be started" *(Mid-Day 10 August 1994*). Obviously, such universities will help in developing and consolidating existing status of Mumbai as the Commercial Capital of India; will attract NRI & PIO families to send their children to study in India and increase interactions between Indian students, with foreign students which will open up new vistas for both.

Next article in this collection "Lost cause" *(Mid-Day, 31 August 1994)* argues to streamline medical facilities by then made available by the Maharashtra Government in 1985. Teachers' health is an important factor in providing effective education in all institutions. But if they are made to run to government hospitals for medical emergencies, they have to face delays and corruption in sanctioning expenses by the Director of Hospitals where treatment is taken. Instead, it advocated scrutiny and sanction could be assigned to Colleges or Universities where teachers work.

On the occasion of Teacher's Day of 5 September 1994 "Forgotten Ideal" (*Mid-Day, 14 September 1994)* calls for self-introspection on the part of teachers: Are we in the profession with a commitment as an educator and moulder of character of young citizens? Or are we simply looking at teaching as a profession to provide livelihood? It bemoans the governments ignoring the task of providing everything necessary to make the profession attractive to high achievers. Certain steps are necessary like raising of qualifications for Primary teachers at the entry level; make teachers to consistently update themselves with changes in different fields, provide teachers benefits of LTC, enable them to conduct research at every level of teaching and see that everyone gets avenues for promotion.

Our education has grossly failed to inculcate civic qualities. "Spitter Spatter" (*Mid-Day, 5 October 1994*) emphasised the role school education ought to play to eradicate the national disease of public spitting. With my long association with VPM, I had several opportunities to address students of all levels from Primary to Graduate and parents of students. On many occasions, I emphasised the need for children to inculcate the habit of keeping school environment clean and tidy. The article is based on personal experience in many foreign countries, I had hoped that by 2000 AD, we must have complete eradication of spitting in public. But though programme has drawn attention of authorities, educating nation on the subject and penalty for non-observance of the requirement in public, has to be carried further.

Teachers in the University are the final shapers of the manpower needed by the Nation and simultaneously are involved in seeking truth through research. The article "Paying proposition" (*Mid-Day, 19 October 1994*) makes a case for better UGC scales to these teachers as many university teachers were quitting to join newer companies formed after the LPG. The heart of the matter is, since IAS officers occupy key decision making positions in the federal government; they do not want anyone else to get better paid than themselves! University teachers hold higher qualifications than IAS officers. Some of the professions are intellectually far superior to IAS Cadre, as they chose teaching profession by design.

A similar approach is of paying well to Primary teachers in schools, as it is they who do everything to lay a strong foundation to make the nation literate. The "Primary Need" *(Mid-Day, 2 November 1994*) makes a strong plea on the subject. The relevant question is whether we plan on 'free and compulsory' primary education only for a statistical satisfaction of claiming cent percent national literacy or really prepare every child to be capable of not only reading and writing but even make a decent living even after only passing primary level of education. That goal can only be met when Primary teachers are a highly committed and well paid lot. The payment made to them should be a matter of great envy to majority of people. In the absence of such an approach, a child when goes from primary, to secondary and to higher education, much of the time of teachers is spent in correcting the harm caused by teachers at lower levels! In that case, when a child moves from Primary to Higher levels, it is only further education instead of higher education!

The University Grants Commission (UGC) has never been clear on the question: what is the role of a Ph. D Degree in making an academic or an academic administrator? In 1976, Ph.D. or an M. Phil was made compulsory for a lecturer (now called an Assistant Professor) in an institution of higher education. But later in 1986, possessing an M. Phil or a Ph D was deemed as an additional qualification deserving an extra increment! Later it came out in 1994, with the requirement of National Eligibility Test (N E T) for getting into the profession. Now, a Ph D is a must to be a Principal in Colleges. As a result, "Easy-to-get Ph.D.'s" *(Mid-Day, 16 November 1994)* draws the attention to scams in producing Ph.Ds. in Universities. There is are plagiarism, ghost writers and corruption in sale and purchase of the Ph. Ds. Ph.D. in reality does not make one a good administrator or a good academic. An M. Phil or a Ph.D. has to be merely treated as a licence to conduct research: Training one's mind in conduct of scientific research.

"An active interaction" (*Mid-day, 21 December 1994*), on the other hand urges, in continuation of my earlier articles on need to introduce Defence Studies as a subject in High Schools and Colleges, increased and continued interactions between military and academic institutions. Former Army Chief, General B. C. Joshi was a Votary of such interactions. He was instrumental in instituting the Chatrapati Shivaji Chair for Defence Studies in Poona University. During his inaugural address he had said: "If one hundred such chairs are instituted in other universities in the country, the army would support it." It is a good idea that many such chairs be instituted in all universities after Indian great warriors. Not many Colleges or Universities have taken such initiatives. The article also welcomes a studied initiative for self-reliance in the defence requirements.

"Delink Ph.Ds from Jobs" (*Mid-Day, 4 January 1995*) carries forward the suggestion made earlier (*Mid-Day, 16 November 1994*). It suggests certain clear cut steps to improve the quality of Ph. Ds produced in this country. Prescription of entrance tests, year long course work (done with the effect from July 2009), limit on guides in taking candidates, preferably five, detailed discussion of research topics and compulsory attendance by Ph.D. students at seminars, making presentations regularly and compulsory public defence of thisis by students.

From the subject of admission to Ph. D., I move to the issue of KG admissions in schools in “The KG Rushhh....” (*Mid-Day, 18 January 1995*). Everyone has spoken and written against the interviews of the child or the parents seeking admission. But every alternative has its own limitations. Hence, alternative preferred is to make children to play games and with the help of an expert in psychology, make a selection. Since, stress is on play-way method of teaching it should not be a matter for public agitation! However, long term solution is to enable more of socially minded public trusts to come forward and open schools rather than make providing education also a prerogative, a reserved arena of political leaders and business magnates. But in a liberal society, rule ought to be to limit - government interference regulation in pre-primary to the extent of its contribution. My firm advice, whenever, I have dealt with government officials, has been: “Government control ought to be commensurate with its contribution. No control if no contribution!”

“Why the neighbourhood policy won’t work” (*Bombay Times, 10 June 1997*), more specifically discusses impracticality of neighbourhood policy to make KG admissions. The author also recommends to devote a longer span of life of the child to be in play-way mode by considering Pre-Primary primarily as crèche; schooling should really begin at the age of seven.

The above argument is discussed in detail further in the next article, “New Pre-primary admission policy is unworkable” *(FPJ, 28 July 1997).* As no nation can choose its neighbours, no school can also ensure the nature of its neighbourhood; even if it had fairly a good neighbourhood to begin with, especially in major cities like Mumbai, slums may develop over the time. Today, some schools are surrounded by slums; it will be particularly a problem for Unaided English Medium Schools. Will the slum children be able to pay high fees required to be paid to maintain high quality of education?

Even after 70 years of Independence, fundamentals of examination have not changed; if they have, they have brought deterioration in the system. "Examiners should be men of highest integrity" (*FPJ, 14 August 1997*) brings out certain evil practices which have crept into our examination system. The University examination system has not done anything to minimise the subjective element on the part of examiners. It happens because of appointing examiners without having any reference to teaching experience of a paper setter or examining it in the collegiate level examinations possessed by examiners! Care is to be taken to see that examiners have minimum of five year experience of teaching the paper they are asked to examine. Paper setting has to be done by only teachers who have at least ten years of experience of teaching it; Revaluation of paper has to be done only by teachers who have reputation for creditability and at least 15 years of experience of teaching it. On the other hand, examination section is often under political/public pressure to announce results at the earliest; hence, the bureaucrats in charge of the work get it done by teachers who have no experience at all.

"For better education" (*Mid-Day, 17 March 1998*) brings out the facts, how government of Maharashtra has gradually, since the beginning of 1990's, discovered several ways to reduce its expenditure on education, like reduction in maintenance grant given to aided schools, deduction of grants through audit several years later, denial of matching development grant and creating a new category of permanently unaided educational institutions etc. Hence, the argument that is still valid is: As long as government is not able to aid adequately educational institutions, it should do away with Anti-capitation Act 1987. "Like the government needs money to provide 'services', politicians need money to win elections; school-trusts too need money to provide good education".

"Class Action" (*Mid-day, 13 August 1998*), expresses support to Colleges and Universities in the nation, as there were efforts to dilute and deny salary grades to academics recommended by the UGC appointed Rastogi Committee. It clearly brings out, how the IAS lobby in the Federal Government, which considers its members as the top notch officers in the nation and all the rest including even those who taught them as inferiors–just because officials at every level of education are paid more than teaching community they deal with. Similar is the approach of the state governments since it is IAS officers who Head Departments of Education.

Hence, obviously, their philosophy is no one can come anywhere near to them in pay grades. This in spite of the fact that at the entry point any one can aspire to join the Federal Services if he has an undergraduate degree. But increasingly, because of better pay given to them even at qualifying- entry point for the teachers at the highest level of the University, (earlier it was only a 'postgraduate' degree in the subject but) after every pay revision additional qualifications like NET/SET and M. Phil /Ph.D. were added, making it extremely difficult for anyone to get into it. The teachers' working hours were also increased similarly. The outcome: Top officials would have enough time to go for fishing, playing golf while teachers will struggle to complete semi-academic or administrative work compulsorily assigned to them. It is unfortunate that every time teachers have to fight to improve their living conditions.

Every year after secondary or higher secondary examinations, the Indian nation sees series of suicide cases by students declared as "fail", as though life ends with a fail remark on the marks certificate. "Whose failure is It" *(Mid-Day, 19 November 1998)* makes a case to adopt grading of students – A, B, C, D and take appropriate steps to enable students to re-appear to improve their grade - from D to C or B or even A. Appropriate counselling is also necessary to remove 'fail' remarks from all public examination system.

"Graceless Gesture" *(Mid-Day, 6 May 1999)* highlights deterioration in the working of the Mumbai University because of the government failure to appoint men of character and integrity to the office of Vice-Chancellor. It presents how politicians use the office of Chancellor or the Vice-Chancellor in promoting their own kith and kin through the gestures of grace marks. It is necessary for those who manage education in the field of action, to ponder over how to do away with the system of grace-marks.

"Internalise Post Graduate Examination System" (*OIOP, November 1999*) focuses on irrelevance of current examination system in the universities in testing knowledge assimilation achieved by above average students. It highlights callousness within the University system in appointing any one teaching a subject for five years in an undergraduate College to set a paper and also examine them in Postgraduate examinations. Those who have not taught a subject are also asked to set papers. The solution offered to improve the examination system is to internalise setting and assessing of papers to those who teach the subject in the PG classes.

Should the government insist on a role for Parent-Teacher Associations in increasing the fees? "Government's prescription of PTA's approval for a fee hike irrational" (*FPJ, 8 July 2000*), argues against it. The government in fact not only is trying to mislead the parents but also primarily trying to cover up its own unwillingness in providing primary and secondary education to its growing citizens of future.

"Fooling the Public" (*Mid-Day, 17 July 2000*) has taken the issue further. The Supreme Court had ruled that the approval of the PTA is not mandatory. The crux of the problem lies in the fact that political leaders are not able to see beyond the next election. The parents are a larger voter-block, next is the teachers and the management are insignificant and unimportant. Thus, government of the day has always forced management to lower the fees and increase the wages of staff! In the pursuit of this contradictory approach, the parent-management relationship has become one of permanent conflicts. In reality it ought to be similar to litigant-lawyer relationship. Can a litigant hiring the service of a lawyer claim to fix the fees? Litigant has option of selecting an advocate of his choice! But now parents are insisting on to determine fees their wards will pay and the school they choose to take!

Under the circumstances, will paying peanuts to teachers help reduction of the fees and making pain of parents bearable by charging lower fees? That way society has taken the issue to ridiculous level so argues, "Teachers as contract labourers" (*FPJ, 26 July 2000*). They were appointed for three years without vacation, any benefits or an honorarium! If work is less than of a part time teacher, schools are to appoint teachers on clock hour basis-which monthly may be less than what a Mumbaikar pays to a maid-servant! Any decision–maker with sensitivity, if he faces genuine financial crunch, would first offer similar low salaries to political leaders and bureaucrats! But they think, even if the size of the cake shrinks, they have a first charge on it and all the rest come later! And rest should bear the burden of salary reduction! Readers can recall how political leaders who get elected to Local Bodies, State Assemblies and National Parliament of all hues and colours exhibit a wonderful unanimity in increasing their own salaries and perks and benefits. One governing principle is: it should be much above what is paid to a top IAS official. These are the very people who describe themselves as social workers and also speak of reduction of social discrimination!

Reflecting on the pitiable status of legal education and lawyers so produced by universities, author in: "Footpath Lawyers" (*The Observer of Business and Politics, 8 August 2000*), recommends the remedy of limiting admissions to study law and young lawyers beginning their careers being provided with kiosks at a small rent. This will help beginners in legal profession to work with some dignity. As long as illiteracy still lingers on the country's educational scene, their fees be regulated by the Bar Associations. Even though they make enough money to survive, it is an undesirable scene to see lawyers in their full uniform, seek petty jobs every day on the footpath!

Governments have always stooped to win over parents by siding with them even if their cause is irrational as they are seen only as 'voters'. The government in Maharashtra extended the benefits of V Pay Commission to the school staff. But the then Minister of Education, as 'Modern day Tughlaq' also directed schools not to increase their existing fees by more than 'fifty percent'. "Modern day Tughlaq" (*Mid-Day, 15 November 2000*), highlights this issue to show the impracticability of such a rule. As it is, even before extending V pay scales to teaching staff, the education department was driving schools to bankruptcy by imposing a rule of permitting fee increase only once in three years though expecting schools to pay ever-increasing Dearness Allowances to teachers and subordinate staff. Government is irrational because, school budget depends upon seniority of teachers, student-teacher ratio and also extent of facilities offered by unaided schools to their students!

Unaided English Schools since the 1990's have faced the continuous threats from government, parents and political elements of different kinds. "Unaided English Schools face closure" *(The Observer of Business & Politics, 22 November 2000)* has its focus on various issues faced by such schools. Thus in June 2000 government made it compulsory for the educational trusts managing English Medium Schools to pay their teachers V pay scales, so that teachers' constituency is taken care of. At the same time to keep parents' constituency also equally happy the then Education Minister issued a directive to managements not to increase fees beyond 50 percent of existing fees. However, the factors such as teacher-student ratio or number of senior teachers in school were not taken into consideration by the Education Minister. Thus, many schools needed a higher increase in fees ranging between72% to 90%; forcing such education trusts managing unaided English Medium Schools, to move the Bombay High Court challenging the attitude of the government that was compared to Modern Mohammed Tughlaq!

Children's Exploitations in hazardous industries and in war and terror is the focus in "What crime have they committed"? (*OIOP, February 2001*). "Primary Cause", it argues of such crimes is extreme poverty". It is also a violation of Constitutional prohibition of employment of children below the age of 14 in certain hazardous industries like carpet and fire crackers making. There cannot be any justification for any kind of child labour. Domestically, then it was pointed out that when a girl child from a rich family is given free education (this is prior to the RTE) boys from poor families also be given free education. Education is to be provided by alleviating family poverty by the state.

Internationally, practice of use of children in promotion of terrorism need to be prevented. Nations like Iran, Iraq, Sri Lanka have also used children in their conflicts. Also Economic sanctions imposed by major powers directly impact on children in regard to medicines, food etc. This should be prevented forthwith.

Parents too have perverted approach to School education! They are willing to pay huge amounts as tuition fees in coaching classes while opposing fee rise in schools. This issue is highlighted by

"Schools V/s Classes" (*Mid-Day, 1 March 2001*). There is also an occasional effort made by Governments to register and regulate coaching classes. While as a liberal, I have opposed government's effort to regulate, need is to find out why students and parents find a need for such coaching classes. A majority of teachers who teach in the coaching classes are also teachers in the regular schools. Main reasons as argued in the article are: Overcrowded classes, irregular presence of teachers and students and low quality of teaching by teachers in the government and municipal schools. Examples show that it is possible for a student to shine without going to a coaching class.

"Breathing fresh air into the system of school education" (*FPJ, 13 August 2001)* lauds the efforts made by Unaided Schools Forum by going to the High Court and the latter liberating educational development from the artificial control imposed by the government. As the nation moved to the twenty-first century, it became possible thanks to Bombay High Court decision to appoint better qualified teachers to teach at upper primary level, and provide academically useful extra-curricular activities to seek really all round development of child's personality rather than make it a mere slogan!

The Maharashtra Governments' populist approach to School education in particular, but education in general, is reflected in its Anti-capitation Act of 1987 that prohibits collection of donations from parents. The idea of voluntary donation is a contradiction in terms. Yet government encourages parents to go to any extent to harass school managements for their alleged acts of collection. This on the face of government radically reducing aid to aided institutions like not giving them grants on account of rent, maintenance and development activities. Unaided schools are likely to outnumber aided ones in next five years. How can education trusts survive without donations? These issues appear in "Is collection of donation justified"? (*FPJ, 03 September 2001*). Increasingly private NGO's are vanishing in running schools as social activity, but it is used by the corporations to channelize their Corporate Social Responsibility (CSR) funds into building expensive schools which can cater only to rich class. Now even state governments are clamouring to seek CSR donations from rich business Corporations, thus denying NGOs running schools funds from CSR!

The problem created by the Maharashtra government are further analysed in "Curbing School donations under rules" *(FPJ, 26 February 2002).* The governments have tried to regulate school fees and collection of donations through various ways to please parents. The government has discovered that most of schools in urban areas have pre-primary classes. These are an alternative for the lack of crèche facility as both parents are employed to achieve a balancing of budget in a middle class family. Government tries to control that, though most of the regulations in the field of school education, 'schooling begins from std I of Primary! Parent-Teacher Associations were in existence in the schools long before government thought of them as one more means to empower parents to control (harassment schools) to cover up its own inability to perform its primary task of providing education to its future citizens!

During the notorious National Emergency imposed by Mrs Gandhi there was a big conglomeration in Shanmukhananda Hall called "Intellectuals for Mrs Gandhi". It is used to be said then by critics that anyone having an undergraduate degree is an intellectual. "Priya Tendulkar as a Prosecutor and Judge!" (*FPJ, 18 February 2002*) was an intellectual of that kind as she was in a T. V. Show 'Zimmedar Kaun? Acting as a prosecutor and judge without having an iota of experience with problems faced by trusts managing unaided schools she characterised fundraising by educational trusts as "business". Schools need facilities and all such things can come from fees paid by parents or donations raised by trusts from philanthropists!

Government has always shown keen desire to control fees of unaided schools. At the turn of the century, it was said that only 3 percent of primary children went to unaided schools. Then the government should give up their efforts to control fees in unaided schools. So argues: "Mess of fees, Government must not meddle with unaided schools" (*FPJ, 5 May 2002*). BMC run and aided private schools are in a pitiable condition. The entire effort appeared as though the government is keen to reduce the better quality of education provided by the unaided schools to the level of aided schools.

Then the government toyed with the idea of permitting schools to charge fees on the basis of income of parents. I had opposed it in

"New fee structure discriminatory in Nature" (*FPJ, 28 June 2002*) arguing that apart from being discriminatory, such a system will introduce avoidable social problems causing psychological impact on children and it introduces hypocrisy in fee structure! The governments have often shown to public that they have enough money to spend on foreign tours for MLA's but no money for educating the future citizens of India!

World Trade Organisation (WTO) under the General Agreement of Trade in Services (GATS) has made member-states to open up their education to international investment and interactions. India is a signatory to it. Hence, has to open up the field of education to foreign investment, since it considers education as 'service' as medicine or law. Thus, "Opening up of Indian education to Foreign Universities" (*FPJ, 16 July 2002*) argues that the entry of Foreign Universities compel Indian Universities to rise to improve the education provided by them. Courses need to be upgraded; make them innovative and relevant new courses need to be introduced to meet the challenges to survival. Mumbai University is notorious for worshipping old traditions like rigid Departmental structures without any encouragement for inter-disciplinary studies: that needs to change.

Not only every government, but every politician when he becomes minister for education wants to change system of education, exam or bring about reforms. Often experts in education are not involved in introducing these changes. One such change brought by the Congress Party led UDF government, is an effort to introduce Primary School Certificate for the children of class IV. This was at a time where Federal Government was probing to introduce the concept of "No Failing" children at Primary Level that was extended to cover classes upto VIII. "Primary Certificate Examination Scheme (PCES) can only bring ruin" (*FPJ, 10 August 2002),* is an analysis of this contradictory effort. The Proposal involved holding of examinations of three subjects– languages social studies and Mathematics for PCES. The examination was to be a public exercise. Government linked scholarships to students performing well in the PCES. The scheme appeared to gain over ten crores in fees for government treasury and some work to babus in educational bureaucracy as well. But there was no application of mind on the consequences of exposing a child to a public examination at such an early stage of education.

The next article in this book, "How to achieve the purpose without Board Examinations?" (*FPJ, 25 September 2002)* tries to bring about some changes in the system of education, most often hastily, without adequate discussion with the stake holders. Thus, Government partially modified earlier decision on PCES by making it in place of school examination. This article discusses probable reasons for introduction of PCES, mainly because Government doubts on teachers having taught well. If so, this purpose can be achieved by appointing dedicated teachers as School Inspectors and see that Inspectors regularly conduct their work.

The US as a more powerful of two Super Powers during the post-World War II Period was able to promote American Studies in India by using PL 480 funds available to them. Once, the Soviet Union disintegrated in 1991 the US was not much interested in continuing their efforts to promote American Studies in India. As the only surviving super power, study of the US Society and politics is an absolute need for India as a democratic emerging major power. However, "American Studies losing importance in Mumbai University" (*FPJ, 15 October 2002*) highlights the apathy of those managing University affairs and the Maharashtra Government.

In the US Universities Heads of Academic Departments are normally those in the rank of Associate Professors who normally aspire to be a professor and professors shun away from responsibilities to manage an academic department. Since they devote their precious time, to conduct research and write acclaimed treatises. "Case for rotation of Department Headship in Mumbai University" (*FPJ, 3 December 2003*), brings out contrasting situation prevailing in Mumbai University. As an ancient University, Heads have exercised power life long as was the case with Dr. Aloo J. Dastur's tenure beginning in 1958 and ending with her retirement in 1978. The UGC had introduced rotation system in 1993. But the article clearly shows how it was flouted by the then VC, Dr S. D. Karnik to grant "a privilege" of ruling over the Department of Civics and Politics. In Mumbai University generally position of head is coveted by those who are more non-performers as a Professor. Since Head's position provides them an alibi for their non-performance!

"Inter University Centre for Astronomy and Astrophysics" (*OIOP, May 2004*) highlights IUCAA role as a place which promotes in-depth study of astronomy and astrophysics in India. It is also committed to the idea of promoting study of legitimate contributions to the subjects in Ancient India. Though well funded by the UGC, as in other fields, IUCAA faces difficulties in attracting talented men for study of these subjects.

Return of the Congress through coalition called United Progressive Alliance (UPA) to power at the federal level in May 2004, led under its HRD Minister Shri Arjun Singh, to scrap books on history produced by previous NDA government under the BJP. The BJP had done the changing of history books prescribed earlier which were mostly promoted by the Congress Party. "Let every school decide which history text books to follow" (*FPJ, 20 August 2004*) argues in favour of freedom to every school to decide history books of its choice. History books since independence were written mostly by Marxist historians with their political perspective. For them World War II began, only when Hitler attacked the Soviet Union in 1941 and not in 1939. Marxists supported British rulers in India in their suppression of Indian National Freedom Movement because British were fighting against Hitler along with the Soviet Union! Books promoted by the UPA are claimed to promote secularism while the Congress Party alleged that the books produced by the NDA, promoted Communalism! Why not these multiple versions be allowed to co-exist and let schools to follow their choice and ultimately Government totally withdrawing from book-production! Indirectly it will allow the nation to move in the direction of what Dr. Manmohan Singh, the then PM under UPA stated that education be developed "on the foundation of professional excellence and intellectual integrity" without making it a prisoner of political ideology.

"Is money meant for education rightly spent?" (*FPJ, 26 October 2006*), analyses purposes of the federal scheme of Sarva Shikshan Abhiyan (SSA) and finds that states are actually using the SSA funds to supplement their bankrupt treasury to provide chalks and dusters or prescribe size and shape of it, instead of spending it on universalisation of Primary Education! It makes a strong case for elected MLAs and MPs to examine whether education cess it collects from citizens is used for the promotion of education or not.

Next article in this collection on "Mumbai University-Restoring the lost glory" (*OIOP, October 2006)* was written in the background of University celebration of sesquicentennial in July 2006. Historically, a British creation as an affiliating University, had jurisdiction from Karachi to Karwar, became a source of liberal education –great many stalwarts of initial era of freedom movement like, Mahadev Ranade, B. G. Tilak, G.K. Gokhale and Mahatma Gandhi were its products. Article points out three significant causes for its decline like increasing politicalisation, over centralisation and its culture of sharing responsibility for inaction". Restoration of functional autonomy is suggested as a remedy.

The next article "The World is our lecture room" (*The Hindustan Times, 26 January 2007*) supports the idea of Indian nation establishing at least 1500 Universities, as put forward by Sam Pitroda, then the Chairman of the National Knowledge Commission, in place of the existing 363. But there is a plea for going for the concept of International Universities as well in every major city like Mumbai International University or Delhi International University. These could cater to promote unity amongst South Asian Countries like an International University at Chennai could cater to students from Sri Lanka and Maldives in addition to students from India. An International University at Kolkata can be a hub to aspiring students from south-east Asia. These could reduce temptation of Indian students to go for foreign universities on the one hand while making foreigners to visit India to study for a fraction of cost in the Western World.

"Keep the Channels open" (*Hindustan Times, 23 March 2007*) was written in the context of Indian officials attempting to advise visiting Fulbright Scholars from the US on research topics they could take and inordinate delay practised in granting visa. It pleads for more liberal approach to Fulbright Scholars coming to India. Though a Cold War–related objective was very much behind the Fulbright Programme in initial stage, even during the Cold War periods as per my own experience, Indian Scholars visiting the US Universities were not prevented from studying the Vietnam War or the Iran-Contra Scandal. On the other hand, twice as the visiting scholar, under the Fulbright Programme, I was provided with easy access to classified documents in Presidential Libraries.

"Schools: the way forward" (*Hindustan Times, 30 April 2007*) suggests organising the teaching within the Mumbai University under broad based schools like school of Social Sciences or School of International Relations or School of Natural Sciences or School of Life Sciences to avoid rigid approach against any internal co-operation between existing departments. Unfortunately though this was a concept played upon by the Professors of University during 1990's, idea has remained on paper.

National Knowledge Commission (NKC) in a note in November 2006 spoke of "a quiet crisis in higher education". It said after 60 years of independence, there is not even one university, in India which is the best in "top fifty in the world". My article, (*OIOP, April 2007)* "Need to strengthen research in Universities" analyses causes for lack of research component in Indian universities particularly when it is noted that for every one patent registered by Indian Scholars in India, 30,000 patents are registered by Indians living abroad! Lack of funding, lack of accountability, use of foreign language (English) are identified as causes. These need to be tackled urgently because funding comes from government and Indian bureaucracy is not attuned to accept research as an area which needs to be encouraged in addition to teaching. Shifting of research outside the universities has provided the government an easy patronage to appoint research heads in such institutions.

Be that as it may, today genuinely well-managed law abiding educational trusts find it increasingly difficult to honestly manage educational trusts. "Government should not harass Private School managements" (*FPJ, 20 May 2007)* highlights this problem. Article lists various ways in which audit clerk who visits for audit after several years of incurring expenditure, to deny it as inadmissible or unnecessary expenditure, only with a view to extract some money as illegal gratification!

With growing number of Unaided English Medium schools, Maharashtra Government came out in 2007 a new concept of "permanently unaided" as well as extended the concept to include even regional media schools. "The plight of schools told to close down" *(FPJ, 25 June 2007)* has its focus on such situation faced by many trusts in Mumbai and elsewhere in the state. The problem of schools asked to close down because of High Court decision were forced to approach the Supreme Court as many of them had by then started "Permanently Unaided" regional media schools. Their permissions were restored by it. At least in one area, Indian democracy has come closer to western developed democracies. In the US for instance, every major issue ends up on the table of the Chief Justice of the Supreme Court! That has also become true in India.

The UGC and the Governments in India have already set in a move to devalue the highest academic degrees like M. Phil or Ph.D. Often issues arises as to whether a College affiliated to University is equipped to run courses on M. Phil or Ph. D. "Bidding for an M. Phil" (*Hindustan Times, June 2007*), highlights the erosion of the autonomy of universities as government takes over minute details of granting permissions to start a College or Centres of Higher Learning. The trend has enabled many bureaucrats who control education, themselves enrolling in Ph. D. programmes. The author recommends that serving Babus be debarred from enrolling into Ph. D. programme to prevent dilution of quality of the dissertations so produced.

If one asks to identify two features of Maharashtra Government's Jr. College admission policy, one can say without any hesitation: populism and ad-hocism. Year after year since the birth of the Jr. College concept (XI-XII stds) developed, this has been the characteristic of government policy. Thus, "Admission Chaos: Government must allow more School, College divisions" (*Free Press Journal, 17 July 2007*) highlights pressure created for more seats because of the government's decision to give 30 marks more in Maths paper during the academic year! This boosted passing percentage from 60 of the previous year to 75.2 in 2007. Since the current trend amongst the students, at least in Mumbai City, is to prefer neighbourhood institutions Government will do well to anticipate student strength appearing for X std examinations in a given year and plan accordingly to maintain a level playing field by opening new divisions or permitting new Jr. Colleges purely on merit basis.

Another issue in the field of education that comes to limelight every now and then is transporting children to school from home and back. "Let's say *bus* to this nasty problem" *(Hindustan Times, 12 Feb. 2008*) and "Avoid tragedies: provide School bussing for Kids" *(FPJ, 16 February 2008*) highlight lack of an imaginative policy on the part of government on school bus service. The suggestion worth emulating is: for government to start a bus service to pick up students from different wards/areas and drop them as per their chosen schools. This could have been easily made a part of Sarva Shiksha Abhiyan (SSA) so that children from poorer localities are picked up and dropped at their respective linguistic schools. In the absence of such a policy, poor children are packed in unauthorised mini vans. Whenever, an accident occurs, ministers will promise stern action and strict regulation of bus service. What they are willing to do is imposing more financial burdens on schools or private bus service providers by insisting on 'speed governors' and other protective measurers rather than provide free school bus service! Government is always generous to the parents as long as it is not required to pay for the service provided!

Though the State is charged by the Constitution to provide education to its future citizens, the task of providing primary education to its future citizens is delegated to Municipal Corporations like the BMC. Over the years, educational trusts are also voluntarily sharing the task of providing primary education as a social work. But what is the attitude of the BMC towards such private trusts which are managing the primary education in Mumbai? That is the theme of: "BMC needs to learn a thing or two", (*Hindustan Times 4 April 2008*). It lists various ways in which the BMC discriminates such private trusts which runs BMC recognised and aided or unaided primary schools. Most hurting is the charging fees to primary children despite the directive principle to provide "Free and Compulsory education to all children below the age of 14". BMC provides milk to children studying in BMC run schools, but denies it to children in the private aided schools!

At last after 69 years of Indian Independence, Right to Education became a fundamental Right – under the constitutional amendment carried out by the UPA Government in 2009 when it passed the Right to Education Act (RTE), 2009 that was implemented with effect from 1 April 2010. "Some pitfalls in implementation of Right to Education" (*FPJ, 30 June 2010*) discusses new problems created by RTE. The school managements were not consulted on new legislation on RTE. But were told 'not to fail' any child upto VIII std. Worst still, even though RTE made primary education "free and compulsory", privately managed but aided schools are forced to collect fees from primary children! The continued collection of fees was justified as as a means to force parents to send their children to BMC run schools where education is free rather than to privately managed BMC aided Schools!

Government policies like reduction of maintenance grant from 12 percent to 6 percent and denial of that in reality, policy of permitting unaided and permanently unaided schools not only English Medium but regional media as well and growing corruption in the field of education are the main causes for increasing fees in schools as discussed in "Eradicate Fundamental causes behind rising fees" (*FPJ, 12 July 2010*). The remedy lies in increasing budgetary "allocation for education to at least 6 percent of the GDP and continuously trying to cure growing cancer of corruption in public administration of education.

Fully endorsing former Prime Minister Dr Manmohan Singh's appeal to politicians, "Populism in education augurs ill for quality" (*Free Press Journal, 10 August 2010*) pleads for the removal of populist provisions from RTE. Thus for instance, it provided for School's Management Committees where three fourth of members were to be parents and chaotic structure where some make primary section upto Std IV, while others take it upto V std. While some others limit it to VII Std, RTE considers Stds I to VIII as Primary! The need is to create an uniform system.

"Can we chop off a hand for making a mistake?" (*FPJ, 8 September 2010*), is a response to a journalist's outburst against teachers getting awards on the Teachers' Day every year in the background of some incidents, unfortunate though they are, to do away all together with them! In an environment full of corruption, thugs getting into power and ruling the roost, teaching community cannot be isolated altogether from the social evils! Yet the article rightly points out despite all flaws, people trust a teacher more than his elected politician and a neighbourhood journalist!

My Interview in *Mulund Meet, 6 August 2011,* highlights the fact that regional media schools in Mumbai as well as in the nation do not have good time. The problem is aggravated by the attitude of authorities where they themselves encourage and open English Medium Schools with Pre-Primary attached to it. Is the English Medium good from the Pre-Primary level to the higher levels for the individual's development as a conscientious citizen of the Indian nation, or a good grounding in the mother tongue at the level of Pre-Primary and Primary and then gradually moving to English as the medium is good, is a larger issue that needs to be discussed seriously at the national level.

As an Interview, "Service in Education is my payback to society" (*Speak out, 9-15, December 2012)* highlights a rapidly disappearing fact in the field of education: During freedom movement many eminent leaders like, Mahadev Govind Ranade, Gopalkrishna Gokhale, Bal Gangadhar Tilak, Agarkar and many others started schools to provide education either in one's own mother tongue or in English. These men did this as a genuine social work, without expecting any reward. Today schools, colleges are started in majority of cases by politicians as an arena to invest ill-gotten black-money to begin with but help them to call themselves as "social workers". This also provides a source for permanent job opportunities to politician and his relatives after loss of an election or retirement. Once these politicians get into political positions, like a Corporator or an MLA or a Minister they flaunt the family controlled trust schools to gain voters' support and enrich family members as the Directors or Vice-Chancellors of the institutions started by them. The idea of like-minded people coming together with an agreed motive of providing education as life-long mission does not exist. VPM- Mulund, Mumbai is the one such modern illustration.

"Globalisation and International Schools" (*Teacher 7(3) 2013*), Education in India has undergone several changes because of the fact that country has practiced LPG policy since 1991. Since globalisation has until recently till advent of Trump Presidency in the US-where he has launched a brave campaign to reverse globalisation in favour of nationalisation of investment, employment and movement of people; with that many international schools have come into being to prepare children mentally to move around globally. Students thus graduated from International Schools are well equipped to gain admissions to Universities of their choice globally.

"A report card of the Modi Government" (*OIOP*, August 2015), though highlights a few achievements of the PM in the arena of foreign affairs, primarily it is a report card of Smriti Irani, as the Minister of Human Resources Development in the field of education, during her tenure of 15 months. Her enthusiastic effort to introduce Sanskrit in the Kendriya Vidyalaya was a good, highly desirable move. However, she had to withdraw it, in the wake of media and Congress Party questioning her educational background. She initiated moves to establish new IITs and IIM's. The piece urges her and the federal government to do away certain moves initiated by the previous government like, admitting students in primary school according to age at the time of admission without insisting on having any background in schooling or not to insist age proof for admission and most important on which I personally campaigned is the dictum not to fail any one upto std VIII.

Is Right to pass a fundamental Right? was written in October 2015 and two paragraphs of which appeared in "Pappu eighth class pass hai" in (*OIOP, November 2015*) as a part of interview by E Vijaylakshmi Rajan, magazine's Assistant Editor. It makes clear that "no fail policy" of government must be limited to primary classes but children from Std VI to VIII must be examined. Children have a right to know that there are certain intellectual gradations in human society. Equal opportunity for education is a fundamental right of any child, but they do not have a fundamental right to pass.

Instead of scrapping 'No fail policy' that was introduced by the UPA II government, present Federal government led by PM Modi and state government led by Devendra Fadnavis have introduced "competency test" as an examination devised, executed by the government babus. They have reduced the number of teachers teaching at primary level and strength of bureaucracy to implement it has increased. This happens because, ministers come and go but bureaucrats are there to control education till they retire. Is the Government listening to the public opinion?

Chapter - 1

Democracy and the Standard of Education

(School Inauguration Souvenir, August 1962)

"If we desire to improve the quality of education, first we must attract intellectuals to the profession"

Much is heard and talked about the Standard of Education. The young and the old, academicians and politicians all make use of the standard of education and voice their fear about the falling standards in Indians schools and colleges. Academicians, probably speak of it in their excessive love of Ancient Indian Education and politicians use it to hide the ugly facet of their own creation. No view is, thus a standard view. All these views are full of prejudices, bias, and one sided so much so that as proper analysis of it shows that the entire concept of the standard of education is a fiction.

Those, who love the ancient Indian educational system, fail to understand the fact that because of 'Varnashrama' system the education was limited to a small sect of the society. Secondly, the scope of education was itself limited, since the knowledge was in its blossoming stage. Now the boundary of the knowledge is infinite and no more is it possible to treat the study of the Vedas and Puranas as an end of education.

Another factor, which the advocates of the falling standards forget is the context in which they are speaking about the standard of education. The phrase standard of education being itself a relative term, we do commit a blunder by comparing the standard of education in a democratic set up and the one prevailing in ancient India.

We have accepted the Democratic form of government, and democracy is not only a form of government but a way of life. No democratic government can survive for long if it is not backed by a democratic society. Hence the principles of equality and liberty, are the foundation of a democratic set up. So we have democratised education. The democratic principle of equality has been extended to the field of education in providing equal opportunities for all desiring to get it. The inborn inequality of the human beings in their capacities has been thus overlooked by democracy, and the portals of schools and colleges have been thrown open to all irrespective of genius or dullard. Thus, we cannot expect all to be equal after passing out of school even after a period of equal treatment.

Mass education at the primary level, another feature of democracy, has lowered the standard of education further. Inefficiency, in every aspect is the fate of primary education. When such is the foundation that we lay for a huge structure, the structure is bound to collapse before it is completed. It is said that in France primary teachers receive more attention from the government, than the university professors, since they believe in strengthening the foundation. But what the condition of our primary education is, can be left to your observation since the past alone requires narration.

So we can say that the defects of democracy are bound to enter in the educational field. Since democracy has been accepted as the best form of government after experimenting with all other forms, there is no scope for us to deny it. If we consider the defects in the education brought in by the application of democracy as evils, then certainly denial of education for a vast majority on the ground of their social backwardness and intellectual inequality will be a greater evil. Then we are confronted with choosing between the evil and the greater evil. However, romantic may be the idea of ancient Indian education, we are not prepared to give up democracy and democratic education.

Logically now the problem before us will be how to minimise the evils of the democratic education and to get the best possible product. We should form our own standard of education, under the existing conditions, without bothering much about the ancient Indian glory. Then when we compare the standard, comparison should be with a democratic ideal.

The Mudaliar Commission's Report describes the aims of secondary education as "the training of the character to fit the students to participate creatively as citizens in the emerging democratic social order, improvement of their practical and vocational efficiency so that they may play their part in building up the economic prosperity of their country; and the development of their literary, artistic and cultural interests, which are necessary for self-expression and for the full development of the human personality without which a living national culture cannot come into being". (Page 23 of the Report). Whereas the university education should "train students to become enlightened citizens and potential leaders of thought and action in the learned professions, in public administration and politics, in the social field, in scholarship and scientific research, in industry and commerce, and practically in every important walk of life" (Report of the Medium of Instruction Universities Committee, 1961).

Thus, we have to see how far our present system of education conforms to these aims and if it does not fulfill the required standard then what are the shortcomings and how to remedy them, so that a maximum possible standard can be achieved. Firstly, it is the quality of the teacher more than anything else which determines the quality of education. Much need not be said on the present quality of teachers. The teaching profession attracts none but the non-salable persons in the employment market. It is because of low scale of salaries and lack of promotions in the teaching profession. If we desire to improve the quality of education first we must attract the intellectuals to the profession. Because, only intellectuals can be moulded to the required line, may be in teaching or in industry or in government. He can acquire the practical teaching efficiency within a short period, for which others will have to repeat the one years experience thirty times. This can be done by paying better emoluments to the teachers, compared to those paid in industries and government. It is lack of understanding to argue that the teaching profession is an easy profession with ample leisure. A good teacher, to be good and to improve his quality further, requires time for development. The payment of higher salaries will also curtail the need for private tuitions, which is a consequential evil of low salaries.

As far as promotions in the teaching profession are concerned, as a rule, a teacher is a "dead-ender and a teaching post in nine cases out of ten is a "blind-alley job". Hardly any teacher, once entering the profession, can aspire for any promotion, other than the five rupees increment. Since government has resorted to recruiting directly the personnel required for higher educational services, hardly any can think of being promoted to the higher services. Therefore, it is essential to provide avenues of promotions. A teacher can be appointed as the head of a particular subject in every school, with additional responsibilities and higher remuneration. A combined cadre for promotions as the Headmasters would have provided some scope but for the multi-linguistic nature of our schools.

Since secondary education, for a large majority of students, marks the completion of their formal education, we should consider it as an end in itself. Much scope for employment at this level should be provided so that, students of average type may be discouraged from entering the university education. Government should liberalise its requirement of higher educational qualifications for lower categories, where an S.S.C. can be made to suit by providing post-recruitment training. Even at the secondary level he should be able to maintain a decent living.

Are not our present students burdened with the study of too many subjects with too little knowledge of it? There is no co-ordination absolutely whatsoever in our policies regarding secondary teaching and university teaching. The students are required to study many languages, purely because of our chauvinistic approach to linguism. We talk of national integration and teaching in universities in the regional languages, which are evidently self-contradictory. Because teaching, in regional languages in our universities will hamper the easy migration of students from university to university, thereby compartmentalising the knowledge. This will breed a tendency of separatism in our younger generation, and the national integration will be a mirage. Let our love for regional language stop at the level of secondary education, and let us realise the need for a common medium for university education, with a necessity to teach that common medium from Secondary level as a connecting link to higher education.

The schools in the present days are overcrowded, ill-equipped and unhygienic. It is essential to fix a maximum number to every school and to every class. To my mind a good number for a class seems to be 25 and for a school 500. This will help to create a teacher and taught relation and every student will receive individual attention from the teacher. We tend to give more importance to class teaching than possible practical teaching. The child is to be educated through encouragement of his intellectual and personal assets rather than by punishment for his weaknesses. He should be made to learn in a school through personal experience, and experimentation, because the power of an idea to convince depends finally on the strength and vitality of the idea itself. For this reason every school must be well equipped with all essential requirements. Why the school atmosphere should be hygienic, requires no further elucidation.

Another most distressing feature of the present system of education is the growth of private coaching classes. These coaching classes which run purely on commercial basis should be regulated by the government if not totally abolished. The coaching classes can be permitted to be run for the benefit of those unfortunate students who could not go to the schools and for the purpose of adult education.

The text-books and the guides present a horrifying state of affairs, many text-books are written for profits with many wrong representations and with printer's devils. Many text-books are unsuitable to the age and knowledge of the pupils and thus strain the nerves of the student. Another feature is the guide-books, undertaken for profit and they misguide the students. The trade in guides is the most flourishing business in the educational field.

Those politicians who indulge in the talk of standard of education should note that the schools and colleges, in democracy, are sacred places where the younger generation is trained to be the good citizen and to be able to man the ship of the state. They must keep their hands off such institutions in the larger interest of the nation.

The present system of examination, and the grade system are another feature which cannot be overlooked. Mere memory test, and classification according to the ability to memorise is rather an unsatisfactory method of judging a student's knowledge. Under present conditions we must give more thought to the acquisition of content than to the formal expression of it. With it the students' work, and ability should also be taken note of. How far we will agree with John Dewey's philosophy of progressivism in education wherein he maintains that out would go the system of formal subjects, text-books, recitation examinations, and grades. It would come an education which gives the child a chance to discover things for himself, to gather facts, to draw conclusions to build his own knowledge through experience with life, is doubtful. A synthesis of this progressivism and present system may perhaps prove a more suitable approach to the problems of education, whereby a really high standard of education can be achieved, and maintained.

Chapter - 2

Why Do Our Universities Lack Research Output?

(Free Press Journal, 9 September 1985)

"Whenever I hear that such and such Vice-Chancellor had gone abroad to recruit some talents for his University, I feel that had he only spent his time to create facilities in his University than bringing a talented man he could render a service to University community."

The academic circles and newspaper columnists have often pointed out a lack of any substantive research work being conducted in Indian universities. In the post-independence India there has been a proliferation of universities and teaching facilities in them but there have not been many startling research outputs by them. Hence, the trend has been and continues to be to establish separate institutions for research, outside the university parameters both in natural sciences and social sciences. This has only helped to strengthen the prevailing perception of universities as teaching factories manufacturing graduates for a variety of jobs (or unemployment).

Why has our university community failed to produce any significant research outputs? This baffles many foreign observers, especially when they learn that Indians are doing so well in the Western countries in various research fields. Speaking only in relation to social sciences it appears to me that there are primarily three causes for this phenomenon which has overpowered the university community and weakened their research abilities.

In order of their significance these are: first, absence of congenial atmosphere for research in universities; second, lack of physical facilities, and third, lack of financial resources. It is the presence of these conditions in universities abroad that enable Indian scholars settled there to bring out best in themselves. Hence, whenever I hear that such and such Vice-Chancellor had gone abroad to recruit some talents for his university, I feel that had he only spent his time to create facilities in his university than bringing a talented man, he could render a service to university community. All such exercises have proven futile, because either the Vice-Chancellor returns empty handed or the recruits go back frustrated. For, talented men, without necessary tools and environment cannot produce any worthwhile research work.

Let us examine these three causes at some length. The most important of the causes is the absence of congenial atmosphere in our universities for any in-depth research. Many governments, university authorities and teachers–are responsible for this situation. The most important factor contributing to the creation of non-congenial atmosphere is the attitude of governments–State and Central–which are the financiers of universities. Since the universities have been rejected as the appropriate body to perform the activities of research, State bureaucracies, from the Minister of Education to the director of education downwards, expect university faculty to teach and only teach. Teaching is the only activity they expect. In their calculations, research is not an activity to which time need to be spared. Hence, is their very casual approach to teaching. Whenever they find a teacher doing only four or six hours of teaching, the governments come with recommendations to increase the workload of teachers. If there is not enough teaching work, when the government official desire a teacher to teach courses in which he may not claim any expertise.

On the other hand, within the four-walls of universities, generally the attitude is one which believes that all serious research ends with one's getting a Ph.D. degree. Some universities have devalued their Ph.D. degree to such an extent that social science departments enroll candidates for D.Litt degrees! But after the degree, further research is a luxury, particularly if it involves a field trip, national or international, or unearthing of hidden data or getting study leave for a year or two. In one university, a Vice-Chancellor reportedly thought a professor was going on a vacation when he saw an application for study leave to go abroad (though he was simultaneously trying for a trip abroad himself). It is not that facilities are not misused but in many universities study leave facility is limited and often, arbitrarily decided. If any research needs going abroad on a field trip, particularly by those dealing with area studies or international relations, the problems involved are very acute.

For many amongst the teachers, any effort to deviate from the routine of teaching is unwarranted. And arguing for some changes towards the new directions in research or teaching generally by the younger members of university, is not only unwarranted but would be put down as unrealistic, or laughed at as importing of some foreign ideas! Seniors will narrate their own frustrating experiences in their efforts towards modernisation, when they were young. And they are able to create a negative environment because normally people come to occupy key decision-making positions not because of their ability or achievements but seniority. While in many places seniority is no longer a criterion for decision-making positions, within universities this continues to be so by and large. Sometimes, they go to extremes by putting even senile persons in such positions, as though seniority is more sacrosanct than ability to decide!

The lack of congenial atmosphere for research is aggravated by a lack of supporting physical facilities. In the course of the last six Five-Year Plans, universities have generally added more teaching courses and faculty positions, without necessarily creating supporting staff and other physical facilities to sustain concentrated research activities. These range from existence of a position without a place to sit, to a lack of rudimentary facilities like a typing assistance or a telephone connection. There are instances, when eminent men have left university positions in frustration because they were not provided with adequate room to sit or other facilities.

A university is probably one place where the gulf between the bureaucracy and academics is widest and most visible. Officials connected with the distribution of supporting facilities do not even think that adequate facilities are necessary for the functioning of academics. There are instances, when teachers are asked to conduct their classes under the tree (as in Gurukul system) and not press for rooms! Facilities like microfilm readers (and word processors) are a waste in their limited vision.

Often it is a truism that the bureaucratic functionaries come to believe that universities exist to support them conveniently forgetting the fact that they get their positions in university administration because of, first students and second teachers. For long teachers have been told, "Better not ask what you can get but say what you can give".

Third and last in significance, is the absence of adequate funds for research. For a country of India's size and importance, research in foreign affairs or regional studies like Africa or Latin America, is as important as research in local self-government. But universities do not have their own resources to support research by their teachers, and not much funds are given to them by governments for research by the academics. There is no system of universities raising funds for research through private contributions from the industries and foundations. Any suggestion in that directions is so revolutionary that universities in their present mould are not likely to accept it. Of course, there are institutions like the UGC and Indian Council of Social Science Research which may help. But by and large their funding has been limited and benefits have neither reached all teachers not all universities. In brief, they have done precious little in correcting the three deficiencies and promoting better research in the country.

Thus, the answer to the problem of lack of any significant research outputs from universities is not to create some centres within a university to conduct research without the burdens of teaching. Our nation at the present level of development, cannot afford the luxury of full-time research centres, as a rule not only in social sciences but even in natural sciences. But there should be equal emphasis on both research and teaching.

It is also worthwhile to seriously ponder over the question, how far the institutions like the UGC and ICSSR and others of the kind in the area of higher education and research have serve their original purpose. They appear to be only functioning as additional bureaucracies, without their meeting most of educational purposes for which they were created in the first instance. The funds now distributed by the UGC and ICSSR can be disbursed by the central government directly to the universities. Universities are in a better position to know the kind of research being done by a teacher than a distant bureaucracy in Delhi.

Here, then is an important area where Prime Minister Rajiv Gandhi can act since he has promised a new direction in the nation's education policy. The new education policy should aim at alleviating these major causes which stifle research in universities. Any efforts at short-circuiting them will only prove disastrous.

Chapter - 3

Teachers or Qualified Clerks?

(Indian Express, 21 December 1988)

"A teacher in a College is not merely a teaching machine.....He is, while imparting education to the youth expected to be an intellectual thinking ahead of times' for the good of the Society. Can a qualified clerk, do it?"

On October 5 when the college and University teachers in Maharashtra went on one-day strike, it was reported that about 70 per cent of teachers had joined to protest the Maharashtra government's failure to implement the UGC scales which they are supposed to have won after being no strike for over 40 days last year. The teachers, this year, though they had joined the one-day strike, were very reluctant and shy to be on strike once again after last year's long-drawn strike and its aftermath. It is unfortunate they are on strike again for the same purpose. They seem to have resorted to the strike weapon only because of the attitude of Maharashtra government towards their pay revision. The other day I overheard a teacher remarking in disgust, that "there is no merit, only workload in Maharashtra". This accurately sums up the present situation in Maharashtra as far as the government's policy towards teachers in the higher education is concerned.

There are two parts in the teacher's above mentioned remark: First, there is no merit in Maharashtra and second, there is only work load. To take up the first part first, the UGC under the Sixth Five Year

Plan had offered to university and college teachers promotional avenues by introducing merit promotion scheme. It was continued by the UGC under the Seventh Plan as well. The merit promotion scheme was adopted practically by all states for implementation in their respective universities. The central government too implemented it in the universities and the institutes under their direct control. As a result, those lecturers who were qualified to be readers and readers qualified to be professors but were slogging because of absence of promotional avenues, became readers or professors, respectively. In one institute, according to a reliable source, over 20 persons became professors overnight. The colleges in many states got readers positions; some colleges as in Delhi, even got professors positions. But Maharashtra remained the only state which refused to accept the merit promotion scheme. The apparent reason given was lack of resources to accept the additional burden involved in granting merit promotion to a few hundred college and University teachers in Maharashtra. But the argument of additional burden on the state exchequer is not really very strong as for each University it would not have been a matter of more than a few lakh rupees.

But in Maharashtra there is only workload. The very term "workload" indicates teaching is no longer an intellectual activity performed for its high purpose of imparting quality education but performed as a routine activity. This unfortunate attitude among the teachers has developed because unlike in other states where the pay revision of 1973 was implemented to neutralise inflation which had eaten away a sizeable portion of their even otherwise meager pay packet, the Maharashtra government succeeded in substantially raising the workload of the teachers in colleges and Universities. Now the government once again, desires to link the implementation of new UGC scales to a further increase in the work load of college and University teachers. According to the union sources, the government proposes to increase the present 20 periods of 45 minutes (15 clock hrs). to 27 periods of 45 minutes (20 clock hrs.)

Maharashtra, which others say is a progressive state, has taken a very regressive attitude towards teachers, as evident in their attitude towards the merit promotion scheme and pay revision conceded by the central government last year.

Teaching is a dead-end job. Unlike in other vocations like jobs in the government or industry, there are no promotional avenues for almost 99 per cent of the teachers. In the absence of promotional avenues and periodic neutralisation of increase in the cost of living and efforts to improve the status of the teachers in the country, teaching cannot be made an attractive profession. Hence the question of optimum hours of class-room teaching one should do, should entirely depend upon the quality of the education the government intends to provide to its youth and not linked to periodical, nationwide revisions of pay-scales in view of the prevailing double digit inflation.

Then, why have we reached this sorry state of affairs? I believe bureaucracy which advises the political leadership in Maharashtra and the teachers unions–in that order–both seem to be responsible. This is not a piece of investigative journalism. But my own personal readings, conversations with the people in bureaucracy and academics associated with it and observations of union activities in Bombay for the last 20 years only confirm my belief.

The bureaucratic advisers of policy-makers in the State are envious of so-called leisure enjoyed by the academics. Before 1976 the college teachers did about ten to 12 clock hours work; enjoyed three months of summer vacation. (this remains the work load of teachers in the developed world even today.) Since the implementation of 1973 scales in 1977, summer vacation has been cut by one month and teaching has become really a "workload" as actual teaching went up to 15 clock hours, that is, 20 periods of 45 minutes. Still the bureaucrats feel that compared to 40 hours of work they put in at their place of work, teachers are spending shorter hours at their place of work.

It is forgotten that for every one hour of teaching, they have to spend a minimum of two hours to prepare a lecture. This minimum is for those who have been teaching for a long time with considerable knowledge and experience in their subject. The time required to prepare a lecture increases sharply for those teaching at higher level classes and new comers to the teaching profession. The teachers spend, like bureaucrats, 40 hours in colleges provided they have proper facilities of office. However, colleges neither provide an office space nor other facilities to teachers. This is true of colleges in the cities as well as rural areas. In the absence of adequate facilities, teachers tend to prepare their lectures at homes. In contrast to this, in government offices, even an office superintendent or an Under Secretary would have place to sit and work and a telephone extension to communicate with the external world. Bureaucratic perks of the higher officials in the government of course, include quarters to live, cars to drive to work.

Now regarding the long vacations enjoyed by the teachers, I am sure, teachers might also prefer like bureaucrats, 30 days privilege (earned) leave which they can accumulate and enjoy whenever they want and if necessary with additional money they can get by en-cashing part of their leave. The point is, in the present system of examinations the universities need at least three months time in summer to conduct the examinations and announce the results before a next academic session could begin. The bureaucrats envy of college teachers having long vacation is therefore, based on erroneous understanding. The vacations are linked to the present examination system and not per se for the benefit of teachers. As a matter of fact, reduction of vacation from three to two months, has resulted in colleges and universities reopening in June without having students in the class-rooms to teach; and before the end of March students do not attend the classes though college teachers are at work, as they need time to read before appearing for the examinations. Some examinations even commence before the formal closure of the academic session. (This revelation might add to bureaucrats, envy that teaches are at work in colleges without teaching in the class rooms for at least a month in every academic year.)

The net gain of the 1977 pay revision has been an increased bureaucratic control over educational system in Maharashtra. Then, the teachers unions in Maharashtra also have contributed a great deal to the present bureaucratisation of the education.

First, by insisting on the government as the direct pay master rather than through the college managements, the college teachers have provided a great deal of control to the bureaucracy over the questions like appointment, salary fixation, increments etc. When we say government, what does it mean? In effect it means, a remote control by a clerk in the bureaucracy who, within his limitations, specialises in applying standardised procedures irrespective of any academic considerations. This has resulted in delayed salaries for teachers for several months and denial of increments on flimsy grounds. The discretion of managements in appointing talented teachers with additional incentives like advance increments etc. has been completely done away with.

The Unions have also shown scant respect for need to improve quality of education and achieve excellence in teaching and educational institutions. They have run so much after their demand for a "running grade" for all teachers in the institutions of higher educations from junior colleges to the postgraduate institutions that they have down-graded, if not degraded, the need for teachers to remember excellence and continuously work to maintain high standards of instruction. The Unions have also not shown any interest in introduction of "merit promotion scheme" and have actively opposed, in all forums, introduction of autonomous colleges. All their actions so far have been aimed at standardisation at the lowest common denominator where bureaucratisation is not an unacceptable risk.

To be fair, these are important enough grounds for the teachers to agitate against any increase in their teaching hours. But what is equally important is its effect on the quality of education the teachers can impart. In the countries which value quality of education like the US and UK the teachers in the institutions of higher education do 6 to 12 hrs. of class room teaching, depending upon whether they teach only graduate classes or only undergraduate classes or a mix of the two. Increased teaching hours for the college teachers will not only deny them adequate time to prepare their lectures but make it impossible for them even occasionally to write research papers. A teacher in a college is not merely a teaching-machine; he has other responsibilities for extracurricular activities, which are equally important in shaping the education of the youth. He is, while imparting education to the youth, expected to be an intellectual thinking ahead of times for the good of the society.

But there is an anti-intellectual atmosphere in the corridors of power. Some years ago, an Under Secretary in the Sachivalaya told me that he, after Matric, joined as a clerk and rose to be the Under

Secretary without any degrees. He was trying to prove that to rise in bureaucracy, college education is not necessary. (Often he failed to distinguish 'season' from session in his notings on the file.) By increasing "work load" of college teachers, government will only succeed in reducing them to a status of qualified clerks loading and unloading information from text books in the class, without even having any time to analyse the information they load and unload.

However, he will remain a clerk, without any opportunity to rise in the hierarchy as it is possible for a clerk to be the Under Secretary in government bureaucracy. Hence, whenever government sacrifice quality in the name of economy and unions do it in the name of employment opportunities, the society at large ought to think loud as to what kind of education they would like to receive.

Chapter - 4

Unaided Schools Get Raw Deal

(Free Press Journal, 9 August 1990)

"English medium Schools started prior to 1980 receive grant-in-aid, another school in the nearby, an aided school is denied aid, just because it was started after 1980. Is it fair?"

The government grant-in-aid to schools is a means to social development and should not be seen as doles to poor. However, since the 1980s the Government of Maharashtra has started a policy of permitting schools on unaided basis. There are today in Bombay alone 138 unaided schools (as against–194 aided) providing education to over 37,000 students. This policy of permitting recognised but unaided schools is discriminatory on many grounds.

Need for new schools is much more in suburbs and extended suburbs than in the city. According to the 1980 census, the suburbs house 61 per cent while the city only 31 per cent of Bombay's population. Since then the population growth has been more rapid in the suburbs and extended suburbs while the population in the main city has been declining. But the established schools in the city proper and some schools in the suburbs receive grant-in-aid. The new schools in suburbs and extended suburbs do not receive any aid. Hence, a student studying in the unaided school has to pay 8 to 10 times more for his education than a student studying in the government aided school. Wittingly or unwittingly this amounts to subsidizing education to a section of children in the metropolis while making another section of children to pay the actual cost for their education. In many cases it may be paying less fees than a student studying in another school.

It is a suitable case for public interest litigation as the state is practicing unreasonable discrimination against one group of students vis-à-vis another.

Then there is a discriminatory treatment given to English medium schools vis-à-vis schools of regional media. The state of Maharashtra in the 1960s began the policy of permitting new schools on the condition that they would be eligible for grant-in-aid after two years. But now regional media schools are technically held eligible for grants after seven years of their commencement. But English medium schools are asked to accept the condition that they will forever function on an unaided basis. There is the fallacious argument that those who want education through English medium can afford to pay for it. But even poor would like to send their children to English medium schools because it could help them to get better jobs. Recently at least two auto rickshaw drivers sought admission to an English medium school through my help, though I tried to dissuade them. But their ambition is that since they remained uneducated, at least their sons must get the best education so that they will not have to become drivers. Even those who politically oppose English medium schools, send their own children to English schools. The ministers and their political hangers-on who do not justify grant-in-aid to English medium schools, however do not hesitate to issue chits to those who seek admission into these schools. Whether educational instruction through an alien language is a desirable thing for the psychological development of the child and his faculties is an altogether different issue.

But not all those English medium schools are denied aid. Those which were started prior to the 1980s continue to receive aid. Can a section of the children be treated discriminatingly just because it is going to a school started after 1980? If this policy is continued, it would mean that a large section of the society today would get subsidized education at the expense of future generations.

It is here that the ugly question of donation enters on the scene of school education. Not all trusts are endowed with huge corpus funds which could meet the recurring deficits in the running of a school. The government rightly insists that the school staff be paid salaries according to the government prescribed scales and ever increasing DA rates because of stagnation in the country.

Chapter - 5

Saving Education from Bureaucracy

(The Observer of Business and Politics, 12 May 1992)

"Education is too important to be controlled and guided by bureaucrats who have lost touch with education ever since they came out from their Schools or Colleges".

The federal government under the leadership of P.V. Narasimha Rao has taken several initiatives to liberalise the Indian economy from the government (read bureaucratic) control since it came to power in June 1991. It is immaterial whether these steps were almost forced upon India by international lending institutions like the World Bank and the International Monetary Fund to meet the balance of payment crisis or the new thinking in economic field arose indigenously as a result of the Congress Party's reassessment of the economic mess in the country–in that these changes of liberalisation in economic field are irreversible.

However, an ideal environment for the success of a liberal economy, free of 'permit-licence-quota Raj' as Rajagopalachari described it, cannot be ushered in unless there is a liberal attitude in other fields of social and political life of the country. Education is one such important field where alone the attitude of genuine liberal outlook can be inculcated amongst the students which they can carry on later in their life.

However, educational administration is one important area which today suffers from initiative-curbing and quality paralyzing burden of government control. As a matter of fact, for the long-term success of economic liberalisation, we need to begin by reorienting the educational field without any more delay. We need to take independent charge of educational administration for the benefit of future citizens where the governmental interference is negligible.

What is the situation today? First, for instance, let us survey the textbook scene. State governments have entered the field of textbook manufacturing in a big way. There are undue delays in bringing out books and children often have to go without books. Monopoly of textbook production enjoyed by the government has brought in all the evils of monopoly. The government should limit itself to prescription of syllabi and permit private initiative in production of books as per the government approved syllabi. Let the schools enjoy the freedom to choose one book or the other.

Second, there are so many regulations in the matter of appointment of teachers that no institution really gets an opportunity to select the best. At every stage, government interferes in the form of quota, and licences and permits so much, that recruitments, in effect if not in form, are made by the government.

Third, the government has taken upon itself to pay the salaries to the teachers in schools. This was introduced as teachers in many schools were not paid on time and adequately as per the scales. However, in such instances government should exercise powers to discipline the school managements rather than take over the task of distributing salaries to the teachers. But most of the erring managements are those which are run by the politicians. As the government is unable to discipline politicians, they instead indulge in taking over one function after the other in the administration of education.

Finally, the government leaders are never tired of the phrase that 'education is national investment'. But what is the preference of successive governments in this country? The government spends less than three per cent of its resources on education. The New Educational Policy of the Rajiv government and later V.P. Singh government spoke of investing at least six per cent in education. But that has been a distant dream. In the meantime, government grant-in-aid is mainly used by it as a means to control the educational administration rather than to promote education.

A majority of governments in the country treat their grants-in-aid as loaves of bread thrown at a beggar. There is no grace in distributing grants. Schools once permitted to be started, do not get grants-in-aid for five to seven years. The government has no policy on the medium of instruction in schools education. Governments permit English medium schools to be started but refuse them grants-in-aid, on the pretext that those who seek English education can afford to pay for it. But in reality quite contrary to it, even taxi drivers, peons in government offices seek admissions for their wards into English medium schools. When you ask them for reasons, they reply "We lacked an education and have to do the job of driving a cab; at least let my child get a good education so that he can become a clerk". Leaders of parochial, regional, chauvinist groups who propagate the regional language as the medium of instruction send their own children to English medium schools. But they are very vocal in advocating regional media for others.

If the English medium schools are denied aid, they should be permitted to charge fees equivalent to the cost of education. But in this respect governments are still following populist measures. They would like to control fee rates in such schools to please parents, but they would like to compel the managements to disburse government prescribed pay scales to please the teachers while at the same time legislate to ban donations to please the parents. Then where will the money necessary to run the school come from? It is high time the government realised the basic lesson that its control over the educational administration is ideal only when it is commensurate with its own contribution in providing that education.

In the forty years of semi-socialism that our governments claimed to have practiced, they have acquired a bureaucracy that is least qualified, almost illiterate in effect, recruited to fulfill its goal of social obligations rather than for its commitment to the cause of education. Some of the people working in educational directorates in this country like education inspectors or assistant inspectors will never be able to get even a clerical job in a private firm. But it is this poorly equipped bureaucracy that has acquired arrogance of power, because of excessive control given to them by the law-makers.

Many of those who have acquired power to regulate educational administration from ministers, law-makers and bureaucrats are themselves guilty of crimes they are supposed to control in the interests of community.

How can for instance Education Inspector, an Assistant Education Inspector institution running an educational institution on a commercial motive and not as a social action exercise powers of checking abuse of power?

This plea for Liberalisation in the field of education, however, does not mean that government should lay its hands off the field altogether. But it should only be concerned with education to the extent of laying down the broad purposes of education, syllabi, minimum wages, qualifications of teachers etc. without involving itself into minor details of educational administration.

In this direction we need to have a totally new thinking in exercising government supervision over the educational administration. The entire idea of direction of education through a directorate, is a colonial hangover and it must go. The British needed to direct the education, towards their own purposes. But Indian democracy, to be liberal needs a community group, call it an 'Education Commission' consisting of teachers and educational administrators, selected on the basis of their merit and commitment, to exercise discipline in educational field. It should be the function of this educational commission to visit the schools periodically and see that larger goals of the community are fulfilled.

An Education Commission should be created at the level of every district and there should be an apex body at the state level to provide broad guidance at the state level. The members of this body should be drawn from amongst the educationists, teachers and administrators of educational societies for a fixed term with a ban on appointment for more than two terms.

Education is too important to be controlled and guided by bureaucrats who have lost touch with education ever since they came out from their schools or colleges.

Chapter - 6

Decentralise Education

(Mid-Day, 13 August 1992)

"The way out from this cancerous corruption is to extend the newly-introduced liberalisation policy to secondary and higher secondary education and minimise government control".

The Report 'College admissions at a price' (Mid-Day, July 24, 1992) carries a shocking revelation by Principal M S Kambli that students pay ₹ 15,000 to 25,000 to government-managed admission centres for colleges of their choice. This shows the rot that has set in the field of education because of over centralisation of control by the government. What exactly is meant by government? In reality, it means some semi-educated clerks and teacher-bureaucrats who lost their 'teaching spirit' long back. Today government controls every minute detail of school and junior college education. The grant-in-aid to junior colleges is in effect controlled by some clerks and education authorities. This gives them scope to make a fast buck often by arbitrary exercise of power.

You want appointments cleared, grants disbursed, arrears paid or qualification approved, causing inordinate delays or raising doubts is their way to make some easy money.

In this corruption-ridden atmosphere, the 'admission centres' are another avenue for more money. If it is true that admission centre staff collect bribes from willing parents, there is another side to this rotten system. This is revealed by a long list, published in newspapers, of junior colleges attached to high schools which still have vacant seats. In a recent policy statement the government made a case for attaching more higher secondary classes to schools.

Students will find a more congenial atmosphere in schools. But in Bombay, more students are absorbed by colleges. As a result, students and parents clamour for admission there.

In such a situation, schools face a problem in reverse. If the junior college facilities are not fully utilised, schools will face an additional financial burden. But the admission centres are not concerned with such problems of school managements. If schools offer some incentives to staff at the centres, they could get some students with good percentages. Otherwise, they will send only those who have passed the Secondary School Certificates with two or three attempts but still seek admission to junior colleges.

This avenue for corruption is in addition to more durable methods, such as appointment of peons, clerks or laboratory assistants in government-aided schools and junior colleges. The education authorities will send their nominees, and principals feel obliged to accept them as they fear a penalty for defiance. The way out from this cancerous corruption is to extend the newly introduced liberalisation policy to secondary and higher secondary education and minimise government control. Firstly, the directorate of education must be abolished. The directorate is a colonial concept. Education must be directed by active educators on the government's behalf, that is the community at large.

This does not mean that there will be absolutely no government and public control. This community control can be exercised by the secondary and higher secondary education commission. Its members and education officers under its supervision should be drawn from educators strictly on contractual terms with a proviso to go back to their schools or colleges without loss of seniority or emoluments.

All collective functions on behalf of society and state should be exercised by it. The state education commission needs sub-commissions on a zonal basis so as to be closer to schools.

In a decentralised system, there is no place for admission centres. Admissions should be left to educational institutions under guidelines laid by the commission.

Of course, it does not mean that under the new system there will be no corruption. There could still be some principals, managements or politicians trying to make easy money. But in all these cases, school committees, parent-teacher associations or officials at the decentralised levels can act as a check on corruption.

The proposed system will have immediate gains. Corruption will not be attributed to the government. To that extent, with its credibility restored, it can act as a supervisor when schools or junior colleges are involved in gross abuse of trust reposed in them by society.

Chapter - 7

Are Aryans Original Inhabitants of India?

(Free Press Journal, 4 January 1993)

We need to follow the words of Vivekananda: "Everything that come from India take it as true until you find cogent reasons for disbelieving it".

School books in history introduced by the now dismissed BJP government in UP received much attention in the English newspapers. These reports mainly acused the BJP government of having distorted Indian history to subserve its political goal of promoting ***Hindutva***. Other headlines have charged the UP government of making history or indoctrinating students.

What are these distortions? From various press reports, it is clear that ancient Indian history of the Vedic times was given more emphasis in these books. Let me take one clear issue of great importance: these history books in UP have incorporated the theory that Aryans were natives of India and did not come from across the Himalayas. This, the government's new text books did only after giving other theories as well, though the emphasis is on the theory that Aryans are natives of India.

Are these new distortions of Indian history or merely corrections of old distortions introduced by the western scholar during their imperial rule of India? It has been argued by some scholars that the western historians deliberately distorted ancient Indian History. ***Ithihasa Bhushana,*** Dr S.D. Kulkarni, a Sanskrit Scholar, retired administrator-turned historian, for instance, in his first volume,

Beginnings of Life, Culture and History (1988) his projected 18 volumes on Indian History and Culture provides, very convincing arguments with evidence as to the motive of these western scholars in distorting ancient Indian history.

He provides ample material on the subject. Take for instance Professor Max Mueller, doyen amongst foreign Indologists, has ulterior motives in translating the Vedas. In a letter to his wife in 1896 he wrote that "the translations of the Vedas will hereafter tell to a great extent on the fate of India and on the growth of millions of souls in that country. It is the root of their religion and to show them what the root, I fell, sure, is the only way of uprooting all that sprung from it during the last 3000 years". What he wished to take the place of uprooted roots in India becomes clear in his letter written in 1898 to the then British Secretary of State for India when he said "the ancient religion of India is doomed and if Christianity does not step in whose fault will it be?"

It is clear from the research of Dr Kulkarni that the Aryans were the original inhabitants of India and there were no hordes or Aryans invading and destroying Indus Valley Civilisation. However, this theory that Aryans were outside invaders was very handy to subserve British Imperial designs of establishing that Indians are incapable of ruling themselves. They were always conquered and ruled by foreigners. Thus, the British were the only recent ones to rule; before them the Muslims and scores of other invading foreigners, going back to Aryans who came to India from Central Asia. This theory not only helped the British to impose their political rule but cultural and religious hegemony over Indians as well.

Like projecting Aryans as outside invaders, western imperialists also promoted a theory of the Aryans and Dravidians as separate races to perpetuate their rule in India by adopting the doctrine of 'Divide and Rule'. Dr Kulkarni again traces the Aryan Dravidian hypothesis to a meeting of the Royal Asiatic Society on 9th April, 1866 in London. "As a result", Dr Kulkarni concludes, "the seeds of schism between the Tamilians of the South and the rest of Indians has been sown and developed".

With the Western education, we have lost our soul. Generations of historians educated and brought up in the Western style have only pursued what the western scholars wrote without even bothering to check it with reference to the authentic Indian source.

It is time we base our ancient Indian history on our sources to check the Western writings. If all these years under the British and then under their imitators, history books said that Aryans were invaders and now if the history books try to counter it by giving another version that Aryans were the original inhabitants of India, should our secular pundits try to give it a Communal colour? Probably we need to follow the words of Swami Vivekananda, "Everything that comes from India take it as true until you find cogent reasons for disbelieving it."

Chapter - 8

Another Indian History

(The Weekend Observer, 17 July 1993)

"Indian history was tailored to suit the British, claim Indian scholars. So is the new version a distortion of Indian history or is it a correction of earlier distortions?"

History books introduced by the UP government in their schools received much attention in the English newspapers. These reports mainly accuse then Bharatiya Janata Party Government of having distorted Indian history to subserve their political goal of promoting 'Hindutva'.

Other headlines have charged the Uttar Pradesh Government of 'making history' or "indoctrinating students"! What are these distortions? From various press reports, it is clear that ancient Indian history of Vedic times has been given more emphasis in these books.

Let me take one clear issue that these books in UP have incorporated the theory that Aryans were natives of India had not come from across the Himalayas.

This, the government's new text-book has done only after giving other theories as well, though the emphasis is on the theory that Aryans are natives of India.

Are these distortions of Indian history or merely corrections of distortions introduced by the Western scholars during Imperial Rule of India?

It has been argued by some scholars that the western historians deliberately distorted ancient Indian history.

Dr S D Kulkarni, a Sanskrit scholar turned historian, for instance, in his first volume, Beginning of life, culture and history (1988) in his project of 18 volumes of Indian History and Culture provides very convincing arguments with evidence as to the motive of these western scholars in distorting ancient Indian history.

He provides ample material on the subject.

Take for instance Professor Max Mueller, doyen amongst the foreign Indologists, had ulterior motives in translating the Vedas.

In a letter to his wife in 1896 he wrote that 'the translations of the Vedas' will hereafter tell to a great extent on the fate of India and on the growth of millions of souls in that country.

It is the root of their religion and to show them what the root is, I feel, is the only way of uprooting all that sprung from it during the last 3000 years. What he wished to take the place of uprooted roots in India becomes clear in his letter written in 1898 to the then British Secretary of State for India where he said, "The ancient religion of India is doomed end if Christianity does not step in whose fault will it be?"

It is clear from the research of Dr Kulkarni, that, Aryans were the original inhabitants of India and there was no horde of Aryans invading North and destroying the Indus Valley Civilisation.

However, this theory that Aryans were outside invaders was very handy to subserve British Imperial designs of establishing that Indians are incapable of ruling themselves. They were always conquered and ruled by foreigners.

Thus, British were the only recent ones to rule before them the Muslims and scores of other invading foreigners, going back to Aryan who came to India from Central Asia.

This theory not only helped the British to establish their political rule but cultural and religious superiority over Indians as well.

Like projecting Aryans as outside invaders, western imperialists also promoted a theory of separate Aryan and Dravidian races to perpetuate their rule in India by adopting the doctrine of 'divide and rule'.

Dr Kulkarni again traces the Aryan-Dravidian hypothesis to a meeting of Royal Asiatic Society on 9th April 1866 in London. "As a result", Dr Kulkurni concludes, "The seed of schism between the Tamilians of the South and the rest of Indian has been sown and developed". With the western education, we have lost our soul. Generations of historians educated and brought up in the western style have only pursued what the western scholar wrote without even bothering to check it with reference to the authentic Indian sources.

It is really shocking to read that many eminent men were brought up in this tradition. R C Dutt, who has to his credit first History of Civilisation of Ancient India, writes in its Preface.

"I have freely quoted from them (western translation) and I have seldom thought it necessary to consult those original Sanskrit works."

By and large, after independence, secularism meant following in the footsteps of the western scholars for journalists, historians and intellectuals alike.

It is time we base our ancient Indian history on our sources to check the western writings. If all these years under British and then under their immitators, history books said that Aryans were invaders and now if the history books try to counter it by giving another version that Aryans were the original inhabitants of India, should our secular pundits try to give it a communal colour?

Probably we need to follow the words of Swami Vivekananda; "Everything that comes from India take it as true until you find cogent reasons for disbelieving it. Everything that comes from Europe take as false until you find cogent reasons for it".

Unfortunately, at present many commentators think that Indian history begins either with the Muslim rule or the British rule in India. For them everything, history included, is linked to electoral politics.

Chapter - 9

Corrupt Campuses

(Mid-Day, 9 February 1994)

"..... a Rotarian confronted me with a question: Is the corruption in Universities, less severe than that in Politics?"

In the early 1970's the rot was setting in nation's higher educational system, particularly in the north. By the early 1980's northern universities had become notorious for underhand dealings in the educational administration. You could get marks enhanced to pass, buy degree certificates, ghost writers were available to write PhD thesis, and faculty positions were freely auctioned.

This was done by ministerial sycophants appointed as vice-chancellors, who created their own circle of sycophants. This was particularly true of Bihar, Madhya Pradesh and Rajasthan.

But now, over the decade, the gangrene seems to have moved down to the west of the country, to Maharashtra. Today all universities are in trouble. It is not necessary here to catalogue the corrupt practices in each university to make a convincing case to describe the deterioration in the universities.

There are reports of degree certificates being sold with costs varying depending upon the faculty, hikes of marks, in direct proportion to the few thousand rupees disgorged and the faculties; academic appointments on non-academic considerations, and the all-pervading corruption in the higher educational administration.

This has put students and teachers alike in a quandary. Some begin to doubt the genuinueness of the degrees, while the rest of the world casts doubts on the degrees awarded by Indian universities.

I learnt this the hard way. Speaking at a Rotary Club meeting the other day, I made highly critical remarks about corruption in Indian politics, and how some elements have gnawed away at the integrity of political processes. I ended with a fervent plea to individuals to take up the cause to fight against corruption; since all state institutions and their leaders have lost the will power to check, let alone eradicate, corruption.

Under these circumstances, can one even hope a prime minister, an education minister, or a chief minister will take up cudgels on behalf of the public, I asked. During the question-answer session, a Rotarian confronted me with a question: Is corruption in the universities less severe than that in politics? For a second, I was ashamed that I too am a part of this rotten system.

But I recovered sufficiently to suggest that the nation observe a year a weeklong event, where people would publicly confess the corruption they have undulged in.

But, however badly they behave surprisingly teachers are still held in high esteem. According to a recent news report, teachers enjoy the highest position on the basis of their integrity.

In view of this, teachers in Maharashtra have a duty to check the deterioration in the standards of public morality in our society. If the temples of education in Maharashtra go the northern way, we will never be able to bring them back to the saner path.

The northern universities are living proof of this: examinations are not held regularly and teachers do not take classes politically-connected academicians continue to become vice-chancellors by provide lots of money and, once in the saddle, auction faculty positions. They are just recovering what they have invested. Recently there was a report that a physics readers were selected as professor of physics in the Patna University on the strength of his PhD in Hindi literature.

This has started happening in the universities in Maharashtra in a small way. Unless teachers and teachers unions, take up the task soon, it will be too late. Is this happening? There are no signs at least at the level of teachers organisation. For instance, the Bombay University and College Teachers Union has sent out a notice, asking teachers to join a morcha to Mantralaya on January 11, 1994.

Nine demands are listed, all relating to improvement of service conditions. It is regrettable that nowhere does it demand efforts to check corruption at high places. In the absence of priority, probity and integrity in educational campuses, teachers will not be able to enjoy any monetary benefits they may win.

It is the time that teachers speak out and retrieve higher education from the pits of corruption.

Chapter - 10

Funding Progress

(Mid-Day, 23 February 1994)

"Pouring funds into education can be a national investment which will improve the all-round quality of life. Has the government's recent decision to increase the allocation for education come too late?"

Prime Minister P V Narasimha Rao announced in Pune last month that government allocation to education will be raised from 3.8 per cent of the gross national product to six per cent in the Ninth Plan which will begin in 1997.

His promise is similar to many others made by politicians who have never tired of saying that expenditure on education is always a national investment. But when it comes to actual investment, defence, agriculture and industry get preference over education.

Since Independence, investment in education in the form of Five Year Plan allocations has shown a decline. In the First Five Year Plan, it was 7.5 per cent of the total outlay. In the Seventh Plan it was only 3.6 per cent – less than half of what it was under the First Plan.

Since the Rao government assumed office, in the name of liberalisation and encouraging individual initiative, public investment in education has considerably declined. Three instances will make this statement clear.

Earlier, schools received matching contribution from the government towards the development fund. But since 1992-1993, they were informed that there would be no funds forthcoming from the government. But the schools are expected to raise the necessary funds towards development.

To add insult to injury, heads of schools were threatened with stoppage of salaries–since paid directly by the government–if they did not manage to pay the school's share to the development fund.

Secondly, government audit squads were sent to schools and colleges to check their accounts of the past 10 years. The negatively trained auditors denied maintenance grants to schools knowing fully well that as long as teachers' salaries were not directly affected there would be no hue and cry. Loss of science apparatus or chemicals was secondary priority.

Thirdly, there were unsuccessful efforts by the administrative officers to disallow grants to the colleges for remission to college teachers for teaching at the postgraduate departments of a university.

The administration failed to understand that in the absence of college teachers sharing the postgraduate work, the universities would be required to appoint more teachers. Many postgraduate departments might even have had to be closed if college teachers did not share the work.

After all, universities are aided by the state and college teachers employed in the postgraduate departments are less expensive to the state than universities appointing more teachers in the postgraduate departments.

Whenever educational reforms, are implemented, the bureaucrats' aim is to reduce expenditure which is always at the cost of improving the quality of education.

Now, there is a move to consider the eighth standard as a part of upper primary rather than the secondary in the initial ten stage. If this is done, more undergraduate teachers can be appointed to teach at upper primary levels. This works out very convenient for the government as undergraduate teachers are paid less than the graduate teachers.

Some universities in Maharashtra, with great fanfare in the 1970s, introduced internal-cum-external scheme of assessment. Under the scheme, students are continuously assessed for 60 marks and only appear for an external examination of 40 marks rather than appear at the end of the academic year for 100 marks.

The aim was to keep the students on the move, make them read, discuss and develop their reasoning faculties rather than rely only on their memorizing abilities. A small number of students–those who were academically inclined–used to opt for this scheme.

However, someone in the bureaucratic setup considered setting up two sets of examination papers–one in 40 marks and another in 100 marks in the same subject as a more expensive proposition.

The need to increase the resources for education is urgent. The promise to hike the GNP percentage in the Ninth Plan, in 1997, has come too late, Action must be taken immediately.

Investment in education could eventually help the nation to reduce its expenditure on healthcare and family planning, to mention just two areas.

Rethink Needed

Certain populist measures adopted in the past must be reconsidered. For instance, education is free to girls till higher secondary. But should this also apply to girls from affluent families who can afford to pay for their education? It would be more pragmatic to impose an income limit on parents if girls are to receive free education, so that some resources can be diverted to provide free education to rural or urban poor boys.

Chapter - 11

Towards Breaking the Language Barrier

(Mid-Day, 9 March 1994)

> *"Instead of imposing a uniform language educational pattern, the government must give parents and schools the leeway to go in for their own formula. This will ensure that students do not lose their roots while learning both the national and regional languages".*

The Maharashtra government has introduced a new high-school syllabus which comes into force from June 1994 for Standard IX and June 1995 for Standard X.

The chairman of the Board of Secondary and Higher Secondary Education says the syllabus is based on the suggestions received on a widely circulated draft. But enquiries with a few school heads and managements reveal that they never even got the draft syllabus.

The revised syllabus in effect, introduces a new language pattern in the state within the broad national three-language policy. The main feature is the pre-eminent position given to the study of Marathi in the examination scheme for classes IX and X, either as first language (wherever it is the medium of instruction) or as second (wherever it is not), irrespective of the student's mother tongue. Some educationists and educational institutions have already protested against this.

English medium schools are affected worst by the new pattern English as the medium of instruction is prevalent not only in Bombay or Maharashtra but throughout the country, notwithstanding Uttar Pradesh Chief Minister Mulayam Singh Yadav's anti-English postures. So why do parents send their children to English medium schools?

Some, of course, prefer these schools because they hold jobs in which they can be transferred anywhere in the country. But the main reason is the perception that an English education helps improve economic status.

Many parents, even those without an English speaking environment around them, like taxi or autorickshaw drivers, have come to me seeking assistance to secure admission for their wards in English schools.

Whatever arguments are advanced to persuade them to send their children to schools where they can learn in their own tongue, be it Marathi, Gujarathi or Kannada, their standard response has been that they did not study and so ended up where they were; but they would like to provide their children a better education so they can at least get a white-collar job. Is it not a fact that employment opportunities are better for those who know good English?

For English medium schools the government has provided the following scheme: English as first language, Marathi as second and Hindi (100 marks) or a composite course of Hindi (50 marks) with any one of the following: Sanskrit, Pali, Ardhamagadhi, French, German, Russian, Urdu, Arabic or Persian (50 marks).

Thus, teaching of Marathi is compulsory as a second language. In the new scheme, there is no scope for learning one's mother tongue. As a matter of fact the entire scheme is based on the medium of instruction and not the mother tongue.

An exception to this is the case of students whose mother tongue is Urdu but medium of instruction is Marathi. Such schools can drop the teaching of Hindi altogether by offering a composite course of Urdu with Persian or Arabic.

Apart from convents, there are many schools run by south Indians, Gujaratis, Sindhis, and others in which the medium of instruction is English. As it is these students study Marathi from Class III or VIII. This formal knowledge of the language and the fact that they live in

Maharashtra should be enough to provide them a working knowledge of Marathi.

But what about the study of a child's own tongue in an English medium school? A provision must be made for a formal study of such languages, preferably from Class III to X. In its absence, children will be cut off from their roots.

This makes even economic sense. Many non-Marathi-speaking people come to Bombay in search of employment or because they hold transferable jobs, as indeed do many Marathi-speaking people. In the absence of a formal education in their own languages, they will be forced to remain in Bombay, contributing to further congestion in the already bursting city. This will put additional pressure on the state government to generate jobs through industrialisation, aggravating urban problems.

On the other hand, a formal study of the mother tongue will leave the door open for the next generation of migrants to find jobs in their own states, as wider industrialisation increases employment opportunities there.

Another adverse feature of the new language pattern is that it makes it impossible for an English medium school to provide for the study of Sanskrit as a full subject, while Marathi medium schools can offer it.

Under these circumstances, what needs to be done is to give the widest possible choice to parents and schools to go in for their own formula for the study of languages. English-medium schools should be allowed to offer a second language in the form of a composite course of any modern Indian languages or a single modern Indian language, depending upon the students' mother tongue from Class III to VIII, with Sanskrit or Hindi as the third language. This will not be too much of a strain as children are adept at picking up languages quite easily.

In Class IX and X, under the three-language formula, it should be made possible for schools to offer any three languages (of 100 marks each) or one language (medium of instruction) and two other composite language papers of the student's choice, rather than straitjacket the languages into fixed patterns. This will make the imparting of linguistic knowledge more student-friendly.

The state, in the process, will ensure that the regional and national languages are taught to the extent that the student can acquire a working knowledge of both to help him/her be a truly 'national' citizen.

Chapter - 12

Language Muddle

(Mid-Day, 30 March 1994)

"Is it not necessary that they (linguistic minority schools) also be given an opportunity to study their mother tongue either as a second language or at least as a part of a composite course either with Marathi or Hindi?"

The state government's decision to make Marathi compulsory in English medium schools as the second languages has been widely and rightly criticised. The bias becomes apparent when we note that other language schools like Hindi or Kannada have at least the option of studying Marathi (100 marks) or Marathi (50 marks) as a part of a composite course. If this bias was incidental to the principle of prescribing a language policy strictly on the basis of medium of instruction, irrespective of student's mother tongue, one could understand it.

But that is not the case. The government is aware that child's mother tongue may be other than the medium of instruction. However, this recognition is limited only to Urdu-speaking children studying in Marathi medium schools.

An Urdu student in a Marathi school can offer Marathi and English as first and third language respectively and can study his mother tongue as a composite course with Hindi.

Second, he can drop Hindi altogether for a composite course of Urdu with Arabic or Persian. Third, and more importantly, while studying in a Marathi medium school, because his mother tongue is Urdu, it is also possible to study Urdu as the first language and Marathi as the second.

Fourth, even while studying in English medium those whose mother tongue is Urdu can offer it as composite course with Hindi while denying this privilege to others.

Naturally the government needs to explain these exceptions, while providing a language pattern on the basis of medium of instruction to other groups. It is such actions which provide a handle to politicians to charge the government with appeasement of the minorities.

Probably the minorities never asked for it. However, government can claim it as a reflection of their sensitivity to religious minorities. In that case why does it not show similar feelings for other linguistic minorities?

In cities like Bombay or Poona, not only those whose mother tongue is Urdu go to Marathi schools. Even those who speak Gujarati and Kannada send their children to them. Is it not necessary that they also be given an opportunity to study their mother tongue either as a second language or at least as a part of a composite course either with Marathi or Hindi?

These shortcomings not only cause political problems but are also legally discriminative. The best the government can do is to postpone the introduction of its new policy by one year and hold consultations not only with MPs and MLAs, but also with school authorities.

This will help restore a sense of justice and fair play without creating any linguistic chauvinism or jingoism.

Chapter - 13

In Defence of

(Mid-Day, 4 May 1994)

"Providing a course in defence studies will help instil a sense of discipline and nationalism in the younger generations".

After reading two of my critical articles on government's new language policy proposed to be introduced in the school curriculum from June 1994, a friend called to ask whether I see anything good in the government's new syllabus for standards IX and X. I had a fresh look at the syllabus going beyond the language policy. I would like to write today on the introduction of defence studies–a subject in which I have developed considerable interest over the last 20 years as a part to a course in health and physical education.

The objectives of the course covered in two years are set clearly in the syllabus. The five objectives may be summarised as:

- To acquaint students with the aim of national defence and the role of Indian defence forces;
- To familiarise them with the defence organisation and its structure;
- To teach about the National Cadet Corps, territorial army and civil defence organisation;
- To promote emulation of defence men as role models for students' and

- To inculcate qualities of discipline and leadership and an understanding and appreciation of the national defence force and create a sense of national loyalty among students.

  Teaching of defence in schools will have at least three advantages:

- The course will help inculcate an appreciation of significance of national security in a nation's life. There is undoubtedly a lack of appreciation in the country of functions performed by the national armed forces under extremely trying conditions.
- The course should also help those who intend to join the forces by giving them basic knowledge on the purpose and organisation of the Indian armed forces. By and large service in the armed forces is looked down by parents, unless there is a tradition in the family to serve in the armed forces.
- Today, it is rarely that one comes across young men and women stating their life ambition as to join the forces. Everyone wants to be an engineer or a doctor and eventually run away to the United States for a lucrative job.
- It will help instil a sense of discipline and nationalism in the younger generations. Today, everyone in India thinks of taking away a slice of the nation's wealth without caring a bit for it or having any pride in being an Indian.

However, it is not enough for the government to provide a course on the paper on defence studies. Because, it was there even in the earlier syllabus. But hardly any school in Maharashtra is known to have seriously implemented it. Hence, the educational authorities should create sufficient and necessary conditions to see that schools introduce it in their curricula seriously.

Some of these conditions are:

- School intending to start the course ought to be provided with extra grants to buy equipment and material necessary to teach the course in the right way.
- There should be proper liaison between schools teaching the course and various wings of the nation's armed forces.

Teachers of the course should be well trained with the provision for regular refresher courses. Students offering the subject should also be exposed to men drawn from all branches of the armed forces.

- Examinations in the subject should be taken more seriously. As per the previous and present syllabus, exams are to be conducted by schools internally. Thus, every school tends to give marks in the medium range and every student scores on average a 'B' grade.

  While continuing to hold these examinations internally, the government should prescribe the need for the presence and participation of external examiner, preferably those in service or retired from the armed services.

  An imaginative course like defence studies taught with a commitment and concern for the nation, will go a long way in creating generations of young men and women imbued with a spirit of nationalism always willing to place the national interest far above self-interest. That is the need of the hour.

Chapter - 14

No Defence

(Mid-Day, 25 May 1994)

"The importance given to defence studies a subject critical in the present security environment is pathetic"

IN MY article (Mid-Day, May 4), I had said that defence studies must be part of the school curriculum.

But what is the status of defence/security studies in Indian colleges and universities? Dismal. Though there are more than 100 universities in the country only four offer courses on defence/security studies.

For obvious reasons of security, British rulers were not interested in introducing sensitive subjects like security studies in the preindependent India. But efforts after independence, have been halfhearted and haphazard.

In 1963, the Bihar education commission sent a proposal to the Union government to introduce military science at the undergraduate level. The proposal was accepted by the then Education Minister, Late M C Chagla in 1964.

Since then the proposal has been examined by more than half a dozen committees of the education and defence ministries and the University Grants Commission.

They suggested the following:

- Military studies could be an optional subject like political science or economics at the undergraduate level. Later the

UGC felt that it should be designated defence studies and limited to the postgraduate level.

- It should be treated as an academic study unrelated to the NCC or practical aspects of military training.
- There should be close and continuous interaction between teachers and the defence forces.
- There should be regular monitoring of the teaching by the UGC.

Nearly 30 years after the concept was mooted, only four universities provide either some courses or a degree in defence studies. In Maharashtra, Poona University is the only university that offers the course. The subject is taught at the under-graduate level since 1964.

At the post-graduate level students can obtain MA, MPhil and PhDs in defence and security studies. Other universities which provide these subjects are Allahabad, Madras and Jadavpur.

For a nation of 900 million people this is inadequate. It is necessary for every educated person to have some knowledge of what constitutes national defence or national security.

In India it is particularly necessary, as despite the improvement in the security environment in many parts of the world, South Asia has not seen any decline in security tensions.

A UGC committee had made some important observations in its December, 1987 ***Report in Defence/Strategic Studies***. It suggested the introduction of a paper on national security as an additional part of existing courses. The natural discipline where it could be added is political science.

An introduction of a course on national security at the undergraduate level will, according to the report promote a general awareness for national security in the country.

It will also enable students who opted for defence studies, to continue it at the postsecondary level. They would provide the basic intake to postgraduate departments of defence/security studies.

It would help strengthen their interest in armed forces in general. Such graduates, can do well in recruitment for the armed forces.

The report observed that "teaching and research in defence/ strategic studies" as a specialised field should be limited to postgraduate level in universities and not in colleges. This was because of the limited expertise available in the country as well as lack of job opportunities. There is however an urgent need to introduce courses in defence/national security/strategic studies at the PG level in a few more universities, in addition to introducing an optional paper on national security.

Today vital national security decisions in government are made by generalist bureaucrats and opportunistic politicians. There are not even enough commentators in the country who can tell politicians–whether they care to listen or not–where and why they go wrong in managing national security of the country.

Chapter - 15

Harsh Realities

(Mid-Day, 8 June 1994)

"After HSC, medicine or engineering need not be the ultimate goal. There are other equally rewarding courses"

The 1994 Higher Secondary Certificate results are out. Thus, begins another mad season of parents and student trying to get into the best professional course and college.

What are the harsh realities of the post–HSC world for those who are in this mad season in 1994? Unless these realities are properly understood by the parents and their wards, they may create a world of illusion which may lead to delusion and end only in disappointment.

There are three major realities:

- There can be only one Abhijit with 96, 17 per cent who could top in the city. The board should explain why and where he lost 3.83 per cent! Though every parent wished his offspring to be Abhijit, not everyone can be. President J F Kennedy's brother-in-law Sargent Shriver often used to tell his son that at his age he was jogging several miles a day. Having heard it many times, the son one day told him. "dad, at your age uncle Kennedy became the President."
- Not all can and need to become a doctor or an engineer. It is necessary to know the aptitude of the child before choosing the career. In recent years, those who topped the list in the Indian Administrative Service have had medical or

engineering degrees. They could have scored even better if they had gone to the Arts stream. Should therefore, those who desire to go eventually to management courses or appear for the IAS, waste their and the nation's resources by going to a professional college?

- Even if one's aptitude is for a professional course, not all will get admission in aided colleges. If you do not succeed in getting into an aided professional course, you may pursue diploma courses in engineering or other equally important professional courses. But do not knock at the door of an unaided college, where the fees are ₹ 32,000 for engineering and ₹ 1,17,500 for medical, though the minimum percentage required for admission is 50. With that low a percentage a student will simply not be able to complete his or her professional course regularly without failures and ATKTs. A product of such a process will not shine or even survive in the job market.
- In the 1950s even those with 50 per cent marks in inter-Science, could get admission in medical colleges. A friend, with little over 30 per cent got a medical seat in a donation college of the South. After six or seven years in the college, he completed his MBBS. He is practicing medicine in a dispensary run by a trust. But he is good in investing little money that he makes in the share market. Thinking of him, I always feel that if he had gone into commerce, he could have been a well known share broker and made a lot more money, as well.
- India, with her vast economic potential now being opened for humane exploitation, parents and students must realise that we not only need doctors and engineers but managers, administrators, educators, researchers, scientists and journalists as well. We have left these fields to mediocres for so long, it is time that the best and the brightest come to occupy nation building occupations through a study of liberal arts and science courses. That happening, India can emerge as a major economic and political power in the twenty-first century. Think.

Chapter - 16

Free For All

(Mid-Day, 29 June 1994)

"Should the government try to aid and provide professional courses, when even after 47 years of independence we have not succeeded in providing free and compulsory primary education to all as mandated by the Constitution? It is time to get our priorities straight. The provision of free and compulsory primary education to all should be the first priority of the government".

In my article on Harsh realities (June 8, 1994), I had suggested that students should not waste scarce resources of their parents by pursuing wrong courses. Today, I would like to make a suggestion to the government in the overall context of economic liberalisation on optimal utilisation of scarce resources.

Undoubtedly the governments-national and states–face a resource crunch. On the face of it, the government is trying to spread its limited resources to all sectors of education from KG to PG. Such thin spread of scarce resourced on a wide canvas only evaporates without creating any impact.

But should the government try to aid and provide professional courses, when even after 47 years of independence we have not succeeded in providing free and compulsory primary education to all as mandated by the Constitution?

Hence it is time to get our priorities straight. The provision of free and compulsory primary education to all, irrespective of caste, creed, religion, sex or medium of instruction or date of establishment of a primary school should be the first priority of the government.

The fact that English medium schools are discriminated in matters of aid is well known. But what is not so well known is the fact that in the same area one English medium school may get aid while another is deprived of it. Second, resources permitting, secondary education should also be provided free as some states have already done.

This only means that all higher education ought to be made to pay for itself. The college and universities should charge fees sufficient to pay salaries of staff and meet their other recurring expenditures. The government aid to the higher educational institutions should be limited to capital expenditure.

This will have two advantages which will make higher education, including professional, value added and socially well-committed.

First, at once it will obliterate the present distinctions between aided and unaided institutions on the one hand, and on the other, paying and free seats in the professional colleges.

This way those who now pay will pay less and those who get free seats in the professional colleges will pay substantially more. Then, everyone will strictly get admission on merit with the exception of those who come under the reserved categories. The choice of college will strictly be on the basis of merit.

Some may argue that this will make meritorious students to pay more. This is an erroneous notion. Each pays for the cost of services he receives; nothing more, nothing less, irrespective of his ability to absorb what he receives.

On the other hand, present distinction of 'paying' and 'free' creates anomalies of the worst kind. A child of poor may get a paying seat while a child of a multimillionaire may get into free category thereby making poor to subsidise the education of rich.

But under the new dispensation, for those who are poor but deserving, provision must be made for concessional lending by banks, a social obligation better served than their lending money at two to four per cent interest to their employees for house building as at present. If banks are still contrained by limited resources, they need not write off loans of politically poor or ministers be prevented from holding loan melas.

The second advantage of the suggested reform will be that it will limit brain drain. Today cheaply educated graduates and postgraduates emigrate to foreign pastures, mainly to the US. This was described as an asset in foreign bank by late Rajiv Gandhi, while a former American Consul General in Bombay called it as foreign aid in reverse-from India to the US.

The economic gains or losses involved in brain drain can be a subject of study. But on the face of it, it is a net loss than a gain. But if someone still wants to go, he could go once he clears the loan he has incurred in getting his higher education.

However, so far there has been a strong belief amongst the informed public, that the proposal for higher education to pay for itself will not be acceptable to our rule-making social elite, as they are the largest beneficiaries of low fees and brain drain. Manmohanomics should prove it wrong if economic liberalisation is to work successfully.

Chapter - 17

Down with Groupism

(Mid-Day, 13 July 1994)

"interstate mobility of teachers.......Let law ensure stipulating that service in one state be counted in another for retirement benefits"

Experts at different level agree that promotion of national integration is an important goal of education. Thus, for instance, Curriculum for primary education: 1988 highlights promotion of the spirit of national integration as a goal of primary education. The higher secondary education board has recently introduced an education subject at the higher secondary level. The syllabus emphasises promotion of national integration as a role of education in life.

That is the way it should be. In a developing society education is a powerful instrument to mould the character of the younger generation so as to point them in the desired direction. However, the authorities seek to achieve it through the contents taught in subjects like history, language and culture. Has it been achieved in the 47 years after independence? Actually we have miles to go before we can confidently say yes.

This hesitation arises from the fact that all these years, educational policy-makers while trying to promote national integration through textbooks, have acted to negate the goal in practice.

Let us take one example of easy mobility of student and teacher population. Certain actions of educational bureaucracy are positive hurdles in the mobility of students and teachers. Mobility in search of good or appropriate education and employment has been an important factor in the process of national integration.

The regionalisation of medium of instruction at the secondary and higher secondary levels has restricted mobility of students. Only those who belong to linguistic minority groups in cities like Bombay can move to their own states. Those who go to English medium schools also have a better mobility.

Even in these instances, Maharashtra has acted to check teachers mobility by prescribing arbitrary rules of equivalence. This is particularly the case with certain special subjects in schools. The government wants drawing teachers teaching in linguistic minority schools to possess the training qualifications acquired within the state. This is done by not recognising training qualifications from other states.

If linguistic minorities are allowed to provide education in their mother tongue, teachers teaching drawing or craft or any other special subject, ought to be in a position to explain the subject through the mother tongue of the child. But often it is difficult to get teachers in these subjects with qualifications acquired from within the state.

Take for instance, Maharashtra's rule which regulate the service conditions of lecturers who come from outside the state. Until recently, it did not consider service rendered in a college or university outside the state for fixation of scale in the state. But now after prolonged pressure from teachers', unions, the state has agreed to count it.

Yet, the state has refused to count service outside the state for retirement benefits. The general argument is that more people come to Bombay than people from Bombay or Maharashtra go outside. That is to say the teachers mobility increases the burden on the state exchequer. Even if we grant that is true, is it not a fact that these outsiders also contribute more to the state? It is a well known fact, that Bombay contributes one-third of the total income tax collect in the nation.

If the state finds it an unbearable burden, the time is ripe for the centre to intervene. As it is, for those who move to the centre from a brief service in any state, a provision exists to count the service for retirement benefits provided the institution where the teacher worked has been in receipt of grants-in-aid of at least percent. A similar law to cover inter-state mobility of teachers is necessary stipulating that service in one state be counted in another for retirement benefits.

It a state like Maharashtra still finds the burden unacceptable, the law could also make it obligatory for the precious employer to transfer an equivalent contribution to the retirement fund when a teacher moves from one state to another.

Another alternative could also be considered. It is to form a separate national educational pension fund to which teachers retirement entitlements are transferred irrespective of where a teacher commences his service or retires. The equation involved here is between the state's parochial consideration of financial burden and considerations of strengthening the process of national integration through easy movement of teachers from one state to another. The consideration of national integration outweighs the consideration of financial burden to the state.

Chapter - 18

Black or White?

(Mid-Day, 27 July 1994)

"There have been reports of racial discrimination against black African students in Bombay University. Considering that they could play a crucial role in relations between their country and ours, it is vital that their experience here is made pleasant".

More than one newspaper has carried the story of racial discrimination against black African students in Bombay University's International Students' Hostel, I do not propose to discuss the veracity or the otherwise of this complaint. What I propose to discuss here is that there is a need to create a positive atmosphere in our university to attract foreign students.

First, UGC Chairman Dr G Ram Reddy has very rightly advocated a need to market education by our universities in the light of economic liberalisation. In this regard, many universities have already increased the fees for foreign students. We need not be apologetic about it as even developed countries like Britain, for instance follow a similar policy. In the US federal structure state universities charge more fees to students coming from outside that state.

Second, many foreign students come to India on a bilateral programme of international exchange of students. An advantage of this is that it helps to generate goodwill and understanding between India and developing countries of Asia and Africa.

Eventually, foreign students act as a group of citizens sympathetic to the country that acted as a host to them. These students, when they go back to their country and occupy position of power in politics, bureaucracy, business or education, will be able to explain the policies of our country to their countrymen. In brief, they are the ambassadors of goodwill for India.

However, if these students carry a negative image of Indians, it would defeat the very purpose of this international exchange of students. Thus, it is saddening to read that African students are annoyed with Indians, by and large.

Why should Indians suggest that Africans should return to their countries as early as possible after completing their studies? The feeling, as expressed by a Sudanese student–"there are so many Indians in our countries. Remember, our song when we return will be, 'Finish your business and go',"–is harmful to India's long-term interests.

What can be done to create a positive impression among the foreign students in our universities? A university system can think of several steps without much financial investment, given the leadership and will to improve our image.

First, special attention can be given to the National Day celebrations of various countries, either in the university or the hostel where the students live. It is better that such days are celebrated in the university campuses as other students can also participate.

Second, the faculty should be encouraged consciously to invite foreign students to social get-togethers, home parties and Indian National Day celebrations. Faculty members specialising in a particular area can be requested to take the initiative to invite students from their region.

None of these activities cannot be conducted without an academic acting as a full time or at least, to begin with, a part time foreign students adviser in the university campuses. This functionary ought to be sympathetic to foreign students and without a bureaucratic outlook. He should himself have not help from foreign student advisers abroad at some time or the other.

These advisers can also act as liaison officers for foreign students intending to enroll in different universities. He should enable them to get all information, arrange for their accommodation, and help them to get acclimatised to India. It must also be his task to help foreign students to see India during their stay, with concessional facilities from the railways, tourism development corporations, etc. Exposing them to Indian cultural shows should constitute and added responsibility.

Unfortunately, no such institutional arrangement exists in our university system at present. In this scenario, a professor showing a sympathetic approach to the problems of foreign students is occasionally interpreted as a special favour done with some ulterior motive.

In the 1980s, I had an occasion to suggest the appointing of a foreign student adviser to a vice-chancellor. After a few days, I was informed that the officer on special duty, appointed to conduct examinations, had been named foreign student adviser.

The rationale behind this move was not that he had anything to do with foreign students but that he happened to be the warden of the international students' hostel.

This will not work. Putting an official in charge of foreign students because it is convenient for the person concerned or because makes financial sense to the university, is not the way to promotion international goodwill and understanding.

In an increasingly interdependent world, in our plans to market education to sustain our liberalised economy, we need to be forward looking to learn never ways of improving international relations.

This can be done through making India a memorable experience for the foreign students who come to study here whether on their own or under an international student exchange programme. We cannot afford to make them feel that living in India was like living in a hell away from home.

Chapter - 19

Global Varsities must be Started

(Mid-Day, 10 August 1994)

"....an international university, called the Maharashtra International University, could be located in New Bombay... though Bombay is the nation's economic capital it has compared to other state capitals, fewer universities and deemed universities".

International universities must be set up in different parts of the country to attract foreign students for higher education in India as an alternative to the United States or Europe.

I had suggested the appointment of a foreign student advisor in universities as part of marketing education and for creating international goodwill and understanding between Indians and foreign nationals ('Black or white' **MID-DAY**, July 27, 1994).

Actually, this is only the first step in marketing education in a general way. More specifically, to attract foreign students, we need to think in terms of establishing the international universities, preferably on a regional basis.

India has surplus talent in all fields of social science, the humanities, medical science and technology. Such varsities need recruit only the best talent in India as teachers. They should provide undergraduate and graduate courses.

Since an international university is for catering to the educational needs of foreign students, at least 50 per cent students should be foreigners. Indians selected on a regional basis and on merit can be a bridgehead between foreigners and the rest of India. There are three nationally important advantages of such varsities beyond marketing education and goodwill:

They are an innovative way to equalise higher fees to foreign and Indian students. Though regular varsities charging a higher rate of tuition fees to foreign students are justifiable, they generate a feeling of differentiation if not discrimination among foreign students. But international varsities will charge the same for all students.

Many non-resident Indians of the first generation, accounting for nearly a million in the United States alone, are passing through a period of agonising reappraisal regarding their children's future as they are more American than Indian in their attitude and understanding of India and its culture.

They are looking forward for ways to have the American cake and retain the Indian cultural heritage too. As it is, many send their wards for medical and engineering education in India, as it is cheaper. International varsities providing courses in other disciplines too will help their wards learn more about India and retain a degree of Indian-ness as their parents by studying in international universities in India.

What is true of the non-resident Indians in the US and Europe is true of people of Indian origin in various countries in Africa, Asia and the Caribbean. They have only a romantic nostalgia of India with very few having any direct interaction with India and Indians. It is estimated that there are over 12 million of them scattered worldwide. An opportunity to study in India and acquire indepth knowledge of Indian society, polity and culture alone will help them become a strong pro-India voice in world affairs as well as in their own national lives.

With the liberalisation of the economy, there is bound to be a greater presence of foreign nationals on Indian soil as employees of multinationals or as trade representatives of various foreign companies in addition to employees of embassies and consulates.

During their brief stay, many may like to acquire specific skills through an Indian degree. These foreigners will find international varsities more akin to their educational need.

Bombay is the obviously a natural site for setting up an international university in the western region. It has been playing a critical role in the globalisation of Indian economy by acting as a gateway for foreign investment.

Such an international university, called the Maharashtra International University, could be located in New Bombay. As it is, though Bombay is the nation's economic capital, it has, compared to other state capitals, fewer universities and deemed universities.

Hyderabad, the state capital of Andhra Pradesh, has Osmania University, the University of Hyderabad and the Jawaharlal Technological University in addition to the Central Institute of English and Foreign Languages, a deemed university. Though Bombay's population is almost double that of Hyderabad, it has only the University of Bombay and a deemed university in the Tata Institute of Social Science in addition to the SNDT University.

The Maharashtra University should be provided land and infrastructure by the government and it should continue to provide state assistance to expand and improve infrastructure of capital expenses. The university however, should meet recurring expenditure through tuition fees and endowments.

Maharashtra has a reputation of being progressive in all fields other than education. Whenever educational issues have come up for consideration, the government has been very inept.

However, Chief Minister Sharad Pawar has been pro-liberalisation even when the Congress was officially trumpeting its commitment to socialism. He has taken several steps to attract foreign investment and said to believe in making Bombay, India's Hong Kong.

This idea is particularly relevant because after three years, Hong Kong's fate as a hub of financial activity is uncertain as it turns to be Chinese territory. The establishment of the Maharashtra University is complementary to Pawar's efforts to make Bombay the nerve centre of International economy.

Chapter - 20

Lost Cause

(Mid-Day, 31 August 1974)

"Teachers are entitled to medical benefits. But the procedure is so tedious that most forgo them, thus negating the purpose of the facility"

Until, the mid-1980s teachers did not enjoy the benefit of any medical facilities in cases of emergencies. Things changed in 1985 due to the driving efforts of the Bombay University and College Teachers Union. The BUCTU compelled the Maharashtra government to extend medical facilities to college and university teachers as available to government servants. It is time to evaluate if this is working. Has the extension of facility of medical treatment in government hospitals to teachers been effective in the face of growing medical expenses?

Based on various experiences it is reasonable to state that the scheme has been ineffective in securing medical treatment for teachers or in meeting their expenses.

There are several reasons for this state of affairs. First, government hospitals are not many and authorised hospitals are still fewer. In a city like Bombay there are three government hospitals and all three are in south Bombay.

Teachers living in the suburbs find in physically inconvenient to go to these hospitals which are otherwise overcrowded. It simply amounts to a loss of a day if they want to avail of the facilities.

Second, the procedure to get reimbursement of expenses in case of emergency treatment in private clinics/hospitals is so tedious that most prefer to forgo the claims that go through untold hardship.

The facilities provided on paper are negated in practice through the cumbersome procedures implemented by an unresponsive bureaucracy. The university or colleges should have been authorised to scrutinise bills for reimbursement to teachers. Instead, at present, the claim forms are scrutinised by an authorised superintendent of government hospitals.

He has to certify that the emergency treatment received by an employee of a college or university is one approved in the government resolution. Since teachers and employees of educational institutions are non-government employees they receive a different treatment. Normally such claims are rejected by the government doctor without assigning any reasons.

Third, if the claims are fortunate enough to get past the superintendent, a tougher battle awaits to get payment from the administrative officer of the region.

And this hurdle is not merely a part of general bureaucratic inertia. Majority of teachers do not belong to the government servants category. Hence, they do not possess any powers to render reciprocal favours which one government servant can extend to another.

Additionally, the officers of AOs are dens of corruption where teachers find it extremely difficult to get any payments authorised without an incentive. An employee whose claim has been approved by the medical superintendent will have to visit innumerable times before he can get the cheque.

It is time for the BUCTU and other teaching and non-teaching employees unions to take up this essential cause of making this facility real. The first step is to authorise the university or the college as the case may be, to decide whether a claim is within the purview of government resolution. If the claims are approved by them, they should also be authorised to make the payment.

This expenditure should be held eligible for hundred per cent grant by the government. It will help employees of educational institutions to get their money cleared with greater speed than at present. But it is only a short-term measure to effectively enjoy medical treatment on an emergency basis. On a long-term basis, it is necessary for the government and the BUCTU to demand some new measures so as to see that the employees of educational institutions do not waste their time commuting long distances to reach government hospitals to receive medical aid for general ailments.

In this regard it should be possible for the government to reimburse medical expenses to teachers and non-teaching employees up to one salary in a year without asking for production of any bills. Over and above this reimbursement should be on the basis of bills submitted with a limit up to one month salary. Similar provisions exist at present in Delhi University.

Chapter - 21

Forgotten Ideal

(Mid-Day, 14 September 1994)

"Unless the status of teachers is elevated and they are made to feel proud of their profession, Teachers' Day will continue to attract nothing more than a formal nod".

Teachers' Day was celebrated on September 5. On the occasion, President Shankar Dayal Sharma gave away national awards to teachers; similar award must have been given at the state, city, district, taluk and village levels, too. From the President down, dozens of official must have extolled the noble role played by teachers in society.

Teachers' Day commemorates the birth of former President S. Radhakrishnan, who was an eminent teacher. But there was no mention of him either in the newspapers or on TV (like, for instance, leaders garlanding his portrait or going round his Samadhi). It is clear that the President downwards, none remembered him. That is a reminder that teachers will be forgotton once Teachers' Day is over.

The day ought to be an occasion for thousands of teachers to do some self-introspection and evaluate themselves. Are they in the profession with an ideal commitment to be an educator and moulder of character of the young citizens? Or are they simply looking at teaching as a job, livelihood, to feed themselves and their families? Are they well equipped in their own field?

I must say that often we come across teachers who lack commitment and are poorly equipped. Sitting on the interviewing committees to select teachers, I have often found that aspirants to teaching positions could not even recall a single book they had read in their chosen discipline. Once, one candidate even told me that he had appeared for the interview because he was directed by the employment exchange to appear for it!

Hence, it is often said-that the teachers of today are not as committed as those in the past. They don't have the burning desire to achieve excellence. Many prefer to speak about the falling standards in the educational field. Of course, one way of looking at it is to think and there is an element of truth in it that it is an age old cliché. In this sense, the late V V John had written that if the standards have fallen, they have not fallen from a great height.

Many others, looking at the current academic scene in the context of the decline in ethical values in the contemporary society and polity, would say that teachers alone cannot be expected to maintain high standards, while it is true that a corrupt society cannot leave the teaching community untouched, the teachers have to rise above society to mould character. For this, they have to be made of better timber than others in society.

How do you get teachers with total commitment to manage the growing number of schools in the country? It may be difficult to attract committed people but once recruited, it is possible to create commitment in them.

The government needs to take certain concrete steps to make the profession attractive to talented persons. Some important steps may be listed here.

First, raise the minimum qualifications of teachers at the primary and secondary levels to that of a second class graduate with a training qualification.

Second, enable the teachers to keep abreast of the latest in their subject. Teachers are useful to students only if they can give them the knowledge they seek. The significance of this factor of utility in the student teacher relationship increases as the student moves to higher classes. Therefore, institutions must encourage teachers to buy books in their respective subjects by giving them a substantial book allowance every year.

Third, of all the people, it is teachers who should be able to visit different parts of the country on educational tours. This can be done by providing them leave travel concessions which, though given commonly to government employees and those in the corporate sector, has been denied so far to teachers on the excuse that they would utilise their LTC during the vacations instead of on educational tours.

Fourth, teachers should be encouraged to undertake research projects relevant to their teaching and field of academic study. The government should provide necessary and study leave facility to enable them to bring out the best of their creative abilities.

Fifth, teaching is a dead-end job. The majority of teachers retire as teachers unlike in the government, where a person joining as a clerk can hope to retire as a deputy or even a joint secretary. Hence, school teachers have to be paid adequately to maintain their self-respect and dignity.

If these steps are taken, I am sure the teaching profession will attract capable persons who can be torch-bearers of the highest values in society. No longer will a person come to the profession because he or she was asked by the employment exchange to do so.

Teaching is more than a job. It is a part of the nation-building process. Unless society at large takes this character of the profession seriously and is prepared to uphold its spirit and dignity, Teachers Days will come and go without making any lasting impact on society.

Chapter - 22

Spitter Spatter

(Mid-Day, 5 October 1994)

"There's more to getting an education than burying one's head in impressive tomes. Practicing good, clean living would do just fine".

Education should not be perceived merely as a means of instruction about useful skills or transmission of knowledge in a formal setting, but also as development of general and special abilities of the mind and contributing to the collective good of society.

Unfortunately, our educational system has failed to inculcate certain civic habits, the most glaring testament to which is the disgusting habit of spitting in public.

We have adopted the peacock as our national bird, the mango as our national fruit and the lotus as the national flower. Why not then dub spitting as our national disease, not with a view to preserving it but with an aim to eradicating it, by say, 2000 AD.

Recently, while travelling by bus, I wondered what would happen if the person sitting in front of me were to spit through the window. Then, before I knew it, my nightmare came true, and there was this awful patch of sputum on my hand, carried by the wind courtesy my co-passenger!

People sitting in the upper deck of buses often spit out of the window a habit which reminds me of the following poem:

I saw a sparrow in the sky,
It dropped some whitewash in my eye,

I didn't swear, I didn't cry,
I just thanked the Lord,
That cows don't fly!

The fact that spitting is an Indian national disease was born out of my observation in areas in the United States where Indians predominate, like Jackson Heights (New York). In places like these, public spitting is very common.

Even in a country like Singapore, where a habit like this is prohibited by law, the condition of public utilities in a temple confirmed my belief that Indians possessively cling to their habits.

Paan chewing is what contributes to the perpetuation of this sickening trait. If one needs any confirmation, one need only look at the lower three feet of the huge pillars on the platforms of Victoria Terminus in Bombay. Here, the garish red hue of the structures tells its own story.

The floor and walls at the booking counters and waiting rooms of railway stations are further proof, not that this is necessary. Which tempts me to believe that if persons in the habit of spitting carry certificates proving that they do not carry germs of contagious diseases can be employed to clear public places of graffiti by spitting uniformly!

It is absolutely imperative that the state government and the Bombay Municipal Corporation take serious note of this habit and consider ways to eradicate it on a war footing. Here are some steps that may be taken:

- All schools ought to devote at least one period a week exclusively to inculcate the importance of good manners not only at home but also in public places.

Such instruction should begin from the kindergarten itself and continue through all levels of education.

I have made enquiries with primary school teachers who tell me they do teach children cleanliness-personal and environmental. And a perusal of the syllabus shows that as a part of the 'Work Experience' subject, children are to be instructed "to cultivate good hygienic habits necessary for healthy life...".

That is has not made any impact so far is all too clear.

- Second, Doordarshan should use the National Network to start a campaign against public spitting as they have one against rash driving or smoking. Flashes should be shown not only on the news bulletins, but also between songs in all film-based programmes.
- Third, there should be a law whereby persons spitting in public places are fined.

State Chief Minister Sharad Pawar has vision of Bombay becoming another Singapore. This should not be taken to mean in terms of economic power only.

In Singapore, the roads are spanking clean and no one spits in public places.

In that country, there is a continuous campaign against this habit on television, radio and through posters, which say that persons who spit or throw rubbish on the streets will be made to clean it personally and fined too.

A law of this kind is urgently required in India. Of course, laws should be applicable equally to those who administer them as they do to the public. I have seen policemen in uniform urinate in public despite this being prohibited under the Bombay Police Act, 1950.

Fines should be collected on the spot and officials of all public utilities like the BEST, ST and railways in addition to the police, should be authorised to impose fines.

This piece was begun before news of the plague epidemic in Surat broke. I am completing it at a time when the disease has claimed at least 47 lives in Gujarat alone, with many cases being reported in Maharashtra.

Besides plague, many diseases spread through spitting. In the past, according to religious custom, upper castes made untouchables hang a bowl around their necks so that they did not spit on the ground in public. Strong cultural traditions ensured that the norm was followed voluntarily.

These are the days of equality and we cannot propagate such inhuman practices. But it would suffice to cultivate the practice of carrying paper tissues to blow our noses and to avoid eating *paan* in public. If some people cannot avoid eating *paan*, the least they can do is to carry a spittoon in their briefcases!

Chapter - 23

Paying Proposition

(Mid-Day, 19 October 1994)

"The parity of pay scales between (University) teachers and IAS officers can help bridge the gulf between theory and practice".

The University Grants Commission announced the appointment of a pay revision panel for university and college teachers on August 26, 1994, under Professor R P Rastogi, former vice-chancellor of the Benares Hindu University.

The R P Rastogi Panel, in addition to pay revision, will also consider a total packet of benefits including medical, housing facilities and retirement. The panel will perform its task in light of the existing pay scales and entry level qualifications keeping in view the need to promote quality of education.

With economic liberalisation and several new industries coming up in the country, academics are leaving to take up more lucrative jobs, particularly in banks, industries and multinational organisations.

Undoubtedly, the money one makes in the teaching jobs, particularly at university levels, is not the sole criterion for judging the importance and status of the profession. Teachers are the final shapers of the manpower needed by the nation and are themselves involved in seeking truth through research.

Even so, they are affected by the disparity between their wages and those of equally or less qualified persons in other professions.

This gulf cannot be bridged by the contention that teachers are instrumental in nation-building.

A colleague, just before retirement, stated her son was bringing home a fat pay packet with his B.Sc Tech in the very first year of service. His salary was much higher than her own ₹ 10,000 a month after 30 years in teaching!

It can be suggested that teachers associations must relate their pay revision proposal to the pay demanded by the IAS Association.

College and university teachers must demand a parity of pay scales with appropriate levels in IAS cadres, though they hold higher educational qualifications in comparison to IAS officers at the entry level.

All these years, IAS officials holding key decision-making positions in the higher educational administration have been able to prevail with the political decision-makers in regard to two points.

First, to deny teachers parity, of pay scales with their own. Second, whenever new pay scales, approved by the UGC have been implemented, the government has increased working hours for teachers.

Teachers in colleges are overburdened, lecturing for 20 periods of 50 minutes each a week. This leaves them with practically no time for reading, reference work or research in their fields of interest. Each revision of pay scales, therefore, has resulted in retrenchment and this has been justified in the name of economy, while the number of IAS official holding top positions in the government multiplies simultaneously.

The IAS Association has reportedly asked for a minimum pay of ₹ 8,000 per month as against the present ₹ 2,200. At the middle level (joint secretary) the scale demanded is one of ₹ 27,000-1,300-40,000 as against ₹ 5,000-200-67,100 and higher level (secretary) ₹ 37,000-1,500-50,000 per month as against ₹ 7,300-100-7,600.

They have also demanded that the chief secretaries in the state be paid ₹ 45,000 per month and the cabinet secretary at the centre, ₹ 50,000 per month. The association of IAS officers has also demanded liberal perks like free telephone calls, petrol, house building loans and medical facilities etc.

The IAS lobby has based its demands on the fact that the liberalised economy has been attracting talented men into the private sector even while existing pay scales in the teaching industry are far more attractive than those of the IAS. These scales or any other scales finally accorded to the IAS cadres in the rank of deputy secretary, joint secretary and secretary should be given to lecturers, readers and professors respectively in higher educational institutions. Vice-chancellor should be given salaries equal to that of the chief secretary.

Additionally, perks given to the IAS officers should be extended to college and university teachers. College teachers are badly off as far as essential requirements go with barely enough space to sit in other than a common room. Even if the parity of pay scales between college/university teachers and IAS officers is accepted, teachers in higher education are at a disadvantage on at least two counts.

First, their minimum qualifications at the entry level are higher at master's degree to that of IAS officers, which as a graduate degree. In several cases teachers have also spent four to five more years to acquire a research degree like M Phil or PhD. Hence, there is a strong case to raise the retirement age of college and university teachers to 65 from the present 60 years.

It is likely that the IAS lobby may put forward the argument that they are selected by tough national competitive examinations. However, the National Entrance Test or State Entrance Test has been made compulsory for teachers from 1993 making these equally competitive.

Further, unlike IAS officers teachers do not enjoy time bound promotional avenues without any fresh applications or having to face a selection committee.

Hence, once the UPSC declares a candidate as the best and the brightest amongst those available he remains the best and the brightest as he grows in age. If there are not enough posts of secretaries, the IAS fraternity knows how to create posts of special secretaries and additional secretaries in addition to a secretary in the department.

However, lecturers and readers in university, aspiring for higher posts of readers and professors must wait for an advertisement of a vacant post and appear for a fresh national selection.

On the other hand, a pay scale parity between teachers in higher education and the IAS cadre can help promote better interaction between the two.

Government bureaucracy has a general notion that teachers have much leisure with their three months vacations every academic year. Hence, those IAS official who possess a post graduate degree can occasionally go to university on a sabbatical (instead of going abroad) and teach the subject of their academic interest.

Similarly, academics can be invited to work in the administration for a year or two. This will help teachers acquire practical knowledge.

Today, there are professors of public administration, who have never administered anything in their life or professors of diplomacy known for their hot tempers. The parity of pay scales between teacher and IAS officers can help bridge this gulf between theory and practice.

Chapter - 24

Primary Need

(Mid-Day, 2 November 1994)

"The state needs to give adequate attention to primary teachers. For, they are doing everything at their end to see Maharashtra literate".

The state government has decided to universalise education before the end of this century. The programmed has to be achieved in reality and not symbolically. In the 1970s, when the federal government spoke of rural electrification it was meant providing one connection at village panchayat office. Primary education should not merely mean ability to read alphabets. It should be taken as the completion of first eight standards to make a person able to conduct his or her life without dependence on others as well as earn his livelihood.

The programme must succeed because many other problems afflicting our society like population growth, poverty and inadequacy of health facilities are directly linked to eradication of illiteracy.

The magnitude of the problem can be understood when we realise that half of the world's illiterate live in India. Thus, universalisation of primary education not only make these Indians better citizens, but education will contribute directly in reduction of population by bringing in better awareness of advantages of a small family. The spread of primary education will also help reduce the expenditure on public health as many of health problems are related to filthy living environment which itself is the result of lack of education.

The programme of universal primary education can succeed only if primary teachers are well qualified and highly committed. As far as the educational qualifications are concerned, all SSC or HSC trained teachers have to be phased out gradually and replaced by graduate (at least 11 class) trained teachers.

This is necessary as the state government as per the national education policy, has already decided to consider classes upto eight as the primary section instead of class upto seven.

But the most important thing is to make teaching primary classes more attractive than at present. Three steps are needed to be taken to achieve this aim.

First, is to give them an attractive pay packet. It is absolutely necessary to increase the salary of the primary teachers to lay a very strong foundation for our entire educational system. At present, much of the time is spent at higher levels of education to correct wrong or incorrect ideas acquired by pupils at the primary level. As of now, primary teachers are poorly paid.

In Bombay, where primary educations is the responsibility of municipal corporation, teachers are paid a total starting salary of about ₹ 3,500. How do they compare with private sector salaries? Even a peon gets paid better than the primary teachers. I feel there is a need to give these primary teachers what one gives to IAS probationers.

Second, teaching is a dead end job. Hence, they need to be provided with opportunities for higher grades at certain intervals. After some years of service, teachers should be given higher grades on par with IAS officials.

To enable them to accept higher responsibilities, the concept of subject-wise, head teacher should be introduced. Head teacher with some reduction in his/her teaching hours should be asked to supervise classwork and homework of pupils. Teachers in the primary schools, should also be able to move easily to secondary section or higher secondary depending upon their abilities and qualifications. As the pay scales or all teachers are on par with IAS officers, it should not be difficult.

Third, certain fringe benefits, which are too common in government services, but unknown in primary school, should be extended to them. These include attractive post-retirement benefits of pension and gratuity, in-service benefits of leave travel concensions, housing loans etc. This year in March, primary teachers in Bombay had to go on an indefinite strike to demand some of these benefits.

Even after these steps are taken to improve the status of primary teachers, quality of primary education is bound to suffer unless we reduce the strength of students in the class from present 60 to 70 to 35 to 40. With a classroom to 60-plus students, it is extremely difficult for the teachers to pay individual attention to every student. Unless teacher student ratio is brought to the level of 1:35, quality of primary education is unlikely to improve.

Chapter - 25

Easy-to-Get-Ph. Ds

(Mid-Day, 16 November 1994)

"In the age of ghost writers, plagiarism and corruption in acquiring Ph. Ds, author recalls, what he learnt in the US: Ph. D is a license to practice research and not to make one a great teacher or administrator."

Several reports have appeared recently highlighting malpractices involved in obtaining a PhD degree, such as plagiarism, ghost writing or purchase by payments in cash or kind. More specifically, the report that Lalit Narayan Mithila University produces an PhD degree holder every six hours is an indication of the shocking state affairs as far as this highest degree in the field of higher education is concerned.

But I was not surprised. In 1975, when I appeared at an interview for a Fulbright pre-doctoral research fellowship, I met a lecturer from Bihar. In a casual conversation, he told me that he had enrolled for a D Litt degree since everyone gets a PhD in Bihar. A wide variety of people in the northern universities have told me about ghost writers who write others dissertation for a fee either in cash or a fridge or a microwave oven will do the trick. While this phenomenon is widespread in north, it does not mean the south or our own region is free from the malaise. In a southern University, the authorities lost faith in native examiners and laid down that at least one examiner to be a foreign expert on the subject.

Since then, there has been a collaborative effort by the university staff, printers and guides and/or candidates to print letterheads of different foreign experts and get a report without the thesis ever crossing the borders of the town.

Authorities, even in universities which have not altogether lost their credibility, often appoint examiners not for their competence and expertise in the field of research, but as a reward.

Hence, it is not uncommon that a thesis in international relations is examined by a person who has spent his life time in studying municipal government. Thus, the fundamental question is: why are we in this sorry state? The primary reason is that those at the helm of affairs in higher education are not clear as to whether to treat a PhD as a necessary licence to conduct research or it is merely a teaching qualification like the B Ed degree. Part of the blame at least could be laid at the doors of the University Grants Commission. The decision-makers charged with the responsibilities to maintain quality of higher education in Colleges and Universities have themselves shown an ambrivalent attitude.

In the 1976 pay revision, qualification of PhD or at least M Phil was prescribed as minimum qualification at the entry level for a college or university lecturer. Further, those who were already in service but did not possess these qualifications were required to acquire them within five years to be eligible to draw increments in the new scales. Many teachers, who had neither of the two degrees, were in a hurry to get at least an M. Phil degree. Many universities introduced crash programmes to award M Phil degrees to teachers on a "sympathetic consideration".

Otherwise they would have been denied their annual increments. The result was the programme was not taken seriously either by the teachers or by the taught. The Bihar phenomenon is the byproduct of that mad rush combined with a self-protection of devaluation of higher degrees like the M Phil or the PhD.

When the pay was revised for the second time by the UGC in 1986, the PhD or M Phil was considered an additional qualification deserving additional monetary benefits. Stress was laid on refresher courses and orientation programmes to continue earning increments and further promotions.

Meanwhile, the UGC laid down the National Entrance Test from January 1, 1994 as a minimum requirement for a college or university teaching job. The states have followed it by giving their alternative, the State Entrance Test. But in the process, they have wittingly or unwittingly questioned the credibility of first class or higher second class awarded by universities as a proof of eligibility for selection as a teacher in higher educational institutions.

But the UGC had provided a corrective factor when taking the decision on NET those who acquire M Phil or PhDs before December 31, 1993, are not required to appear for NET or SET. That explains, at least partly, the production of instant PhDs.

What is the place of a PhD degree in the life of teacher? Does it make a good teacher?

In my opinion, a PhD does not help a teacher acquire teaching skills or makes him good at his job. It is essentially a tool, licence to practice research as a serious avocation. In the Johns Hopkins School of Advanced International Studies in Washington DC, the first thing I learnt is that PhD is a licence to do research. But, in India, most PhD holders end their research interest with the acquisition of a PhD degree.

Chapter - 26

An Active Interaction

(Mid-Day 21 December 1994)

"The armed forces have realised the need for collaboration with industrial organisations and academic institutions to realise the goal of self-reliance in defence and development".

General B C Joshi, a scholar to the core, was the first army chief to die in office. He was the only person who recognised the need for continuous interaction between the armed forces and academics. I had met him briefly, when Prime Minister Narasimha Rao inaugurated a seminar on "Panchasheel and global diplomacy" in the last week of June in Vigyan Bhawan, New Delhi. He was to visit China in the first week of July, the first army chief to have done so.

In retrospect, the last major academic function he attended was the University of Poona function to honour him and where the army has instituted the Chatrapati Shivaji Chair for defence studies.

While speaking on this occasion, he called for greater interaction between the military and academic institutions. He also stated "that if one hundred such chairs were instituted in other universities in the country, the army would support it".

Reading this news on November 15, I wrote to him the same day to express my complete agreement with him on the need to promote defence security studies at every level in our educational system schools, colleges and universities.

I also added that if I were in a decision-making capacity in some university, I would have grabbed his offer. The news of his sudden death on November 18 came as a shock. He is no longer with us to continues his mission. However, his worthy successor, General Shankar Roy Choudhary will no doubt, keep alive the gaol of academic military interactions for the national good. In his own exposition of national priorities after formally amusing office, the new army chief emphasised the need for indigenisation. Indigenisation is another name for self-reliance, he stated.

This call for self-reliance is necessary at a time when economic liberalisation is being misinterpreted as encouragement to foreigners to have a greater say in our trade. The fact that it provides greater encouragement to Indian entrepreneurs is overlooked.

It is a recognised fact that the Indian armed forces suffer from a resource crunch. This is also clear from General Chowdhary's statement and the recent comment by the Naval Chief in Bombay. In these circumstances, it is necessary for enhanced collaboration between the industry and the armed forces to overcome this crunch. General Choudhary, who has worked with defence, research and development organisations, and is aware of their strengths called for a trilateral cooperation between the armed forces, industries and academic institutions. This may invite decision from leftists who may not be able to visualise a military-industrial-academic cooperation. But if the goal is self-reliance in defence and development, there is no alternative to such a collaboration.

This type of collaboration between the three important segments of the nation, in turn, calls for a new liberal atmosphere in the country. While advantages of such collaboration are known to the armed forces and the industries, the universities and their decision-making bodies have yet to realise the benefits of such cooperation. They have depended for too long on the state for their academic sustenance, which has resulted in sapping their individual initiatives. They have depended for too long on the state for their academic sustenance, which has resulted in sapping their individual initiatives. There is an urgent need for them to look at alternate resources and shed their dependence on the government. The military-industrial-academic cooperation is an answer to that problem and the best academic tribute to General Joshi's departed soul.

27

Delink PhDs from Jobs

(Mid-Day, 4 January 1995)

"In these days, when Ph.D degrees are thought of as merely a way to get ahead, it is imperative to delink degrees from jobs."

I had argued in favour of delinking PhD from the job market (MID-DAY, November 16, 1994) as a first step to restoring a degree of credibility to the highest academic achievement.

The PhD should indicate a scholars' ability to conduct serious research. It should not be linked to teacher's qualification at the entry point. This is difficult in many universities as they have for long been accustomed to looking at the degree in terms of a teaching qualification and teachers have been looking at it in terms of increments or job confirmation.

The universities will have to change their approach to the entire question of the PhD degree. Here are a few steps which universities can take to enhance the credibility of a PhD.

Entrance test

First and foremost, select candidates for PhDs only once or twice a year through entrance tests. This will help select the best. The universities can also give merit fellowships strictly on the basis of performance in the entrance test. This will help prevent the chances of guides scouting to register candidates under them so as to claim certain advantages, as happens now. In the past, even administrators have used a PhD registration to demonstrate their credentials as academics.

Course Work

Second, every student enrolled for a PhD should be made to go through at least a year's course work. The course work should include two streams: one, attending seminars in the candidate's area of research to help the candidate acquire in depth knowledge; and two, a thorough grounding in research methodology. At present, many candidates think-and wrongly-that philosophic depth in a subject is essential but abilities to organise those thoughts systematically are non-consequential. Often, they end up as the most confused thinkers in university campuses.

Guide

Third, a guide should not be allowed more than five candidates under him at a time.

Discuss scheme

Fourth, candidates should be permitted to work on their dissertations only after successful completion of course work. Before a candidate selects a research design for his dissertation and decides upon the methodology, he should discuss his scheme before his colleagues. For this, a committee for research guides ought to be constituted in every discipline.

Presentations

Fifth, candidates working on their dissertations have to be compulsorily made to present their research findings even if they are tentative. Now, the guides often do not see their students for months together. As such participation is not compulsory, average students or students working on their PhDs as a matter of convenience think such a requirement is an unnecessary imposition.

Sometimes, even guides who are least interested in academic work themselves think this is an imposition. If a senior professor insists on holding such seminars, these 'misguides' fall back on rules to show that such a thing is not required under them.

These are days when university vice-chancellor are scientists but may not know the difference between 'fusion' and 'fission'. When a scholar was introduced to a vice-chancellor as one working in the area of 'operation research' the vice-chancellor reportedly asked him as to how many operations he did per day! Such vice-chancellors are willing to confer honorary degrees not necessarily D Litts but even PhDs-on eminent and not so eminent people in public life.

What is of interest is that even those who are not in academic life, or were in it decades ago, clamour for a PhD degree as a status symbol. These are the people who normally have lots of money and are willing to donate it to universities in return of a degree. For others, conferring a honorary degree on eminent people is a step in their search for more power or fame.

Though the academic environment in the country is as polluted as the political environment, there are still people who treasure academic excellence. This piece is addressed to such people. A beginning has to be made to improve the quality of the dissertations written in the universities so as to enhance the stature of a PhD degrees.

Chapter - 28

The KG Rushhh

(Mid-Day, 18 January 1995)

"A child learns to hate learning by the time he finishes KG"

Every winter high schools with attached kindergarten classes complete their admissions. Each year, we read the views of critics on the KG education. In particular, there has been loud criticism about the method of interviews and tests adopted by the KG schools to decide admissions. A noted educationist, Professor Ram Joshi has been instrumental in organising Maharashtra Bal Shikshan Parishad. I happened to attend the conference held by the founders of this organisation on November 15, 1994.

One pertinent point that came out during the conference was their opposition to the prevailing practice of tiny tots being introduced to formal teaching of three "Rs". As Professor Joshi very rightly observed that because of an over emphasis on formal teaching in KG classes, a child learns to hate learning by the time he finishes KG.

On the other hand, the emphasis should be on play, learning techniques and preparing them to learn together. Even according to medical sciences, a child should not be made to write before he/she has completed four.

Professor Joshi has also pointed out that the Yashpal Committee appointed by the central government has asked for total ban on tests and interviews to admit the child to the KG classes.

Bal Shikshan Parishad wants Maharashtra state to accept the recommendation of the Yashpal Committee and enforce it. It is said many states like West Bengal, Kerala and Karnataka have enforced this ban. It may be educative to find out how these states actually enforced the ban of admission tests and interviews. In reality, it is very difficult to enforce such a ban when schools have fewer seats than the number of admission seekers.

Let me illustrate the difficulty in enforcing the ban. I will limit my discussion to strictly English medium KG classes. It is a fact that parents prefer to admit their children to KG classes in a regular school.

The reason in: once admitted, there is no need to think again on the question of child's admission for at least the next 12 years.

Then the question is how do the schools decide on admissions when they have limited seats. Depending on number of schools in the area, reputation of individual schools, the schools receive at least five or more applications for every seat available in the school. What is the alternative to screen and select children to be admitted to schools, if tests and interviews are to be banned?

Let us discuss some possible alternate methods

One method that can and has been tried by many at different times is to give admission on the basis of first come, first serve. In such schools I have seen and heard about the long queues in front of school gates during the night itself so as to be the early bird to get forms. Is it a scientific way of deciding the fate of a child? What happens to those children whose parent were unlucky?

Second, the schools can give admission to those who give the highest donations. We will be sorry for the promising children whose parents cannot afford to pay a big donation.

Third, admissions can be given on the basis of personal contacts, recommendation letters from influentials– a spoils system.

Fourth, it can be argued that interviews of parents could be taken to find out their ability to pay high fees and teach in English at home. What, if parents are matriculates but the child is brilliant?

Fifth, schools can give forms to all and then draw a lottery to decide admissions. A parent can give forms filled in three schools and if he turns out to be unlucky in all three, is it not as traumatic an experience for the child and parents as interviews and tests?

Sixth, schools can adopt friendly neighbourhood policy. Those who are closest to school will get a seat. Then, for 100 seats, the school can limit its neighbourhood radius to a kilometer or even less.

The entire exercise of thinking of alternatives shows that there is no satisfactory solution for admission to KG classes so long admission is a matter of selector's choice.

However, having said this, it must be made clear that a school will do well to take into consideration all psychological limitations of a child and take interviews and tests as a part of games children play but with a difference. Some win and some try elsewhere. But it is only a short-term remedy.

On a long-term basis it is the responsibility of the government and society to see that admission become a child's choice by liberally encouraging setting up of more schools.

Chapter - 29

Why the Neighbourhood Policy won't Work?

(Times of India, 10 June 1997)

"In the context of KG admission policy it is argued that neighborhood policy will not work; let pre-primary be considered as creche and primary education begin only at the age of seven to give a child more time to play."

Following the recommendations made by Prof Ram Joshi, the government has banned, schools from interviewing children for admission to nursery and KG classes. This decision may, however, adversely affect educational trusts which are in the field for the good of society and not for profit-making. Reputed English-medium schools (I am limiting myself of English-medium schools) receive at least five to ten applications for each seat in their KG sections. How are schools going to select children, if their intake is barely one-fifth the demand?

It is true that young tots should not be subjected to the rigours of a written test as they cannot be really assessed on that basis. There could, however, be a social interaction with the family to determine whether the child hails from a background that is receptive to English education. I know many instances of children of watchmen, shopkeepers and rickshaw drivers who dropped out of English-medium schools after three or four years as they were unable to cope with the syllabus.

The alternative suggested by the anti-interview lobby is to "restrict admission to the neighbourhood level". Can a government force a school to restrict its admissions to a particular neighbourhood? The point to be heeded here is what constitutes the neighbourhood of a school? If a schools is located say in Mulund, is one to gather that the entire Mulund area will be considered as the neighbourhood? Or should the neighbourhood concept be restricted to a 1 Km radius? Schools in thickly populated suburbs could have over 100 children within a 1-km radius. If the neighbourhood is the principle for admission, why should colleges admit children from far and wide? Is it because they can travel?

If a school is unaided (as many English schools started after 1982 are), how will it support the students? In fact, one wonders what the government's contribution to social upliftment would then be. The government's policy has decided not to give aid to English primary or secondary schools. Education minister Sudhir Joshi was frank in admitting that if aid is extended to English-medium schools, many Marathi-medium schools may face closure.

However, the government is right when it says the playway method should be used to educate young tots in the KG classes. Here, the purpose of nursery and KG become relevant. Should they be viewed as crèches as the child has working parents, or should they as acknowledged as preparatory education? Somehow, parents, schools and government have tended to see them in the latter mould. It is for this reason that there have been efforts to regulate them. However, education in the true sense should begin in Class I when the child is six years plus if not 7 plus and not 5 plus as at now. In fact, the pre-primary exercise should be viewed as a crèche where some education is also provided through the play-way method. Hence, do-good lobbies must ask the government to make it compulsory for employees to provide crèches and bus facilities to parents. In this respect, the government should be a model employer. Then the existing schools can only cater to parents who do not have crèche facilities. This will considerably reduce pressure in the existing schools.

Chapter - 30

New Pre-Primary Admission Policy is Unworkable

(The Free Press Journal, 28 July 1997)

"Author highlights problems inherent in neighborhood policy as many schools in Mumbai are surrounded by slums and will not be able to work with government forcing English medium schools to work without aid"

The government of Maharashtra has recently banned all interviews for admission in Pre-Primary Schools and asked them to admit children from the neighbourhood. This was largely in response to the recommendations made by a Committee appointed by Maharashtra Government under Professor Ram Joshi to improve Pre-Primary education. After the committee submitted its report, Prof. Joshi also was vocal in lobbying for the acceptance of his committee report.

For a variety of reasons, neighbourhood policy is unlikely to work for admissions to Pre-Primary classes attached to regular schools with Primary and Secondary sections. First, because, reputed English Medium schools (I am limiting myself here to only English Medium Schools in Mumbai city though many of my observations are applicable to reputed Marathi Medium schools as well), receive at least five to ten applications for each seat in their KG sections. How are you going to select children, if the school's intake capacity is five to ten times less than the demand?

It is true that young tots in the age group of 30 to 48 months should not be subjected to the rigour or written test. They cannot be really assessed on that basis. However, there could be social interactions with the family to find out the social backgournd of the child, to determine mainly whether child has cultural background to be receptive to English Education. I know many children of watchmen, petty shopkeepers and rickshaw drivers, who were admitted to KG classes by ignoring their social background have become dropouts after third or fourth classes largely because of the medium of education.

But you cannot state it to parents who will consider it as snobbish and socially demeaning. There are also people who fight with the school managements to be admitted on the specific plea that they have become rickshaw drivers as they did not get good education. But they do not want their children to be deprived of it. It is also true that if the child is on an average caliber but able to pass XII standard examination in English-medium, he can hope to get a better job opportunity in contrast to a student of the same caliber from any regional media schools.

Second, how can a government force a school to restrict its admissions to neighbourhood? What constitutes the neighbourhood of a school? Who defines it? If a school is located, say in Mulund, is entire Mulund the neighbourhood of the school? Or is it a radius of ten kilometers? The schools in thickly populated suburbs could provide for even 100 children within a radius of one Km. If the neighbourhood is the principle for admission, why should a College admit children from far and wide? Is it because they can travel? Parents are eager to send a child beyond neighbourhood because a school's objective reputation is good. There are cases where parents are eager to admit their children in the KG Section of a school and continue there till SSC, but do not want to keep them in the same school's Junior College! If the principle of choice is to be provided to parents, why deny it at KG level? Why not the educational institutional also exercise similar right to choose?

Third, for many schools, KG is the main feeder for their Primary and Secondary sections. Should a school sacrifice its reputation to the kind of neighbourhood it has come to acquire? As you cannot chose your neighbours, schools too do not choose their neighbourhood. By the misfortune of the School, if neighbourhood is blessed with slums, should it take all children or even eighty per cent from the neighbourhood? Finally, can the government impose such a policy of restricting the admissions to neighbourhood on unaided but recognised schools? Many English Medium schools started in Maharashtra after 1982 are unaided. What is the government's contribution to the social upliftment through better opportunities for education of the people through English medium? The government's policy is not to give aid to English Primary or Secondary schools. Education Minister, Shri Sudhir Joshi was frank in admitting that if aid is extended to English Medium schools, many Marathi medium schools may have to be closed down in Mumbai.

However, government is right when it says playway method be used to keep young tots in the KG classes fully engaged. Here the purpose of Nursery and KG become relevant. Are they to be seen as mainly crèche, as both the parents of child are working, or is it preparatory education for admission to the primary school? Somehow, parents, schools and government have all-and wrongly-tended to see them in the latter mould. Hence, the effort to regulate them. However, education in a true sense should begin in the Std. I when the child is 6 plus if not 7 plus and not 5 plus as is now. As a matter of fact, a case can be made to raise the minimum age of admission to Primary from the present 5 years to 6 years.

On the other hand, the entire pre-primary exercise ought to be viewed as a crèche where some education is also provided through playway method. Hence, do good lobbies must seek the government's help to make it compulsory for employer to provide crèche and bus facility for all parents and their children to reach their place of work. In this respect, the government should be a model employer. Then the existing schools can only cater to parents who do not have crèche facility. There is also a need to increase number of schools with pre-primary classes. This will considerably reduce pressure on Pre-Primary admissions in the existing schools.

Chapter - 31

Examiners should be Men of Highest Integrity

(The Free Press Journal, 14 August 1997)

"University examination system has not done anything to reduce the subjective element on the part of examiners in the absence of examiners being men of highest integrity corruption is inevitable"

A recent report in a newspaper said that a third-year LLB student who secured only 14 marks in a paper applied for revaluation of the paper and received 54 marks, while another revaluation of the same paper by another examiner assigned him only 24 marks. Why is it that there is such a wide variation in the marks assigned by three different examiners?

First, the appointment of examiners without teaching experience in the papers they examine, though they are technically qualified to be examiners. In the past, examiners were appointed after great scrutiny. Though, according to rules, the requirement is five years of teaching experience at the graduate level, very rarely a person was appointed as the examiner just because he had requisite experience. A person appointed as the examiner not only qualified as per the rule book but also possessed actual teaching experience of the particular paper.

Speaking from personal experience in the subject of political science at post-graduate level, I can state the deterioration in the appointment of examiners in the Mumbai University took place in the mid-eighties. While working as the chairman of an examination panel, I had a few examiners who had never taught a political science course at the post-graduate level. Yet, when I would ask such a person whether he would set a paper on International Law, he would say yes: the same would be his reply for any other paper. He even agrees to set a paper on Development Administration or Marxist Political Thought. What gives them the confidence to set papers in any subject? A paper setter is provided with papers of at least the last three years in all subjects. All a paper setter has to do is to select questions from different papers and reproduce them including mistakes in the original paper, if any. Such questions continue to be vague and open to several interpretations.

Second, after the students have answered the paper, there is no guarantee that it goes to an examiner who also has taught the paper. Hence, if the paper goes to an examiner who has never taught a particular paper, he would not like to risk an opportunity of being on the examination panel. Hence, he will give the candidate marks in the middle range-45/55-to be safe. A few years ago, I had a unique experience, a student, whose paper I had examined had merely reproduced all the questions in the answer format. Naturally, he failed. However, another paper of this student had gone to another examiner who assigned him 52 marks, though the candidate had played the same trick.

Third, when the student is unhappy with the marks he has secured in a particular paper, he applies for revaluation. But again there is no system of sending it to an examiner who has either the teaching experience or the expertise in that particular paper. In theory and even rationally, for revaluation, a paper ought to be sent to an examiner who has experience of teaching the subject. However, universities again goes by the rule book. It appoints examiners for revaluation irrespective of an examiner's knowledge on the subject. This happens primarily because universities do not have ready information on the examiners' specialisation, and subject they are teaching. Often, the examiner, in the first instance, may be more qualified than the examiner who does the revaluation. Whenever, I have received a paper for revaluations I have invariably returned it if I have not taught the paper.

However, not all examiners will do so. In such a situation, the examiner will take recourse to assigning safe marks. The cumulative effect of a paper being set by an examiner who is not well qualified to do so, and examined by teachers without teaching experience in that particular paper leads to such wide variations as 14-54-24. If all those who are involved in the examining process are fully qualified to do their jobs, and the questions are clear and sharply focused, variation in marks would hardly be around five per cent.

What needs to be done under the present system is for universities to appoint only men of highest integrity as paper setters and examiners. Papers need to be assigned for setting as well as examining to only those who have taught it for a long period and or are teaching it at that point of time. If the appointment is on the basis of past teaching experience, the gap between teaching, setting or examining the paper should not be more than two years. This rule should be applied rigorously for revaluation as the student is approaching the university for revaluation as he is not satisfied with the marks secured by him in the first instance. But these steps can be taken only if men of character are appointed/selected as chairpersons of board of studies and their recommendations are vetted by a competent authority. Of course, the real solution for the long-term is to internalise the paper, setting process as well as assessments. But that is a theme which requires a separate treatment and will be covered at a later date.

Chapter - 32

For Better Education

(Mid-Day, 17 March 1998)

"While unaided schools are badly affected as they have no hope of getting government aid, the aided schools too are not affected".

School education is the worst casualty of the economic policy of liberalisation, 1991. With the states being required to reduce budgetary deficits to fall in line with the Central Government's policy of the deficit not crossing five per sent of the budget, have been forced to cut their education expenditure and other social welfare schemes. While unaided schools are badly affected as they have no hope of getting government aid, the aided schools too are not unaffected.

Thus, in Maharashtra, for instance, the government without any consultation, reduced the annual maintenance grant of 12 per cent given to the schools to six per cent. This is done at a time when the cost of educational accessories, like stationery and everything else, has gone up steeply. But the bureaucrats in the education ministry, insensitive to educational needs, found that such a step alone could not decrease the bill.

Hence, the government devised certain additional ways to save money on education. First, it decided to send audit squads to check past accounts of schools so as to enable them to deny the grant-in-aid to many schools, at least, for a year or two. But schools are given their annual grants only after their accounts are audited. However, since the government is the pay master of teachers' salaries, school heads are too deferential to the government representatives to impress upon them the unreasonableness of their exercise.

The result has been that auditors, at the government's bidding found out several items of expenditure already incurred as inadmissible, hence recoverable from the grant payable for the next one or two years. Many schools were denied even six per cent of their non-salary grant between 1993-1996.

Second, in the 1980s the government used to give a small sum of money towards the school's development fund on the condition that the management contributed an equal amount. The funds are supposed to be used with the government's prior permission for major repairs or development plans like creation or expansion of laboratories. But since the early 1990s, the government stopped this payment; however, compelling the management to set aside a fixed amount in the development fund.

Third, schools are paid a nominal rent by the government according to the year of construction. They are expected to maintain the buildings from the rent collected. Older the building, greater the maintenance cost. But older buildings get only few thousands as rent. I know a suburban school which gets an annual rent of approximately of ₹ 35,000. But if it paints the school building, it spends over ₹ Two lakh; if it repairs the toilets, it has to spend over ₹ one lakh.

Even this paltry sum is reduced under administrative rules. Thus, for instance, if a management gets a rent for running an aided school, and if it also runs an unaided school in the same building in a second shift, its rent is cut by 50 per cent. The government with even minimum sensitivity to the needs of school education which is the primary responsibility of any democratic state would have thought of indirectly aiding the unaided schools by not deducting 50 per cent from the rent due to an aided school.

School managements have to raise funds for their social commitment to run good schools. Barring a few notorious school mainly run by active or retired or rejected politicians, a majority are run by registered societies. At least in Mumbai, a majority of schools are run by minority linguistic or religious communities, which were founder to provide educational facilities to children of their own linguistic or religious group.

Then, where can the schools get money? School trusts are continuously involved in raising funds. But most sources are not under any legal compulsion to donate. However, if there is one group which ought to give, it is the parents. As beneficiaries of educational activities, they ought to give for the good of their own children.

The State Government, however, as a populist measure, has prevented schools from collecting donations, linked to admissions. Every year some management or the other is dragged to court, some teachers are arrested for accepting donations, and generally management is painted as corrupt and anti-social. Ironically, real culprits go around as Shikshan Maharshis!

Further, this stance of the government is particularly ridiculous on two counts. It has been selectively sensitive to the needs of managements of institutions and uses these managements as a source to collect funds for their activities.

Until the government is able to provide education to all, it needs to scrap the Anti-Capitation Act and permit school trusts to take donations by issuing proper receipts for the amount. Like the government needs money to provide services it ought to provide, politicians need money to win elections, school trusts too need money to provide good education.

Chapter - 33

Class Action

(Mid-Day, 13 August 1998)

"The striking teachers' demands are justified"

The striking teachers' demands are justified

College and university teachers have gone on strike to demand pay scales recommended by the University Grants Commission (UGC). What are the demands which have made them take such a drastic step at the beginning of the academic year? And what is the government response?

The Bharatiya Janata (BJP) led government was prompt in announcing new scales for teachers. Though the previous government implemented steps like pay hikes and raising the retirement age, it did not implement recommendations of the Fifth Pay Commission which would be opposed by the staff, like reduction of staff strength by 30,000 in the Central Government. The I K Gujral regime didn't bother about revision of pay scales for teachers in institutions of higher education.

Be that as it may, teachers, led by All India Federation of University and College Teachers' Organisation (AIFUCTO) are concerned about issues touching immediate monetary gains, which are meant mainly to neutralise the financial burden of inflation. The Rastogi Committee was appointed by the UGC to make recommendations on teachers' pay in light of the Fifth Pay Commission. It had recommended grades which were upwardly revised by UGC while forwarding them to the

Human Resources Development (HRD) Ministry. The ministry has ignored UGC recommendations and accepted scales recommended by the Rastogi Committee with minor changes which further affect teachers adversely.

Lecturers were, thus, given a scale on par with the entry grade of Central services and the Indian Administrative Service (IAS) of ₹ 8,000-13,500 as against UGC recommended scale of ₹ 10,000-15,200. While in this regard, both the Rastogi Committee and UGC had recommended annual increment of ₹ 325, the ministry has quietly reduced it to ₹ 275.

Similarly, professors have been given the scale ₹ 16,400-22,400 by equating them with the selection grade of ₹ 14,000-18,300 given to Central employees while UGC had recommended ₹ 18,400-24,500. The government, on the basis of this, had claimed that revised scales not only maintain parity with organised central services group 'A' but amount to higher total emolument at some levels.

This is totally misleading for a variety of reasons. Four important ones are listed here. First, the government is offering a lecturer a scale offered to an entrant in the IAS cadre. But minimum qualifications for entry into IAS is an undergraduate degree, while that of a lecturer is a postgraduate degree with a score over 55 per cent.

Thus, a lecturer puts in minimum of two more years of academic performance in comparison to IAS entrants. Since UGC has made the National Educational Test (NET) or State Educational Test (SET) a must for lecturers, competition has become equally tough for new aspirants. I have seen quite a number of young PhDs and MPhils failing in NET or SET, though these are set at the level of postgraduate examination.

Second, in the academic field it is unlikely that every entrant will retire as professor, it is more likely he will retire as a senior lecturer/reader. To this middle grade the HRD Ministry has offered ₹ 12,000-18,300 which is lower than the UGC recommended grade of ₹ 14,300-18,300.

Third, a few lucky enough to be selected as professors, have been given according to the government scales higher than the selection grade offered to IAS cadre. But the government has not informed the public on the 'Revision of Pay Scales of Teachers in Universities and Colleges: Some Basic Facts' the fact that an IAS officer does not end his career at selection grade. There are at least four more levels of scales to which he can aspire to senior administrative grade (₹ 18,400-22,400), additional secretaries (₹ 22,400-24,500), Secretaries (₹ 26,000) and chief secretary (₹ 30,000 consolidated).

Why this situation? The IAS lobby is so powerful that it has seen to it in the last three decades that several posts of additional secretaries and secretaries are created in government departments. If in the 1950s and 1960s there was only one secretary, today every department has several secretaries designated as secretary 1, secretary 2 etc, in addition to numerous additional secretaries. Hence most IAS officers have reasonable chance of becoming additional secretaries while not even one per cent in the academic field can aspire to the government's new offer of professor of eminence, created for meritorious teachers (₹ 22,000-24,500).

Fourth, the concept of perks is unknown in the academic field. An entrant to the IAS begins his career with a chauffeur driven car, a telephone and fairly decent accommodation. In the academic field, even a telephone extension is a luxury.

But it is not merely a matter of monetary gains for which teachers are fighting. What the HRD Ministry has done while offering the new scales is to undo the gains to teachers in the last two decades, where they were able to get an all India uniform grade in the field of higher education. But now the HRD minister has informed states that they are free to offer their teachers Central pay scales or reduce them; they have also been given freedom to decide date of implementation, though the scales are supposed to come into force with effect from January 1, 1996 as with other beneficiaries of the Fifth Pay Commission recommendations. The rationale for this decision is not clear. My surmise is that since different parties are in power in the states, the Central Government wants them to realise their commitment to higher education.

But the Centre can achieve this goal by making it obligatory for the states to implement scales by offering them financial assistance as recommended by the UGC. The latter had said the Centre should bear the total burden of additional pay in 1996 and reduce it annually by five per cent to arrive at 80 per cent by the year 2000. Instead, the Centre has provided an alibi to states to offer teachers scales lower than recommended by the Central Government by reducing Central assistance to 80 percent in 1996 and limiting it to the the next three years with an annual reduction of five per cent.

This is a retrograde step, as because of uniform national scales in the field of higher education there was a degree of mobility of teachers, which as it is constricted by different media of instruction and inability of universities and colleges to offer mobile teachers accommodation.

It is unfortunate that teachers have to strike every time Central Government employees' pay scales are revised. It only shows that teachers have no clout in the social system. It is also an indication that the HRD minister does not enjoy much clout in the Cabinet either.

Chapter - 34

Whose Failure is it?

(Mid-Day, 19 November 1998)

"The present education system whereby students are classified into those who have passed and failed is at the root of their non-performance and dissatisfaction"

According to a report in **(MID-DAY)** November 14, 1998 a 16-year old girl Yamunabai Laxman Salvi, an eleventh standard student of commerce in Ghatkopar committed suicide. Reason: she had failed in the examination. Yamuna is not alone. In Chandigarh last June, 15 year old Sukhdev, son of a professor in the Punjab University committed suicide as he failed in mathematics.

Every year throughout the country, at least 100 young boys and girls commit suicide because of their failure in one or the other examination. Why do these young students take such extreme steps to end their life? Without going into a psycho analytical study, the single most important factor is parental pressure to do well and excel in studies.

Is education a sound criteria to declare a child as a failure? Several individuals who did not do well educationally have made a name or fortune in normal life without inheriting any ancestral wealth. Then why take recourse to brand a child as a failure? Is it because in this country education is directly linked to employment? Or is it because of the stigma attached to the term failure? It seems to be both.

Education is not merely a process of acquiring skills for a trade or profession; it is also a process wherein a human being acquires general knowledge and abilities for reasoning and judgment. By linking an educational performance to employment in to we ignore the second aspect of education: development of abilities for reasoning and judgment. What can be done? We need to change our present approach drastically.

First, throughout the nation, the purpose of branching out to vocational courses after tenth standard has not occurred. Instead, everyone desires to continue study two more years of the plus two stage. This is because at the end of the tenth standard, at the age of 15 plus, it is extremely difficult for a boy or a girl to decide his/her career plans. Hence, we need to make 12 years of schooling as general schooling and ask a child only to branch to different professional/ vocational courses only after completion of 12 years in the school.

There is a proposal to make the minimum age of entry to regular school to six plus instead of the present five plus. If this is done, at 18 or if not at the age of 17, the student should be in a better position to reason and judge his aptitude for a profession in life.

Second, and most importantly, in the twelfth standard examination, the examining body need to grade students between A, B, C, and D. The word 'failed' should absolutely not appear in relation to even those who receive D grade. Those who get A and B grades must be considered eligible for professional courses while the first three grade holders being also eligible for liberal arts, sciences and commerce courses. The students securing D grade should be held eligible for various courses leading to a proficiency in specialised skills, like accountancy, secretarial practice, technical proficiencies like painting, plumbing, electrical, etc. The government should open and encourage private trusts to open vocational institutions to accommodate all D grade holders. But what is crucial in this system is to enable anyone with a D, C, or B grade to appear again in an examination while pursuing a course or to do so after a lapse of six months and at least thrice in a career the opportunity to improve his grade. Today it is criminal that after 10 years of schooling an examination board declares more than 50 per cent of young boys and girls as 'failures'.

I have often asked my principal friends that after their taking students with very high percentages like 80 or above, as of now, how is it that these students fail in their next class? They offer many reasons, but if a student with 90 per cent marks in the twelfth standard fails in the first year medical or engineering course, something needs to explain.

It is likely that critics may say that the grade system is creating a caste system and those who get D grade are condemned to be carpenters.

However, the present system of awarding I, II, and pass classes to about 50 per cent of those who appear in the examination drives them to despair. It is better to save lives by giving them an opportunity to do some courses according to their abilities, and at the same time give them a chance to improve their grades. Today, if a diploma holder can move on to an engineering degree after fulfilling certain requirements, why can't a certificate holder move to a degree in electrical engineering through a certificate course?

Similarly if one has done a certificate course in accountancy, it should be possible for him to move to get a B.Com degree after exercising an opportunity to improve his grades.

Chapter - 35

Graceless Gesture

(Mid-Day, 6 May 1999)

"It is not unusual for the university to grant grace marks to enable students to get first class or distinction. However, in such cases, action is taken before results are announced".

The judgement of the Bombay High Court by Justices Agarwal and Deshmukh on a writ petition filed by students affected by revocation of eight grace marks in the Preventive Social Medicine (PSM) paper in the final MBBS examination, has drawn the curtain on the so-called grace marks scandal in the University of Mumbai. It is worth analysing of the roles played by major actors in the decision-making on the entire issue. It is also worthwhile to consider whether any reforms are necessary to avoid similar instances in the future.

The facts of the case in brief are: The Board of Examinations (BoE), with the vice-chancellor (VC) in the chair, on their own initiative, decided to grant eight grace marks to all 963 students who had appeared for final year MBBS examination, after the results were announced in January this year. The justification offered by the BoE was that questions worth 15 marks in the paper were out of syllabus. As a result, 64 students were able to clear the examination while 38 students passed in the PSM alone.

The grace marks were granted not out of concern for the career of 64 students or 38 who passed in the subject, but for 15 students who could get distinction because of these eight marks. These students thus became eligible for postgraduate (PG) studies in the medical faculty as distinction marks are the minimum requirement for PG admission. According to sources in the University, of these 15 at least eight were doctors', children. That explains the concern shown by the dean of medical faculty and the VC.

It is not unusual for the university to consider granting of grace marks to enable students to get first class or distinction. However, in such cases, action is taken before results are announced. If it was a genuine case of out of syllabus questions being included in the PSM paper, students would not have waited till results are announced to ventilate their grievances. Hence, the motive must have been to help well connected students to get admission to the PG courses. Therefore, the claim made by the dean of the faculty of medicine, in his resignation letter that the "decision of the board might have prevented frustration, depression and even suicides by some medical students..." is ridiculous.

Thus, grace marks enabled not so bright students to go in for PG courses. Thus, the BoE can be charged with lowering the academic standards. However, when the students are admitted to medical courses, despite their scoring low marks in the entrance test, because they belong to one or the other reserved category, charges of lowering standards are likely to be seen with a degree of skepticism. What needs to be still investigated is whether the helping hand extended to students to get distinction is a humanitarian act or whether any other considerations were involved.

But undoubtedly this case cannot be compared to the scandalous case, where marks were increased before the MD results were announced to pass the daughter of former Maharashtra chief minister Nilangekar, at the instance of the then chancellor Kona Prabhakar Rao in early 1986. In the present case, marks were increased more intelligently by covering all students.

If this unique decision of increasing marks, after the results were announced, was taken out of genuine concern for the students career, the VC and BoE should have stuck to their decision instead of offering to abide by the decision of the chancellor, because he can also go wrong. The VC and her colleagues in the BoE should have placed all arguments before the chancellor and public, and if the chancellor still decided to revoke grace marks, the VC should have volunteered to resign. In such an event, transparency and accountability would have won the case for the VC. But it was too much to expect such a principled stand from the VC.

What has been the role of Chancellor P C Alexander? Alexander has maintained a stance of non-intervention in university affairs ever since he became the governor of Maharashtra. From the experience of university teachers agitation in 1994-1995 against the former VC SD Karnik who after taking charge as VC in 1993 proclaimed that he was a man of guts and not a goody goody VC-the chancellor completely stonewalled himself from the university teachers.

Neither letters of the teachers association were acknowledged nor were they given an appointment to meet him and explain the situation. Then, I had concluded, both by personal and collective experience, that this chancellor has a self-perception of his role that is limited to performing ceremonial functions like laying of foundation stones and cutting ribbons or inauguration of gardens etc. But he was positively not interested in setting things in order in the university.

In this background, his intervention in the grace marks case has surprised many. Advocate and former President of ABVP, Bal Apte, even termed the chancellor's intervention as uncalled for. This feeling was further strengthened by the activities of sideline actors in the university. The grace marks issue was seized by forces inimical to the present VC. In an interview of present VC published in **Mid-Day** (March 28, 1999), it was mentioned that former VC Karnik was using the crisis to enable his protégé, Dr Nawaz Mody to become VC, if Deshmukh was forced out of office. This has really upset the academics in general and university teachers in particular, because of their past misdeeds. For them prospect is worse than the present.

Many misdeeds of the former VC were made public in the contempt case filed by him against the *Loksatta*, a Marathi daily. In the judgement, Justice Deshpande observed that Karnik "also admitted that he personally helped Mody" in becoming a professor in the Department of Civics & Politics. The Judge added: There are however, other instances of some indirect favours to Mody and in the explanation, the plaintiff has admitted that his decision to take Mody on Management Council was wrong. Was the chancellor acting at the behest of the duo?

Before concluding, I would like to mention, suggest at least one important long-term reform here. With a general deterioration of public life, the stature of persons appointed to the office of the VC has also deteriorated since the 1990s. Ever since the office became a paid one in 1974, the political connection has been a prerequisite to get the post of VC. In a democracy, this may be unavoidable.

But it falls on the shoulders of the government of the day to appoint persons of high academic standing and integrity to the post, who can withstand all kinds of political and personal pressures. Alas! Instead of that commitment, politicians are today talking not only in terms of present VC's party connections, but individuals within it. The press is full of stories as to how she was selected by former chief minister Manohar Joshi who is out of grace today with the powers that be. This attitude, on a long-term basis, may disgrace the university much more than the present grace marks scandal.

Chapter - 36

Government's prescription of PTA's approval for a fee hike irrational

(The Free Press Journal, 8 July 2000)

"Are governments using mandatory PTA approval to fee increase as a devise to divert the real issue of failure to provide adequate resources for education?"

Since last year the Maharashtra government and BMC are asking unaided schools to provide, before they approve fee hikes, a resolution from the Parents and Teachers' Association (PTA) approving the hike. Though this has been challenged in the High Court and the HC has held that the PTA approval is not mandatory, the officials continue to insist on such a resolution.

This way the government is actually trying to fool the public and so far it has been successful. It is the constitutional function of the state government to provide primary and secondary education to the children of the state. But in the game of promoting regional languages, the government has consistently denied government aid to English medium schools in the state since 1980s. Now with the steep increase in the pay burden has increased on the school management because of implementation of the Fifth Pay Commission scales and rise in the cost of other government utilities like water, electricity and property taxes.

It is nothing but fooling the public because, the government wants to divert the attention of the public away from their failure in performing the primary task towards the society. In this game of fooling the government has adopted several methods. First, it asked all schools to constitute PTA in every school with a motive to show that it cares for parents.

Many good schools had their well organised PTAs even before the government stepped in. From my own personal experience, PTA has been cementing good understanding between parents and teachers by holding cultural and educational activities. These have also helped parents to improve their own role as effective parents towards their own children. Now the government wants only ₹ Five per year collected as the PTA fees. In Mumbai, one meeting of the PTA would cost ₹ 5 even if one cup of tea were offered, apart from the cost of stationery etc.

But government was never interested in promotion of cause of understanding between the parents and teachers. Their hidden agenda was to use the PTA to protect themselves from the backlash of parents anger. Otherwise, what is the validity of prescribing PTA's approval of fee hike? There is no rational basis for such a prescription. The management and parents have a manager-client relationship or relationship that exists between a provider and recipient of services. Once the need for the service is over, the parents have no interest whatsoever in the good of the school.

It is like the relationship between the litigant and the lawyer. If the law is to prescribe the fees of advocates on the basis of approval of the litigants. I am sure they would not like to pay any fees to their advocates. Or let us imagine a situation where the salaries of the judges are to be approved by the litigant. I am sure again that the litigants are in no mood to pay any increases in the salaries of the judge. In both these cases, litigants feel harassed by the delays in our legal system.

In the like manner, parents as the recipients of services provided by the school, are interested in the best buy at the low cost. According to press reports, the Supreme Court has already ruled in March this year that PTA approval for fee hike is not mandatory. Yet some educational authorities in Mumbai are insisting on the PTA resolution. This could only result in the harassment to the honest management; while providing another means in the hands of unscrupulous elements in the bureaucracy to collect some easy money from equally unscrupulous management.

Third, that the government has limited these requirements of the PTA and its approval for fee hike only up to the school education. Very interestingly, the scheme of PTA approval of fee structure does not exist for the unaided degree colleges. In the case of unaided degree colleges, whether they are medical, engineering or education, government itself determines the fee structure. Why is the government so generous with the unaided professional colleges? Being in the dual position of an educator and educational administrator for the last forty years, I wonder at the government rationale and the parental psychology. What I feel is that the government is generous to the management of these unaided degree colleges, because the politicians control most of them and the class interest binds those who are in the government now with those who were in it in the past. Another plausible explanation is that at the present level of political development, government is not obliged to provide higher education in contrast to the primary and secondary. Parents also expect free or at least cheap education at the secondary level than at the degree level.

In these circumstances some parents become tools in the hands of unemployed politicians aspiring for a role in the local affairs. So come June and July every year, there are good opportunities to such men to exploit the situation and direct parents anger towards the management of schools.

However, it is necessary for the parents to know that these local politicians are only extending their helping hand to the government to cover their failure to provide secondary education for the future citizens of the country. Thus, parents' while agitating against the management are barking at the wrong tree; they need to ask their elected representatives and the government to provide them aided educational facilities in their locality irrespective of medium of instruction.

Chapter - 37

Internalise Post Graduate Examination System

(One India One People, 10 November 1999)

"One of the chief defects of the present higher education in India is the examination system which has hardly any scope for testing the real knowledge of students. The author, here describes the present examination systems and its anomalies on the basis of his personal experiences".

After teaching at post-graduate level for twenty seven years, and guiding successfully seventeen students for their research degrees, I was preparing to retire early in 1997. Then, one day, I encountered a fairly intelligent female student, who had just passed the examination with a first class. When I specifically asked her how much she got in the paper I taught, on International Politics, she informed me that she got 60 per cent without attending many of my lectures.

While I told her that she could have got more marks if she had attended my classes, it has always troubled me as to why students consider our lectures irrelevant to their goal of getting a degree with a good class. If this is the attitude of above average students, average ones are merely interested in passing the examination and having a label of MA before their names that might help them to get an additional increment here and there.

What has contributed to this state of affairs in our universities? The answer lies mainly in the way we conduct our examinations to decide the merit and award a degree though other contributory factors are also there.

The conduct of examination is unrelated to the teacher who has taught a subject in the class room and the content of his lecture. Thus, the university authorities appoint a teacher who has taught a broad sub-discipline, say politics or economics for a period of five or ten years, as an examiner. It is not necessary that he should have taught the specific paper which he is going to set or examine.

To take a concrete example, a person who has taught political science at the undergraduate level in a college, will be deemed eligible to set the papers at MA. Thus, if the person empowered to select a panel of examiners–a dean of faculty here or a chairman of board of studies there, and if she or he is an academic manipulator-there is a good chance of his or her cronies being appointed as the examiners, though there are a few good deans or chairperson as well.

Thus, as the chairman of one of the panels of paper setters, I had the disgusting experience with one head of the political science department in a local college when he was working as a co-examiner on my panel. If I asked him whether he could set a paper on International Politics, he would say yes and he would say yes for a paper on International Law as well, though I knew it well that he had never taught those papers in his life time.

His technique-and that is the bane of our examination system-of setting a paper is very simple. University is expected to provide him with the papers of past three years six sets since examinations are held twice a year. By using the technique of 'cut and paste', he will prepare a paper on any subject in the present system. But a good teacher will refuse to accept to examine a paper that he has not taught in the recent past, let alone set the paper in such a subject.

This trick of the trade is known to enterprising students. Thus, what students will do is to look for the previous papers and prepare for nine to ten questions in a subject irrespective of the topics emphasised in the class depending on the changing contours of the topic in the world, of which he is sure to get at least six questions to choose to write his examination. The next luck factor is the examiner who assesses these papers. If one can set the papers without teaching a subject, he can very well examine it, though he has never taught the subject.

In mid-1980s, I had an experience of how such teachers mark the answer scripts. Out of four papers one writes in a year of an MA examination, I received two answer scripts of one candidate and another examiner got two other answer scripts. The student had through six supplements, reproduced the questions from the question paper as his answers. Knowing that the student has cheated the system, I had failed him. But my counter-part had given this candidate 53 marks. He obviously had gone by the weight of the answer script rather than the weight of answers! If you do not understand the content of the paper, giving safe marks-median marking is a popular way with the examiners.

After twice failing, because I had given this candidate four marks one mark each for four questions attempted, for candidate's sheer ability to translate a questions into a positive statement of fact the candidate asked for a revaluation. I asked the university authorities to ask the candidate to personally appear before me and read the script for me as the paper could not provide any answers. The candidate had to admit the fraud. But if one is lucky 90 per cent get through because of the median marking by examiners.

The above two drawbacks in our examination system at the level of the Post Graduate (PG) examinations, perforce create two types of teachers. One type of teachers let me call them, student friendly knowing the examination system, will give notes in the class, which are attuned to patterns of questions. Since questions asked in the examinations are old, teachers' notes too remain old. I know some teachers who have through their historical notes-prepared soon after they joined teaching profession-sometimes may be based on inputs from their own teachers, have risen to the top position in the professional organisations.

These teachers are always attuned to student passing examination rather than equip him to think independently or analyse the material available on a subject. Dictating notes in the classroom, makes him popular with a majority of average students. There is a perfect harmony between student, teacher and examiner in this system as the student gets ready made answers to learn, teacher can continue to use the notes he prepared earlier and examiner is also happy in his task of setting up papers. Since all have depended on the past knowledge, there is no question of any conflict arising.

In contrast, if a teacher teaches about the latest development, asks a question on the same in the examination, students find it tough and 'out of syllabus' giving rise to student agitation. This is particularly so as our syllabi refuse to change for years together and the rigidity of examination system leaves no scope for a teacher to be innovative in teaching and examining the student.

What can be done to improve the examination system? What needs to be done is totally internalising the examination system. This is not a revolutionary concept unknown to teachers and academic administrators.

It was tried in University of Bombay in the 1970s. In this system, the students are periodically assessed by the teachers who have taught, on the basis of their class room lectures and discussion, for which sixty marks are devoted while for remaining 40 marks, an year end examination is held instead of holding one annual examination for 100 marks at the end of the year.

The system was opposed by the students on the ground that the scheme could be used to penalise them. There was an agitation by them for two weeks. As a result, it was made optional. For nearly 15 years or so, internal system was opted only by serious students; average student preferred to appear for an annual examination.

However, under the general deterioration in the University system in the late 1980s, the scheme was withdrawn by the authorities. Their justification was: setting up two sets of the same subject, was expensive and therefore, PG departments were asked to opt only one or the other scheme. In case the internal scheme is followed, a teacher has to be prepared to teach about the latest developments and exert little more than usual to assess the students in periodical tests. Whether it is humanities, social sciences or physical sciences it will demand additional work on the part of every teacher.

When academic authorities like the Vice Chancellors, are more concerned with economy, heads of departments also toe their line by opting for the one shot annual examination system as it is least controversial and calls for minimum work from them. The PG departments are the producers of ultimate teachers in the undergraduate colleges and even schools. If their students come into society through a scheme of rigorous internal examinations, they will influence ultimately the entire educational system in the nation. If so, no cost to be so high as to sacrifice the benefits of internal examination scheme.

Chapter - 38

Fooling the Public

(Mid-Day, 17 July 2000)

"The government wants to divert the attention of the public from their failure in performing the primary task towards society".

Many good schools in Mumbai had Parents Teachers' Association (PTA) for a long time, much before the government discovered how they could use them to establish their democratic credentials. At the same time they also realised that they can use the PTAs to check management and show that the government is on the side of the parents. The latest news is that the government wants a student representative to be the joint secretary of the PTA.

Since last year the Maharashtra government and the Brihanmumbai Municipal Corporation are asking the unaided schools to provide before they approve fee hikes, a resolution from the PTA approving the hike. The Supreme Court has already ruled in March this years that PTA approval for fee hike is not mandatory. Yet some educational authorities in Mumbai are insisting on the PTA resolution.

This could only result in harassment to the honest management while providing another means in the hands of unscrupulous elements in the bureaucracy to collect some easy money from equally unscrupulous managements.

This way the government is actually trying to fool the public and so far it has been successful. It is the constitutional function of the State Government to provide primary and secondary education to the children of the state.

But in the name of promoting regional languages (siblings of ministers and bureaucrats of course go to English medium schools by and large), the government has consistently denied government aid to English medium schools in the state since the 1980s.

Now there is a steep increase in the pay burden on the school management because of the implementation of the Fifth Pay Commission scales and the rise in the cost of other government utilities like water, electricity and property taxes.

The government would like the teachers to be paid according to new scales. But does not want to bear the burden of contributing even a paisa towards the education through English medium.

The government wants to divert the attention of the public away from their failure in performing the primary task towards the society. In this game, the government has used PTA in several ways. First, it asked all schools to constitute PTA in every school. From my own personal experience, PTA has been cementing good understanding between parents and teachers by holding cultural and educational activities. These have also helped parents to improve their own role as effective parents.

Now government want only ₹ five per year collected as PTA fees. In Mumbai, one meeting of the PTA would cost more than ₹ five even in one cup of tea were offered, apart from the cost of stationery, etc. School management can borrow or beg, which they often do, but they can neither steal nor mint money.

But the government was never interested in promotion of the cause of understanding between the parents and teachers. Their hidden agenda was to use the PTA to protect themselves from the backlash of parents anger. Otherwise, what is the validity of prescribing PTA's approval of the fee hike?

The management and parents have a management relationship or a relationship that exists between a provider and recipient of services. Once the need for the service is over, the parents have no interest whatsoever in the good of the school.

Many parents, who have played active roles in PTA, pay scant attention to schools once their wards are out of it. It is like the relationship between the litigant and the lawyer. If the law is to prescribe the fees of advocates on the basis of litigants approval. I am sure they would not like to pay any fees to their advocates.

Or let us imagine a situation where the salaries of the judges are to be approved by the litigants. I am sure again that the litigants are in no mood to pay any increases in the salaries of the judge. In both these cases, litigants feel harassed by the delays in our legal system. In like manner, parents, as the recipients of services provided by the school, are interested in the best buy at low cost.

Third, that the government has limited these requirements of the PTA and its approval for fee hike only up to the school education.

Very interestingly, the scheme of PTA approval of fee structure does not exist for the unaided degree colleges. The student participation in the management of the PTA is also obviously not there in these high fee colleges. In the case of unaided degree colleges, whether they are medical, engineering or education, government itself determines the fee structure.

The government has been always generous in deciding fee rates in these institutions. Why government is so generous with the unaided professional colleges? Being in the dual position of an educator and educational administrator for the last forty years, I wonder at the government rational and the parental psychology.

What I feel is that the government is generous to the management of these unaided degree colleges, because the politicians control most of them and the class interest binds those who are in the government now with those who were in it in the past. Another plausible explanation is that at the present level of political development, government is not obliged to provide higher education in contrast to the primary and secondary. Parents also expect free or at least cheap education at the secondary level than at the degree level.

Hence, these very parents, who agitate against paying high fees in schools, are willing to pay a huge fee to coaching classes and later in the professional colleges. In these circumstances some parents become tools in the hands of unemployed politicians aspiring for a role in the local affairs.

So, come June and July every years, there are good opportunities to exploit the situation and direct parents anger towards the management of schools by organising a *morcha* or an agitation.

Thus parents need to ask their elected representatives and the government to provide them aided educational facilities in their locality irrespective of the medium of instruction.

Chapter - 39

Teachers as Contract Labourers

(The Free Press Journal, 26 July 2000)

"Author makes a strong case for concept of 'sevak' not only be applied to qualified teachers, but be a common norm applicable to bureaucrats and politicians for a period of three years!"

Maharashtra has never been a progressive state in the field of education. The latest example that bears testimony to this statement is the government's decision to appoint teachers in the schools and junior colleges on contract basis of ten months on a pittance of ₹ 3,000 or ₹ 3,500. Government treasury is bankrupt, on the government's own admission while it took control last year. But it seems that it also suffers from intellectual bankruptcy.

How could otherwise government devise devious device to reduce its financial burden on account of secondary education? How can it imagine hiring post-graduate trained teachers to work on a salary or what government calls honorarium of ₹ 3000 or ₹ 3500? Government pays its Class IV servants around ₹ 4500. Brihanmumbai Corporation pays little over ₹ 6000 to their sweepers.

Most of these teachers would have paid high fees to get their B Ed Degree by joining B Ed Colleges promoted by politicians and influential bureaucrats. The government wants teachers to work on contract basis for five years before they can be considered for a regular appointment. During the five-year period, the contract teachers would not get any vacation salary or any long term benefits.

But nothing better can be expected from a government that has consistently treated teachers as social scum. This is true of all governments in the past irrespective their party complexion. This is because, policy in fact is determined by the bureaucrats and not elected leaders. Thus, for instance, where there is not even work enough to appoint a part-time teacher, government wants the schools to appoint teachers on clock hour basis.

About a year ago, I sat to interview a teacher on clock hour basis. We calculated her monthly total remuneration was only ₹ 250. Hence, we offered to double it by management contributing an equal amount to what the government was offering. The teacher walked out stating that she paid that amount to her maid servant!

The government's shortsightedness and lack of respect of teaching profession can be gauged from another instance. In schools with junior college attached to it, for all these years heads of schools were paid a paltry sum of ₹ 100/pm for holding additional charge of junior college which might have a strength equal to or even more than the school. Now after the Fifth Pay Commission, this amount is doubled to ₹ 200.

But the very bureaucrats who decide these rates for the schools, provide to themselves, 10 per cent of basic salary of a post when they hold additional charge claim a minimum salary of 10 per cent of the basic of the post they are holding as additional charge. As much as the head of school does the entire work pertaining the additional charge, during the office hours as the government officer does. Then, why this discriminatory treatment?

The government has advanced the argument that with the expansion of education and increase in salaries, the burden of educational expenditure has increased on the government. The similar burden has increased several folds as far as the government bureaucracy is concerned. No doubt the population of the state has increased since the state was formed in 1960. But in comparison to the increase in population, the bureaucracy had increased several folds.

Then why not apply the same rule to the bureaucracy in Mantralaya and elsewhere in the state? Newly selected probationers for Indian Administrative Service (IAS) could be appointed on a honorarium same as offered to teachers for a period of five years. This should be much more rational than the case of teachers. Because, in IAS one has numerous opportunities for promotion. Teaching is a dead-alley job, except in rare occasions.

Equally pertinent is the another question; Since the elected representatives of the people are after all social workers, why not ask them to forego, their numerous allowances? Instead, they always are first and fast to pass their own increase in salaries and allowances without much discussion. In performing honorary service to the society, they ought to be first to lead by their own example.

Then, when a regular graduate trained teacher gets a salary of over 9,000 rupees, the contract teacher gets ₹ 3000- one third of a regular teacher, though qualifications of both are identical, their performance is bound to suffer. At the minimum, he is bound to be slack in his work.

Second, these teachers would openly seek tuition to supplement their pittance they get as salary. Third, as it is coaching classes have become inevitable part of educational system involving competition. Now parents and pupils would have added justification since contract teachers teach them.

Fourth, if the idea of contract teachers is not opposed, it will then be introduced to institutions of higher learning as well. Here the government would make the argument that it is not obliged to provide higher education to every one and therefore any one who wants it, has to pay for the same.

Fifth, the management will exploit it in the name of economy. As it is cases of making teachers to sign for higher amounts than they receive is not unknown device. Since contract teacher scheme empowers them to hire teachers in contravention of existing provision of confirmation in a teaching job after two years of probation, some management may as well prefer to have contract teachers on daily wages.

As of now, we see lawyers standing outside the courts and asking passersby whether they need his services. If the contract teachers' scheme is not withdrawn, one might see teachers standing in front of the schools and colleges with a hope that they might be called in to teach a subject!

Chapter - 40

Footpath Lawyers

(The Observer of Business and Politics, 8 August 2000)

"Universities should enroll only a smaller number of students in law faculty than they do now, though it is extremely difficult to know the number of lawyers the nation requires. But the scene of lawyers accosting passersby for work really lowers the dignity of legal profession and also our judicial system".

In my article 'Teachers As Contract Labourers' (The Observer of Business and Politics, 31 July 2000), I referred of lawyers standing outside the courts and asking passersby whether they need their services. It was not meant to cast an aspersion on the legal profession but meant to sensitise legal fraternity, courts and the governments in the country.

Any time I walk through the front of Esplanade Court next to the BMC annexe building on the Mahapalika Marg, what hurts most is the scene of lawyers on the footpath in their full professional dress, offering their services to passersby. However, its not merely at Esplanade Court that this happens but one can see it in most of other lower courts in the city too. This is the scene to some extent in smaller towns also.

Any day, when the court is in session, their number is not less than fifty to sixty. These lawyers accost you, offer to plead your case and get any other legal service you need. It is, in my opinion, a shameful act for the men of this noble profession of law to behave as their own promoters! It hurts for two reasons. First, as a former professor, having served Mumbai University for 25 years in the Post-graduate department, I feel pity for the Law Department that produced most of them, as though to practice on the footpath!

I strongly feel that universities should enrol only a smaller number of students in law faculty than they do now, though it is extremely difficult to know the number of lawyers the nation requires. But the scene of lawyers accosting passersby for work really lowers the dignity of legal profession and also our judicial system.

Second, it directly or indirectly tends to promote corruption in the judicial system in a broadest sense. It does it so directly, because as unemployed or under-employed lawyers, they develop a nexus between the corrupt judicial bureaucracy. Let me give here an example to illustrate the point. Some fifteen years ago when I went to Kurla Court to get my son's domicile certificate, I was swamped by five to six lawyers, who were very keen to offer their services to me. When I told them that I had done my own domicile way back in 1957, as such I can apply for my son as well, they said that without a lawyers, I cannot do it, as I also needed to file an affidavit.

Thus, I was almost forced to engage a lawyer and get the services of a typist and spend a few hundreds. What struck me most was, when I went to get the certificate, after few days. I was asked to pay Rs five (it must have gone up now) to the peon before he could affix the stamp of the judicial magistrate. When I asked him on the need to pay, he simply said it is a routine matter!

In contrast, when I had gone to Esplanade Court in 1957 to get my own domicile certificate, it was a simple affair: Apply and take away your certificate after few days. This shows, how within a period of about 30 years, corruption had crept into lower judicial system, I hold the surplus lawyers, at least partly, responsible for this.

When I talked to my lawyer-friends about the footpath lawyers' practice, they told me that they make good money; I should not think that they are poor starving lawyers. They do make money because in this city, as in this country, there are still 50 per cent illiterates, who can be fleeced by these roadside lawyers.

However, this practice need to be regulated if not totally curbed in the interest of the credibility of judicial system at large. Though corruption has crept into the judicial system even at the higher levels, such cases are far in between; may be, because only a few cases come out in public. Yet, I believe judiciary is less corrupt in comparison to the other branches of the government, like legislature, executive and bureaucracy. The judiciary on the whole can be expected to fight out creeping corruption within it.

Hence, here are two suggestions for the judiciary, government, bar associations or the local authorities-whichever has the responsibility to implement them. First, the authorities need to build small kiosks inside or outside the court premises and make them available to lawyers on some reasonable rent. The bar associations may be the best organisations to enforce this code of conduct on these footpath lawyers.

Second, bar associations ought to also regulate the fees by prescribing them. The lawyers in the Kiosks need to display their fees for different services like notary, affidavits etc. This is necessary to prevent the lawyers fleecing the poor and illiterate litigants. The chiefs of different courts also need to take greater interest to see that their administrative staff does not indulge in corrupt practices so as to uphold credibility of the judicial system. They need to remember that the judiciary is the last bastion of Indian democracy. If it falls, that is the end of institutional support of democracy.

Chapter - 41

Modern Day Tughluqs

(Mid-Day, 15 November 2000)

"The government must have the courage to explain to the parents its policy of not aiding English medium schools, and encourage their voting citizens to go to vernacular medium schools which are aided and where education is free".

Most of us were taught in schools to remember Mohammad Bin Tughluq for his indecisiveness in government and administration. Are these Tughluqs a thing of the past? No. Because, democratic rulers behave irrationally to please their voters and escape from the responsibility of taking hard decisions. The Maharashtra government is behaving like a modern day Tughluq in its societal function of supervising the field of education. Take the unaided English medium schools in Mumbai and their current plight. It all began with the Fifth Pay Commission pay scales, which were implemented belatedly by the government in June 2000. The government has implemented new pay scales in aided schools and colleges. They have also forced the unaided schools to implement the scales. The government permitted these schools to raise fees proportionate to the increase in expenditure because of implementation of commission scales. The schools approached the deputy director of education for approval of the new fee rates. The education department's auditors visited schools and checked their budgets. Then these schools were given approval for new fee rates in May-June. However, some parents voiced their opposition to the fee hike. But nobody bothered to see the reality.

Friends' Education Society School was charging ₹ 175 per month. They were permitted to charge ₹ 400 per month. Smt Vidyaben Gardi High School was charging ₹ 185 per month and was permitted to charge ₹ 400 per month. B R Tol English High School was collecting ₹ 195 per month while its new fee rate became ₹ 440 per month. The educational trusts, which run the schools, are by and large not profit making ventures (like politician-run professional colleges) but are organised to provide education to their linguistic or community groups. These perform a vital function of providing education to the community, which is the primary task of the government. Hence, what was expected of the government is to take the educational trust into confidence and discuss the matter to find a reasonable solution.

On the other hand, the minister of education gave a solemn promise to agitating parents that under no circumstance would the fee hike be more than 50 per cent. This is based on his calculation that the burden on account of increase in salary is not more than 40 per cent. Tughluq had also raised taxes and he too had limited the raise to 50 per cent!

The actual burden on account of salary payment under the new scales alone ranges between 72 to 90 per cent. Just to illustrate the point, the monthly pay bill of B R Tol English High School under the existing scales in ₹ 1,46,873 which goes up to ₹ 2,59,601–an increase of 76 per cent. There are always ever growing expenses on account of water, electricity and other teaching aids. As a result of ministerial directive to reduce the enhanced fees to 50 per cent, the deputy director of education put on the notice board a list of reduced fees as per the new decision of the minister.

The government has been squeezing the unaided schools to financial bankruptcy by imposing a limit of increase only once in three years, though the dearness allowance rates have been going up every six months! As a result, many schools in their second and third year have had to face a huge deficit. Thus, for instance, in case of one school, in the very first year it had a deficit of ₹ 1,70,000. In the second year and in the third year it had a deficit of ₹ 2,60,000 and ₹ 3,40,000 respectively.

One insensitive education inspector told me that trusts should raise funds from industry! He forgets that trusts can raise funds for infrastructure; but not to educate children of parents who want English education. Probably seeing no effect of wallpaper administration of the school, it has issued fresh proforma letters asking schools to reduce their fee rates in such a way as not to exceed 50 per cent. But for their own safety, the Directorate has not superseded their old orders before issuing new orders. But it has reiterated the command that Fifth Pay Commission scales ought to be given to the teachers.

It is a matter of common sense that the fee structure will depend upon the seniority of teachers-longer the service of a teacher in the school, more it costs the school. The number of students in the class is another factor more students in a class mean lower fees and vice versa. Maharashtra government has had a policy of not aiding the English medium schools since 1984, though the present government recognizes the importance of English since it has introduced the subject at the primary stage itself. In the silver jubilee celebrations of an English medium school in Mulund, I had pleaded with the then minister of education, to bring English schools under government aid. The minister was forthright in stating that if the parents want English education, they need to be ready to pay for it. If now, however, government's heart bleeds for the parents who send their children to English medium schools, the sensible thing to do is to aid these schools. But the government says it has no money. It is difficult to believe that government has no money as its deputy chief minister proudly tells the public that government rules provide a whopping amount of ₹ 27 lakhs annually of repairs of his official residence. But he has been kind enough to save ₹ 10 lakhs by spending only ₹ 17 lakhs!

However, accepting the government version, it can extend partial aid to the unaided schools immediately. To begin with, it can come forward to make good the difference in the increase in the financial burden over and above the ministerial fiat of 50 per cent. Let the government audit the accounts of schools and if the burden of increase in pay is 90 per cent, let the government pay 40 per cent. If it cannot do either of the above, it must have courage to explain to the parents its policy of not aiding English Schools and encourage their voting citizens to go to vernacular schools which are aided and where education is free.

Instead of which the government has created ill will between teachers and parents, teachers and pupils, parents and management; thus disturbing peace in the schools, which is a prerequisite for good education.

Chapter - 42

Unaided English Schools Face Closure

(Mid-Day, 15 November 2000)

"It is a matter of common sense, that fee structure will depend upon the seniority of teachers longer the service of a teacher, more it costs to the school. Teachers with continued service of twelve years get senior scales. The number of students in the class is another factor, more students in a class mean lower fees and vice versa. By asking schools to reduce fees and at the same time forcing them to pay the Fifth Pay Commission scales is encouraging management to cheat the teachers".

Are the Tughluqs a thing of the past as we have democracy in the modern time? No. Because, while Mohammed bin Tughluq was behaving in irrational manner as a personal trait, democratic rulers think that they have to behave irrationally too. If necessary, to please their voters and escape from responsibilities of taking hard decisions, Maharashtra government in general and minister of education in particular is behaving as modern Tughluqs.

Unaided English medium schools in Mumbai for instance were asked to pay their teachers the Fifth Pay Commission pay scales. These were implemented belatedly by the government in June 2000. The government having already implemented new pay scales in aided schools and colleges.

The number of unaided English medium schools in Mumbai alone is quite large. The government permitted these schools to raise fees proportionate to the increase in expenditure because of implementation of the Fifth Pay Commission scales. As a result, schools decided to go for a new fee rates which was permitted in May-June.

However, some parents voiced their opposition to the fee hike. It became a populist slogan for the parents that fee hike is more than hundred per cent! Here, are some figures from Mulund schools. Friends' Education Society School was charging ₹ 175 per month. They were permitted to charge ₹ 400 pm. Smt Vidyaben Gardi High School was charging ₹ 185 per month and was permitted to charge Rs 400 per month. B. R. Tol English High School was collecting ₹ 195 per month while its new fee rate reached as high as ₹ 440 per month.

The educational trusts, which run the schools, are by and large not-profit making ventures (as politician-run professional colleges) but are organised to provide education to their linguistic or community group. These perform a vital function of government of providing education to the citizens, which is the primary task of the government worth its name. Hence, what was expected of a government is to take the educational trusts into confidence and discuss the matter to find a reasonable solution.

On the other hand, the minister of education gave a solemn promise to agitating parents that under no circumstance fee hike would be more than fifty per cent. This is based on his calculation that the burden on account of increase in salary is not more than forty per cent. This is nothing but bin Tughluq like dicta totally unreasonable and irrational. Tughluq had also raised the taxes but he too had limited the raise to fifty per cent!

But the actual burden on account of salary payment under the new scales alone ranges between 72 to 90 per cent. Just to illustrate the point the monthly pay bill of B R Tol English High School under the existing scales is ₹ 1,46,873 which goes up to ₹ 2,59,601 an increase of 76 per cent. There are always ever growing expenses on account of water, electricity and other teaching aids.

According to the author, the reduced fees range between minimum of ₹ 180 to ₹ 825 per month. If one school can run with ₹ 180 monthly fee, other can also run with the same. If in case of one school, reduced fee is ₹ 825, how is it that ₹ 440 in case of another school is more? This fact shows that decision is based on the assumption that till fee structure was revised, then existing fee rates were adequate to meet the expenditure. And all schools have a uniform burden on account of increase in pay.

Both these assumptions are factually incorrect. Government has been squeezing the unaided schools to financial bankruptcy by imposing a limit of increase only once in three years. Though government dearness allowance rates have been going up every six months, many schools in their second and third years have had to face a huge deficit. For instance, in case of one school, in the very first year it had a deficit of ₹ 1,70,000. In the second year and in the third year it had a deficit of ₹ 2,60,000 and ₹ 3,40,000 respectively.

The fact that three-year rule was irrational is recognised by the government now when in the new fee rates, government has permitted an increase of ten per cent in the second year and increase of twenty per cent in the second year. If it is so, then the government has to permit the schools to recover the loss made by them because of impossible condition of the increase of fees for three years.

Now, government has issued fresh proforma letters asking schools to reduce their fee rates in such a way as not to exceed fifty per cent. But for their own safety, the directorate has not superseded the old orders before issuing new orders. However, it has reiterated that Fifth Pay Commission scales ought to be given to the teachers. Next to parents, teachers constitute an important segment of voters.

It is a matter of common sense, that fee structure will depend upon the seniority of teachers-longer the service of a teacher-, more it costs to the school. Teachers with continued service of twelve years get senior scales. The number of students in the class is another factor more students in a class mean lower fees and vice versa.

In case of a school, fee rates have been reduced from ₹ 440 per month to ₹ 290 per month. It can only pay comfortably old scales to teachers, as in the fee rate prior to June 2000 the school was making loss of over ₹ 2.5 lakhs. By asking schools to reduce fees but at the same time asking them to pay the Fifth Pay Commission scales is encouraging management to cheat the teachers.

Maharashtra government has a policy of not aiding the English medium schools since, 1984. In the silver jubilee celebrations of an

English school in Mulund, the author had pleaded with the then Shiv Sena minister of education, to bring English schools under government aid. The minister was forthright in stating that if the parents want English education, they need to be ready to pay for it. However, now in opposition, their heart bleeds because of heavy fee burden imposed on parents by the government decision. If now, however, government's heart too bleeds because of the impact of higher fees on the parents sending their children to English medium schools, the sensible thing to do is to aid them. But the government says it has no money.

However, accepting the government version of financial crunch, it can come forward to make good the difference in the increase in the financial burden over and above the ministerial flat of fifty per cent. Let the government audit the accounts of schools and if the burden on account of increase in pay is 90 per cent, let the government pay 40 per cent.

If it cannot do either of the above, it must have courage to explain to the parents its policy of not aiding English schools and encourage their voting citizens to go to vernacular schools which are aided where education is free. Instead of that what the government has done so far is to create ill will between teachers and parents, teachers and pupils, teachers and management, parents and management. Thus, disturbing peace in the schools.

Chapter - 43

What Crime have they Committed?

(One India One People, February 2001)

"Innocent children have to bear the brunt of much pain and suffering. Child labour is a known reason. Children being drawn to terrorism is another. So too is the effect of economic sanctions against poorer countries".

Everyday various crimes are committed against inocent children in different parts of the world. The nature of crimes and their causes vary, depending on the country and circumstances in which they are committed. The Primary cause of such crimes is extreme poverty. Often, because of poverty, children are forced to work at a young age and thus denied education and family care that is essential for full growth. If childhood is spent working without proper care and education, the child grows up to become a burden on the society, rather than a responsible citizen of the State. Keeping this in mind, the law-makers of India, prohibited the employment children below 14 in hazardous labour. But, not withstadning the constitutional ban, children below 14 are made to work and in the process are also exploited by industries. Poverty-stricken families procreate more with the hope of improving their economics status. They believe that more earning hands at home means more income to the family. However, in reality, such families end up increasing their poverty.

Few years ago when I visited Ganapatiphule, I came across a boy of nine to 10 years, working as a cleaner in a hotel. When I asked him as to why he was working in the hotel instead of going to school, he said that his father could not afford his education.

Certain industries in India and other developing countries exploit poor people by employing their children in hazardous industries at nominal wages. Carpet and firecracker industries are regarded as the most prominent among those who exploit child labour in India. Often it is argued that certain carpeting designs can be made only by children through their tender fingers; hence, employing them is justified for the growth of the industry. This is something unbelievable.

Ever since my encounter with the boy in Ganapatiphule. I have been repeatedly questioning the rationale behind providing free education to a girl child from an affluent family, while denying it to a male child from a poor family just because of the gender difference. Now that many state governments have made education upto the secondary level free, it should be easy for a poor children irrespective of their sex to go to school. But, that is not so, because, free education does not compensate the income loss which occurs due to a child attending school instead of working. Hence, the government should think in terms of providing monetary inducement to parents of poor families to send their children to school.

The imperative need is to make the right to education, a fundamental right and enforce it with vigour and national zeal. It will have a telling effect in improving the economic, social and political condition of rural as well as urban poor besides limiting the size of their families.

However, denial of education and forcing the child to work are only soft crimes against children. Soft, not because I underestimate its impact on the growth of human personality, but because, adults have discovered more heinous forms of crimes against children. For want of space. I limit here only two other forms of such crimes internationally practised against children.

One is induction of children in regular or guerrilla warfare or using them to promote international terrorism. During a decade long (1980-1989) Iran-Iraq war Iran used thousands of children to fight the war. In Sri Lanka, the Liberation Tigers of Tamil Eelam (LTTE) have indiscriminately inducted very young children including even teenagers to fight against Sri Lanka forces for their separatist cause.

There were some very disturbing reports of teenagers being trained in mosques and *Madarasas* in Pakistan in the name of religious *jihad* (holy war). In the first week of August 2000 Indian armed forces captured a group of armed teenager-militants, sneaking into Kashmir. The organizers of the Lashkar-e-Toiba, the new incarnation of old Lashkar-e-Ansar, banned by the U.S. as a terrorist organisation also claimed that they are training around 80,000 young men in religious studies and warfare.

The UN Security Council recently estimated some 300,000 children under 18 and some as young as seven to be trained in arms. Other figures are staggering too. In the last decade, two million children were killed, one million orphaned, six million seriously injured or disabled and 12 million were made homeless because of international conflicts and acts of terrorism.

For the first time the UN Security Council, after a marathon debate in which representatives of more than fifty nations participated, passed a resolution of "children in Armed conflict", asking nation and warring groups to protect children and prevent them from turning them into soldiers. However, earnest pleas by the Indian representative Kamalesh Sharma, to add teeth to the resolution by banning the use of educational institutions as recruitment grounds fell on deaf ears. So were his pleas to increase global co-operation in fighting terrorism.

The second area of concern is the growing rate of dying children in Iraq because of imposition of economic sanctions by the US-led UN Security Council. A survey by the UNICEF showed that under-five mortality in Iraq went up from 56 deaths per thousand during 1984-1989 to 131 per thousand in 1994-1999. The UN Secretary General, Kofi Annan supported the view that the UN sanctions were responsible for the increase in the death rate of children in Iraq.

The Clinton administration has rejected the findings. But the linkage between the rise in the death-rate of under-five children and economic sanctions became indirectly evident when the State Department denied permission to the four Congress aides to do an on the spot study of the impact of economic sanctions on Iraq. This cannot be an isolated case of Iraq as it is likely that, in the present unipolar world, the US would impose similar economic sanctions against other nations in future.

The lives of Iraqi children should not be lost because of an ego-clash between the US President Bill Clinton and Iraqi President, Saddam Hussain.

The Americans need to realise the cause of humanity to save the children of the world. On the one hand, US and other developed countries have threatened to boycott of Iraqi goods. On the other hand, American policies in not taking a tougher stand against international terrorism or by refusing to withdraw economic sanctions against Iraq directly, lead to the massacre of children.

To some extent terrorists too are created because of extreme poverty. Reports suggest that the Pakistani Inter-Services Intelligence recruit young children from amongst Uighurs Muslims by offering $20,000 per recruit for six months. Similarly, economic sanctions in Iraq will lead to greater impoverishment of ordinary people, though the ruling elite would continue to survive.

What Americans cannot achieve by imposing economic sanctions or following a dual policy on terrorism can be achieved by promoting a consistent humane policy of helping to eradicate poverty. If Bill Clinton could visit Vietnam to put past history behind, he could also lift economic sanctions against Iraq to save children from scourge of crime, death and impoverishment.

Chapter - 44

School V/s Classes

(Mid-day, 1 March 2001)

"If the State Government is serious about banning coaching classes, it can do so without any draconian regulatory measures-by just reducing student numbers in school classrooms"

The Maharashtra government, it is reported is planning to bring a fresh bill in the ensuing budget session to regulate and control coaching classes. Its earlier ordinance on the subject was stayed by the High Court. It is relevant, therefore, to discuss three questions. First, is there really a need to regulate coaching classes? Second, why do these coaching classes come up and grow like mushrooms? Finally, what can be done to minimise the menace of coaching classes?

To answer the first question first, the government's motive in trying to regulate the coaching classes itself is suspect. Justice Shah had said in the case challenging the ordinance, that it seemed to have been framed "keeping in mind a certain individual." The question of relevance of such regulation needs to be analysed in the context of where the nation wants to move in the next few decades.

The buzzword in Indian politics today is liberalisation. Then why control private coaching classes? The government wants to control and regulate coaching classes. But it is ridiculous to prescribe that coaching classes make provision for "parking of the students vehicles" or provide for waiting rooms. Control means avenues to earn money for the state by means of registration fees. This is welcome for a state that is bankrupt as far as public services are concerned.

For the sake of argument, granting that coaching classes are necessary, what on earth empowers the state to determine the fees chargeable by them? If the state or bodies like All India Medical Council or Bar Associations, for instance, are unable to regulate the fees to be charged by doctor or lawyers-a greater priority in the interest of public welfare-how can it lay down the fee structure for the coaching classes? After all, these provide, group tuitions to students who feel a need for it and can afford to pay for it. The government interference in the working of any profession should be minimum and only commensurate to state's contribution in maintaining such activities.

Now to move to the second, and more important question as to why such coaching classes mushroom, we need to look at the present system of educational administration in the state. A look at the government-aided schools show that these are overcrowded. Teachers are unable to pay individual attention to students. But being the paymaster, the government's single motivation has been to reduce the expenditure on education. Hence, if more students are admitted to a class, the cost borne by the government on account of wage bills, is lesser. Then there are problems caused by the government using the teachers in the aided schools as though they are their employees. So the teachers are detailed for all sorts of government work like conduction census, election duties, campaign for family planning and so on. Often a teacher may be away for such a long time that he might appear as a visiting teacher. The government does not even spare unaided schools. It tries to enforce aided school norms in relation to unaided schools, which stifle any possibility of innovative teaching. These developments have led parents to believe that what is taught in the school is not enough for their wards to get a good score in Standard X and XI examinations.

I have come across instances where coaching class owners critique the teaching styles of certain teachers in public meeting, so as to attract students to their coaching class. Is it really necessary for a student to attend a coaching class to gain a good grade? At the outset it must be made clear that persons who teach in the coaching classes are in no way better than those who teach in schools. The main reason if there is one, for the justification of a coaching class is that these are small and they are able to provide individual attention to students attending them. Parents find these are less expensive in contrast to the individual tuitions.

The government can take certain long-term measures. Reduce the size of classes to maximum 30 and 40 students in schools and junior colleges and compulsorily provide for tutorials. Every year, at the time of school admissions, we see the government permitting schools to admit more children in existing classes rather than permit opening of new schools. Parents are willing to spend thousands of rupees for sending their children to coaching classes while refusing to pay increased fees in schools. If parents spend the same amount in school fee, their children can derive much better education than they get now. Whenever a school gets a rank in the SSC or HSC examinations, it is the coaching class, which claims credit for the feat as though the school has done pretty little for the progress of the child. As an educational administrator, I have come across numerous parents who proudly say that they have spent ₹ 20,000 or more to get a ward into a reputed coaching class.

In contrast, I can cite the examples of students who got into merit lists only with the efforts of schools and without going to coaching classes. Last year, in Vidya Prasarak Mandal's Kannada High School, in Mulund, one Ms Ganagi secured the 16th rank in the SSC Board. I found that the school had a class strength of little above 40 and teachers had given individual attention to the student. However, if the schools fail to maintain an average attendance of 40, the government is happy to deny grant to such a division in a school! If the government is serious in banning coaching classes, it can do so without any draconian regulatory measures by just reducing student numbers in school classrooms.

Chapter - 45

Breathing Fresh Air into the System of School Education

(The Free Press Journal, 13 August 2001)

"High Court directive in March 2001 on the fees issue is lauded as it enabled private unaided schools, appoint graduate trained teacher in upper primary as against government norm of undergraduate teachers teaching at the level"

The cash-starved Democratic Front government in Maharashtra is looking for simplistic ideas to save money. Invariably it only sees the field of education as the rich area where it can save some money. This year in the middle of June, it sent out a circular cutting aid to aided English medium schools by fifty percent. Moment some parents and students came out protesting against the government policy, the State suspended implementation of the policy. Affected aided schools were also preparing to go to High Court against the government policy.

But during the last year, the government was so adamant on the question of granting adequate fee structure to the managements to enable them to pay the Fifth Pay Commission scales, that at last the managements of unaided schools were forced to seek justice from the High Court. Despite High Court coming out in favour of a fair fee structure, following into the footsteps of parents of aided English High Schools, parents of unaided English Schools resorted to a Rasta Roko protesting against high fees charged by Hindi Bhavan School in Marine Lines.

The parents of the unaided schools-whether English or any other regional media-ought to learn to think themselves outside the norms of aided schools. This will serve them to get education of better quality than that provided in aided schools. The High Court interim order of March this year liberates unaided schools to some extent from debilitating norms in the appointment of staff. It permits the management to appoint better qualified staff to teach children in the unaided school. All these years the government forced management to apply government's aided schools' norms in the matters of appointment of teachers to unaided schools too.

The government's single aim is to minimise its budgetary (they call it a burden) expenditure on education and issue norms accordingly. To give an illustration, the government norms say that only trained undergraduate teachers to be appointed to teach lower secondary or upper primary classes (V to VII) attached to secondary schools. In recent years, the government has added even VIII class to the lower secondary stage and asked the aided schools provide trained undergraduate teachers to teach them. Their only logical explanation thus is to reduce the 'burden' and not improve the quality of teaching.

On the other hand, many unaided schools have been appointing trained graduate teachers to teach children in V to VIII classes. So far, government babus invariably reduced the graduate salary scales paid to those teachers to undergraduate salary levels for their calculation of permissible fee rates. Now that the High Court has given a directive, it would help enlightened management to appoint legitimately better qualified teachers.

Second, the idea of including three per cent of the overall expenditure, as development fee in the general fee structure is itself a revolutionary concept. By and large, parents are not interested in the long-term development of the educational institution. What they are interested is best possible education at the lowest cost. They demand clean toilets, cold water and clearly written question papers. But do not bother to know that it costs money. It does not matter for them how socially minded people built educational institutions. Hence, making them pay three percent towards development would help to some extent to inculcate a sense of participation in institution building.

Third, are the schools merely to teach without enabling young pupils to reach out to build their potent abilities? The High Court once again by acknowledging the fees other than tuition fees, whether currently approved or not by the government, legitimizes need for co-curricular and extra curricular activities to achieve an all round development of child's personality. Of course, management has an obligation to see that extra fees collected are utilised for purposes for which they are collected and purposes ought to be directly related to the development of child's personality.

Here also the government and parents cannot demand a veto over such activities. The government simply needs to keep out from such decision-making, as babus are not intellectually equipped to make such a judgement. While the parents being too pluralistic in their approach, management ought to be permitted to determine what is good in the interest of their school activities. This will leave the freedom for the parents to decide whether they can afford education provided in a particular unaided school. Parents can decide to change the schools rather than pressurize the schools to change their goals of providing good education.

Chapter - 46

Is Collection of Donations Justified?

(The Free Press Journal, 3 September 2001)

"Should government or semi-government machinery be used to raise donations, even for good cause like social welfare?....... That is the function of private trusts or non-government organisations"

Now Mayor of Mumbai is out to collect donations albeit for a good cause of helping poor for their medical treatment. Noble thought. He has promised that it "is not forced on any one."

Do people voluntarily part with their money in our society? Do they give a donation to a good cause say providing education to poor children or for giving them free uniforms? In my 45 years of doing a little bit of social work in the field of education, I have come across only one individual who came to me quietly and gave a donation for a College building fund.

Even here, he has because his child studied in our educational institution for 12 years and probably he felt satisfied with the kind of education we provided. So it is necessary to have some correlation between a donor and donee. Without such a linkage no one gives a donation.

As a student I used to go from shop to shop in Fort area in the 1950s seeking small donations for a school building fund. Many of these people from I expected donations, have given me abuses; when I refused to budge, they chose to chase me out of their shop!

Only entity that gets donations without soliciting is the God Almighty. But here too, devotee gives in a moment of stress seeking God's help to prevent unknown from happening or praying for make him cause something to happen. But even here, unlike the Christianity in Hinduism, there is no concept of confession. The system of confession, I suppose can be used by the priests to channelise ill-gotten wealth for good causes. Recently, I came across an instance in the United States where an inspector from Federal Bureau of Investigation (FBI) was caught for providing state secrets to the erstwhile Soviet Union's intelligence agency KGB. He is supposed to have given $20,000 he received, in small amounts to Mother Theresa charities.

I have gone into details about difficulties experienced in India in collecting purely voluntary donations. Therefore, having said that no one will be forced to donate, Mayor in the next breath stated, "each of our officials is expected to collect about ₹ 10,000!".

If Mayor expects a particular amount to be collected by an official, that official in turn would naturally use his position to extract a fixed amount from a service seeker be that an eating establishment license or a birth registration certificate. Big services, like a building occupation certificates or a water connections of course will not be given at all without speed money to every one-from the peon who moves the heavy file, to the head of the department. Now add another ₹ 500 or ₹ 1000 towards a donation card.

But Mayor is not the only one who collects so-called voluntary donations. You go to the collector's or his subordinates' office they will persuade you to buy a printed coupon for contribution to some welfare organisation under their tutelage. You need a property extract, or a sat bara, you end by paying against your will as it is likely that your work might be done in four visits within a week rather than merely visiting endlessly forever without any results.

Then come education officials who wish to promote Savitribai Phule fellowships to poor and deserving students in schools. They print coupons and ask Head of schools to collect a fixed amount from children, teachers and management. If you question the commanding voice of the official, he tells you "after all we have to coexist!".

Then why make a farce of anti-capitation act and say that no donations to be taken at the time of admissions? If the officials in the above three instances are going to collect their donation from their captive clientele, why prevent the schools from collecting donations from the beneficiaries of their educational activities?

Educational trusts too need money particularly when the state and the BMC, which have main responsibility under the law to provide educational grants-in-aid, are bankrupt and are unable to provide legally obligatory assistance to schools like their annual non-salary grants! How can these trusts maintain school or college buildings, provide electricity and other equipments, if the government starve them of their dues?

But there is a more fundamental question. Should government or semi-government machinery be used to raise donations, even for good cause like social welfare? The government or semi-government institutions like the BMC are not the suitable agencies to be involved in charities. The function of the state is to regulate and administer and not indulge in public charities. That is the function of private trust or non-government organisations. If the Mayor can raise funds by using his official position or the government officials can collect funds, what was wrong with Barrister Antulay as Chief Minister collecting money for his then proposed trusts for the development of his village, town, and the state?

Chapter - 47

Curbing School Donations under Rules

(The Free Press Journal, 6 February 2002)'

"The role of PTA, the government visualised as promotion of 'the all round development of child' But is effect,....is using it as a populist rod to regulate fee structure in unaided schools".

Maharashtra Government has prepared draft rules under Maharashtra Educational Institutions Prohibition of Capitation Fee Act 1987 to prohibit collection of donations by schools from parents and children in the state of Maharashtra. The British administration used to hang revenue regulations in English on a village tree inviting objection just a day before they were to come into force. Since the villagers saw these rarely, the colonial administration would implement them on the ground that people have no objection to new regulations. In the British legacy, now government gave these drafts to schools on December 29 asking them to report, if they object, on or before December 31!

Previous Shiv Sena-BJP alliance government had tried to regulate pre-primary education, which had to be withdrawn because of the pressure from the Church-run schools. But now through these draft rules, government wants to control them by bringing the Balwadis, and Kindergarten schools within the purview of definition of "admission" to educational institutions.

Formal education of a child begins only from admissions to primary school. However, because in most of the cases a child's both parents are working to support their families and they live in nuclear families. Hence they are required to take care of their children during their absence in the day. Thus pre-primary education is crèche irrespective of its nomenclature Balwadi, nursery, or kindergarten. In this area the government has no responsibility whatsoever and therefore it should keep out of these activities. The basic purpose of the 1987 Act is to curb the school management from taking donations from parents/guardians at the time of admission or promotions of pupils. Now by framing these draft rules the government intends to regulate the activities of schools collecting donations. However, the meaning and intentions underlying the clause 5 are not clear.

The sub-Clause (b) says: "An Educational Institution proposing to collect or accept donation shall prepare a project or an estimate in respect of the work for which donations are proposed to be collected, and send it to the competent authority for approval. Such donation when collected shall not exceed the cost of such project." It means that an educational institution is authorised to collect donations from parents with the prior consent of the "competent authority." However, the educational institutions are not provided with the income tax exemption by the federal government which acts normally as an incentive to citizens to give a donation. But a reading of clause 5 (c) implies that receipt is to be issued by "the management as per their memorandum of association and rules". Hence, if the trusts/ associations managing educational institutions are to submit the "project" for collection of donations. The government is unnecessarily imposing restrictions on the trust activities, as they are already empowered to collect donations. They are also required to submit their annual budget to the charity commissioner. Hence, the proposed rule appears to constrict their existing powers and functions.

The trusts raise donations from a variety of sources independent of parents, and students and their admissions and promotions. These are subject to Income Tax authorities and charity commissioner. By proposing to control the donation raising activities of the educational institutions, government is creating one more new avenue for corruption in bureaucracy at the lower level. The government control in a liberalised economy has to be commensurate with the contributions of the government to the cause of education. Socially minded individuals largely manage the educational trusts as a social work. In the event of too many fetters on the educational work and fund-raising by genuine trust, only the Business or family promoted trusts-which do not need to raise money from the public-alone might be left to work in the educational field. This might lead to greater exploitation of parents and children.

The clause 6 dealing with the Fee Structure of Unaided Schools does not mention Development fee approved by the Mumbai High Court in their interim judgement of March 2000. Similarly it is silent about the Laboratory fee and deposit. These are necessary for effective, efficient management of education in the unaided schools and colleges.

The Parent Teacher Associations (PTA) have been working effectively in many good schools for many years prior to some one in government discovered the usefulness of PTA. The role of PTA, the government visualizes as promotion of the all round development of child. But in effect, the government is using it as a populist rod to regulate fee structure in unaided schools.

Since the government made PTA compulsory in 1998, it has been anything but a body concerned with the all round development of child. Parents, in the unaided schools, as the recipients of the service of education, like to get best education for the lowest fees. That is the only aim of the PTA in their perspective and they intend to exercise a veto on the increase in fees whenever necessary.

Hence, the PTA has to be seen as an advisory body and not as a decision making body. Only then the parents could see the perspective of "all round development of child." Now it has become a cliché for the parents' leaders to decry commercialisation of education even when they are asked to pay the cost of education in the absence of money coming from the government.

But in reality a few self appointed leaders have made education as a field to emerge as professional agitators and destroy quality education provided by the unaided schools. By encouraging them, or succumbing to their pressure, the government is aiding them in their professional agitation.

Chapter - 48

Priya Tendulkar as a Prosecutor and Judge!

(The Fee Press Journal, 18 February 2002)

"If someone catergorises 'fund-raising' as business, "I have no hesitation in characterising them as 'professional agitators' with an eye for cheap publicity"

Can a person be a public prosecutor and the judge at the same time? Ask Ms Priya Tendulkar, anchorperson of Zimmedar Kaun. She might instantly reply "Yes, of course!" At least that is my conclusion after attending the shooting of her show on education at Nanavati Studio, Vile Parle and watching it on the Sub TV on January 20.

I happened to be in audience at the shooting of her show on education on December 30, 2001 on the personal invitation of Secretary of Unaided Schools Forum, Shri Jagdish Nanavati. I have been basically a teacher since 1960 having taught right from Secondary school to the highest level of education M. Phil and Ph.D in the University of Mumbai. But I attended this programme, as an educational administrator, since 1962. I have been associated with an educational trust that runs schools and a Jr. College at Mulund.

I was given to understand that the issue to be discussed was the implementation of government's policy of compulsory primary education. But sitting through the show, I was highly disappointed at the manner in which it was conducted. Largely due to the fact that the entire show was dominated by cheap populism without even a wee bit of effort to contribute towards improvement of educational standards, facilities or improve academic administration. Let me explain.

First, as in the political meetings probably one panelist had his supporters occupy most of the seats in the audience. As a result, those who held passes had no place to sit. Ms Tendulkar had to ask some of them to vacate their seats as they were occupying them without valid passes. The tone was set by Priya Tendulkar herself by referring to commercialisation of education characterising education as a business. It is only the so-called populist viewpoint that too one on donation that dominated the minds of the majority of the audience.

Second, Ms Tendulkar was unduly harsh on School Education Secretary Mr. Pathak. He was pointing out that 97 per cent of children in Maharashtra study in aided schools and only 3 per cent in unaided schools. He was rightly stressing that the discussion was placing too much of emphasis on the problems of unaided schools. Incidentally, majority of audience came from this tiny minority. There are numerous problems of aided schools ultimately policy of free and compulsory primary education has to be implemented by these schools. For instance, many aided schools have not received their non-salary grant to maintain the school infrastructure; the building rent they receive is so inadequate that the schools having four floors with four toilet blocks will not be able to maintain one toilet block from the rent received! But none of these were articulated.

Third, it is strange but true that these parents of unaided schools only want quality education in English medium schools without paying adequate fees. Mr. Pathak was stressing the point that there is no free lunch any more. If you want Basmati rice instead of ration rice, you have to pay for it. Maharashtra government in the 1980s decided to permit English medium schools only on unaided basis. Secretary School Education was stating that if parents want English medium, obviously they have to pay for it.

Ms. Tendulkar was referring to poor state of Municipal schools and aided schools. Instead of demanding that better facilities be provided in the aided schools, parent want to downgrade the unaided schools to the level of aided schools without any consideration for cost of quality education. When Nanavati by the unaided schools. Vaidya another panelist dismissed it as irrelevant and as a spokesman of primary teachers, he felt that quality of education is an issue after child goes to VIII standard! On the other hand, the spadework for quality education has to be done in the primary level itself. How can one introduce concerns for quality, after 7 years of formal educations?

Fourth, Ms Tendulkar was repeatedly making fun of educational trusts with audience applause for commercialising education and running schools as a business. Recovering cost of education, cost of infrastructural maintenance and development, at least partially, is not business. Trusts, which are founded and managed by socially minded people can beg, borrow but cannot steal or mint money in the absence of government aid.

Hence, what the government has to ensure is that the money raised in the name of education is spent for the purpose. Money cannot only come as fees it has to come through other means like charity either specific or general for building institutions for the benefit of future generations. Those parents who complain that schools raise money under different pretext, who are joined by Ms Tendulkar, however, as a right demand admission for their second or third child on the basis of their one child already studying in a school. If their being a part of the schools system confers on them a claim for admission they also have a moral obligation to contribute in the creation of assets for the future.

If Ms Tendulkar is to categorise fund-raising a business, those men and women who indulge in accusation of management's fund-raising as business, I have no hesitation in characterising them as professional agitators with an eye for cheap publicity. That is how they become 'leaders'. I remember, in one case a judge, once asked a professional agitator whether he has run a school anytime in his life! Ms Tendulkar for a change should join a school and run it for a few years to get the personal experience.

Chapter - 49

Mess of Fees: Govt. must not Meddle with Unaided Schools

(The Free Press Journal, 15 May 2002)

"....education secretary had said that only 3 percent of School going children go to unaided Schools. It is then not clear why the government is so keen to bring them to the level of aided schools, instead of allowing them the freedom to conduct the schools according to liberal norms..."

If the Government of Maharashtra moves one step forward it moves three steps backward in the field of education. The latest example is its submission before the High Court (HC) in connection with the writ petition 2552 of 2000 on the question of fees in unaided schools in the state. After a great deal of bungling and corruption in fixing the school fees, on 22nd July 1999 the government had come out with a resolution to lay down a formula to fix the fees in unaided schools on the basis of their anticipated expenditure rather than on the basis of past expenditures. This was done preparatory to the implementation of the Fifth Pay Commission scales to teachers in unaided schools.

This was a major relief to the schools management and a forward looking step. Because, in the past, fees in unaided school were revised once in three years on the basis of statements of accounts of the past three years. This provided the corrupt bureaucrats to reject certain items of expenditure inadmissible and sanction fee rates lower than requested. It also meant that the management faced the deficit in the very first year of the new fees-structure.

In case of one school in 1997, when it asked government to approve a fee rate of ₹ 225, the government approved ₹ 195 pm. As a result, it had to meet a deficit of ₹ 1,75,000 during the first year while the deficit was ₹ 2,60,000 and ₹ 3,40,000 in the second and third years respectively.

However, if the management agrees to bribe the person/s dealing with the case, the fee rates requested could be restored.

So assume that the school has 400 children and because of reduction of ₹ 30 per child per month its annual loss would be ₹ 1,44,000. So if the institution agrees to pay say half the amount otherwise lost in the very first year, the fee rate could be what you asked. Even if you lose ₹ 70,000 in the first year, the management would at least not face deficit in the second and third years. On the other hand, by basing the fee structure on anticipated expenses, the schools are likely to be able to meet their growing expenses with the fees.

The contents of the resolution were presented to the HC on the basis of which the HC had given an interim order asking the government to follow its own resolution of 22 July 1999 and not limit fee increase to fifty per cent of the then existing one. Now the government increasingly facing the pressure from professional agitators wants to go back on four steps as earlier laid down in the resolution. Thus, first is: instead of basing the fee structure on the anticipated expenditure it wants to base it on previous three years expenditure. This is likely to cause huge deficit in the school budgets.

In the past because fees sanctioned were always lower than the fee rates requested, the very first year the schools could face a deficit. There was also no built in system to take care of growing inflation. The government resolution of July 1999 had proposed to automatically permit the schools to increase the fees during the second years by 10 per cent and during the third year by 20 per cent.

Second, in this case also the government wants to go back on its own resolution and permit only the increase in the dearness allowances (DA) sanctioned by the government. However, the government forgets that DA is the only one of item in the escalation of cost of education.

There has been a steep increase in the charges for the use of water, power and property taxes in addition to general inflation of all items used in a school. The behaviour of the government while increasing the power tariffs or the municipal authorities in raising the property taxes and water charges has been worst than the private traders.

Worst of all, third, the government wants to take into account the aided schools norms to fix the non-salary expenditure of the unaided schools. In the past the government used to limit non-salary grant to the aided schools to 12 per cent of the salary. In 1994, it came out with different rates like 6 per cent for older institutions and 12 per cent for newer ones on the assumption that older institutions would have acquired all their equipments and does not spend much on non-salary account. On the other hand older schools need more money to maintain their school buildings than the new school buildings.

But the aided schools find it hard to meet their non-salary expenditure with even 12 per cent let alone with 6 per cent. Additionally, for the purposes of calculating non-salary expenditure, the state wants to take Fourth pay scales as the basis rather than the Fifth pay scales. Now if these norms are applied to the unaided schools they will find it impossible to meet the expenditure on account of maintenance. If a trust runs an aided school and an unaided school in the same building, the government instantly cuts expenses on account of building rent, water, power, telephone etc. by one half.

Fourth, the schools charge one month's fee in a term as term fee for extracurricular and examination related expenses. The schools are required to maintain a separate account for this fee. The deputy director argues that certain schools do not maintain a separate term fee account. If it is required under rules it is his duty to enforce the rule. Instead, he threatens such schools to divide their total expenditure by 14 months instead of 12 thus reducing rate of monthly fees.

The government today is not able to even pay the aided school teachers on time. Many school teachers get their salaries two month late. It is now trying to collect cost-based fees from income tax paying parents from aided English medium schools. It means some children will be paying higher fees; they consider children paying lower or no fees as inferior. This will defeat the very purposed for which schools children are compulsorily made to wear uniforms.

In another context school education secretary had said that only 3 per cent of school-going children go to unaided schools. It is then not clear why the government is so keen to bring them to the level of aided schools, instead of allowing them the freedom to conduct the schools according to liberal norms as laid down earlier in the Government resolution and upheld by the HC. If the government does not temper its populism, the quality of the education in the unaided schools would also be reduced to the level of the aided schools.

Chapter - 50

New Fee Structure Discriminatory in Nature

(The Free Press Journal, 28 June 2002)

"....discriminating fee structure will wash off advantage of social leveling achieved by School uniforms"

Government has introduced a new fee structure in aided English medium schools in Maharashtra from this academic year based on the parents' ability to pay. Those, whose income is Rs. Fifty thousand or less, will pay no fees, while those who draw more than fifty thousand rupees but less than a Lakh, will pay ₹ 100 per month. But as one goes up in the income ladder to ₹ 2 lakhs, he pays ₹ 200, to 3 lakhs, pays ₹ 300 and those who cross the Rs 3 lakh limit end up by paying ₹ 400 per month.

The entire fee structure needs to be opposed by those who have welfare of the pupils in the schools at their heart. The opposition draws its arguments on three broad grounds. First, it is discriminatory. Second, its implementation is likely to cause many social problems leading to the psychological impact on the children and third, government's reasoning smacks with hypocrisy. Let us examine each of these grounds in little more detail.

Take the ground of discrimination caused by the proposed fee structure. First, those parents, whose children study in aided English medium schools, ask why only apply the principle of 'ability to pay' standard to English medium schools? Why not to rich in other medium schools in the state? However, lower income group parents whose children study in the unaided schools then might ask, why they be made to pay on par with parents in the upper income? If the children of parents with less than ₹ 50 thousand income pay no fees in aided English medium schools, why the same category parents in unaided English medium schools are made to pay a uniform rate irrespective income principle?

Second, it raises another question. Now government has permitted computer education in schools through the investment by outside agencies. However, all children pay a uniform fee. If the government can discriminate on the ground of ability to pay, will the same principle apply to computer education? Why can't management ask for a higher fee rate from the students from rich families?

It is the arguments at the implementation level, which create a strong ground to oppose the new scheme. First, discriminatory fee structure will wash off advantage of social leveling achieved by school uniforms. Children paying no fee or lower fees would be made to suffer ridicule by the children who pay higher fees. The school education is not merely to acquire knowledge necessary to economically be a productive person but also make him a good citizen by imbibing in him concepts of equality, brotherhood and a sense of justice.

Second, the government sanction to discriminate children on their monetary abilities could make management to practice the same or parents to demand a class system in all school activities. The schools with a large number of divisions may even resort to the practice of constituting divisions on the basis of rates fees paid by them. This could cause tremendous psychological effects on pupils.

The governments justification for introducing the fee rates on the principle of ability to pay appears hypocritical. The government argues that it has no money to pay grant-in-aid to the English medium schools on the spacious argument that poor do not any way go to these schools. This is untenable proposition, at least in the city of Mumbai. During my last forty years association with educational trust, I have found very poor parents like rickshaw drivers, petty shopkeepers etc.

approaching me for admission to English schools on the plea that at least their wards could become a clerk or a stenographer. An admission into aided school for such parents could be a great boon.

Government's arguments do not convince any one who is affected by their decision because government's own behaviour does not confirm their feeling of financial crunch. Maharashtra has a jumbo cabinet of 55 ministers. Take education as an area of government activities. Earlier there used to be one minister of education and at the most a minister of state. Today there are three separate ministers for school, higher and technical and medical education, with three ministers of state in each category.

If ministerial positions rise, there is consequent need to increase secretaries positions in the department at the level of IAS cadre; down the line, obviously there is a growing number of joint, deputy, under, and assistant secretaries. Earlier, down the line in the 1970s there used to be only one director of education. Today there are separate Directors for School and Higher and Medical education with at least half a dozen Joint Directors.

According to government sources there are only 265 or 20 per cent of total English medium schools in Maharashtra, which are aided. The proposed measure could bring a saving to the government 30 to 40 crores of rupees. Now this is a paltry sum for the government. Trimming the size of government and bureaucracy can very easily save this. As it is, whenever teachers have been given a new scale of pay, government has insisted on trimming size of teaching staff by making them to bear the additional 'workload' a change let us now trim the government and bureaucracy at the higher levels. Additionally political and bureaucratic class should vow not to accept bribe or pilfer government money as long as the government is faced with the scarcity of resources.

In this background without deviating from the main theme of this article, I can easily ask: where is the need for a foreign study tour for the MLAs now? If they need to be trained-and that is a must-in the art and science of government and public administration, there are hundreds of eminent scholars in this city alone who can inform them on anti-defection act, its use and misuse, parliamentary democracy how it functions in developed countries and comparative ways to improve our working. A rejection of cookies for their loyalty at the time of financial crisis would definitely enhance reputation of elected representatives as well as the government. But a question always bugs me: why is it always education has to be the first casualty whenever government has to think of economy in the administration?

Chapter - 51

Opening up of Indian Education to Foreign Universities

(The Free Press Journal, 16 July 2002)

"......we need to convince our youngsters that every foreign university is not necessarily an excellent degree giver nor every University in India is average in quality."

When I open my daily newspapers what I see nowadays in the front page as well as inside pages are attractive advertisements of foreign universities offering their courses in India. Most of these universities offer courses in management, computers, and hotel management but also various other sciences and social sciences as well. Some of them make it more attractive to affordably ambitious students and their parents by stating that prospective student would spend one semester in mostly US or UK or Australia. Still imaginative ones would add, in addition to these foreign countries, Japan or Singapore. So if the advertisement is from say an American university, student by the time he acquires the degree would have the benefit of visits to three countries.

Why is this happening? The immediate cause is Indian membership of World Trade Organisation (WTO). Under this India is a party to General Agreement of Trade in Services (GATS), which has made India to open up its field of education to foreign investment. GATS consider education as a service like doctor or architect or engineers providing service to their clientele. Providing education is thus a service industry like any other industry and one can trade in this industry as others are carrying on trade in machinery or manufacturing. This trade in service industry globally works in different ways. First, "consumption abroad." It means Indian students can move to a foreign country and a foreign student can come to India to receive the benefit of education. Second, "cross-border supply" meaning enabling one to acquire service in education through distance education. Third mode is of "natural presence" suggesting teachers from one foreign university providing service of education in another country. Lastly, a nation can use the "commercial presence" mode to spread its educational service in another country.

Under these four patterns consumption abroad has been there for a long time. In general more Indian students have been going abroad in search of "foreign" degrees than foreign students coming here to study. A few foreign students have been coming to India either on government fellowship of their own. Indian teachers have been going in a limited way to developing countries. But what is new under the GATS are the facts that these four modes of interaction are part of global arrangement and the fact that two modes "cross-border supply" and "commercial presence" are new.

Hence if the newspapers are inundated with advertisement of foreign universities setting their shop in India it needs to be seriously discussed and its implications properly understood. Unfortunately there is very little awareness on the part of general public even amongst those who are involved in service in education in the domestic market. In the absence of corrective steps taken more money will flow out of the country than coming into the country as a result of opening education as a market for foreign universities.

What needs to be done? Since India has no option but to open up the service in education to foreign, say investment or penetration or competition, Indian needs to take every step to protect domestic service in education. Here are some suggestions. First, India needs to see that only education at the level of graduation and above by correspondence or commercial presence in opened up for foreign universities. At the level of pre-primary, primary, high school and junior college irrespective of the subjects, the foreign universities should not be allowed to compete. Only exception would be foreign nationals having the benefit of starting schools for the education of their own personnel either, from business or embassy on reciprocal basis for Indian in their countries. Already I see the advertisements of visits by foreign school authorities to recruit students at high school level.

Second, we need to improve our present quality of higher education as well as options of subjects available within our own system for study. At present, for instance, if a student studying geography, as main subject desires to offer one or two papers in economics or vice versa it is impossible even if you turn mountains to achieve your goal. In foreign universities it is not only possible for such combinations but it is also encouraged.

In Mumbai University, for instance, there are numerous examples when scholars with M.Sc in defence studies were prevented from doing Ph.D. on topics in politics. But in foreign universities students with M.Sc in Physics or chemistry are given fellowships to do Ph.D in international relations! In brief, what needs to be done is to break the departmental barriers and loyalties and encourage crossbreeding of knowledge. One way of doing it could be bring all science, social science departments or humanities departments under one umbrella like a school under a Dean.

Third, the governments at state and federal levels also need to liberalise their control over universities. Politicians and bureaucrats speak in favour of liberalisation but in practice want to centralise controls in their own hands. Considerable time and energy of academics are lost in universities in securing approvals for academic reforms. In the global scene what I see is that some subjects taught in 2001 are no longer relevant without change in 2002. But in Indian context, an educator in the university is not in a position to design his own course and teach. The government should also permit opening of more colleges and universities to cater to the growing demand from the public.

However, the most important need is to bring about a change in colonial mindset of our people, which believes that anything provided by the white man is good or better or excellent. Even after fifty five years of independence, by and large Indians go crazy for foreign (means in fact, European, American, Australian), education and degree. The fact of the matter is that in these countries there are excellent as well as extremely third rate universities. I have come across in Indian academic field several foreign degree holders whom I would not hire even as teaching assistants. Similarly, I have interacted with a large number of foreign academics in the field of higher education that are average in their abilities. But those who are crazy for a foreign degree would not care much for the quality degree and education so long it is foreign. If one cannot afford to go there and acquire a degree, second best is to have it by studying in them here! Parents, who would come on streets protesting payment of enhanced fees in colleges, would readily pay a fortune to get a foreign degree without going abroad!

The point is: we need to convince our youngsters that every foreign university is not necessarily an excellent degree giver nor every university in India is average in quality. Convincing easier if men and women of calibre are recruited for their competence and not for their connection or corruption.

Chapter - 52

Primary Certificate Examination Scheme can only bring ruin

(The Free Press Journal, 10 August 2002)

"The strange fact is that some parents, who are willing to fight against an increase of ten or twenty rupees in fees, are willing to spend in thousands to get their children through PSC"

The latest educational reform-so does the Maharashtra government at least think-is introduction of public examination, called Primary School Certificate (PSC) for children in IV standard. Under the PSC examination rules every IV Standard child has to compulsorily appear for the examination. Henceforth, school leaving certificate shall carry a remark that pupil had appeared at the PSC examination.

Students have to appear for maths, general science and general knowledge-three papers on one day. The government has even decided the time frame for the examination. The examination will be held in the month of February every year. Of the three papers-Language and Social Studies will be from 11 am to 12 noon, second on Mathematics from 1 to 2 pm and third on Intelligence and General Science from 3 to 4 pm. All papers are of one hundred marks each.

The proposal for PSC has already given another issue to parents to come on the streets. May be, that this time they will bring primary children on the streets as secondary pupil were on the streets some time back in June protesting against discriminatory fee structure based on ones ability to pay in aided English medium schools.

The scheme of examination is quite absurd. Is it fair to make a child of 9 plus to write three examinations on one day that too in the climate of a 'public' examination system? The bureaucrat who drafted to government resolution has been very thoughtful in leaving one hour gap between two papers so the child can have its lunch after first examination and snacks after the second! Of course, it means mother will have to sweat it out that day outside the school building. But bureaucrat has not taken into consideration the mental strain that can cause on the child because of writing three examinations in one day.

On the other hand the previous Shiv Sena-BJP government in Maharashtra had accepted the fact that there is a great and undue burden on the Pre-primary and primary school children and urgent need to reduce burden of books and urgent need to reduce burden of books and learning on the early learners in the Kindergarten schools. Based on Ram Joshi Committee report the government had introduced play-way method at the KG level. Even at the Primary level, extending the same argument, the government had made promotion of child almost automatic rather than examination based.

The PSC examination idea also goes against the modern concept of liberalisation. Of course, so far the government has used liberalisation concept in the field of education to reduce the grants where grants existed and deny it altogether where it is necessary to be given. Under liberalisation government thinks in terms of reduction of their investment in education. Make parents pay more and more towards the child's education. Beyond that the concept of liberalisation in the field of education does not mean anything to the government. Thus, for instance liberalisation also means greater private initiative and absence of government control, government is trying to increase rather tighten its control over system of education. But the government does not want to loosen its control, rather wants to further centralize it. The government has offered a sop to parents and children, Children securing top ranks in the examination will be eligible for government scholarship. But then why make everybody to undergo the exercise of appearing for the examination? It is understood that officials say that teachers in primary schools do not take teaching seriously as there is no evaluation of their performance on the basis of results of the IV standard. This may be true in government, municipal or Zilla Parishad run schools run by private trusts. Then why club good schools with the non-performing ones?

One unstated reason seems to be government's desire to find enough work to the vast bureaucracy working in the Maharashtra State Examination Board. The number of students expected to appear is some where near to 25 lakhs. At an examination fee of ₹ 40 per candidate, government will earn over 10 crores.

The PSC examination scheme will also provide another avenue to bureaucrats at various levels to accept illegal gratification from anxious parents. There will be efforts to buy marks' manipulate results and order in the merit list and various other ways at the Board level. Similarly, at the operational level it will provide another avenue for educational bureaucrats called inspectors and superintendents to make quick money. It is provided that though promotion to V standard depends on the school performance, though appearance at the examination is compulsory. Those who do not appear the PSC can be promoted only with the approval of these officials. While teachers, parents and educationists have generally raised their voice against the introduction of public examination system, one segment of the society will however welcome the idea of PSC. And that segment is those who thrive on running coaching classes. My investigations show that already coaching classes are charging anywhere from six to ten thousand rupees to train the child for PSC examination. Private tuitions have also of course will thrive.

The strange fact is that some parents, who are willing to fight against an increase of ten or twenty rupees in fees, are willing to spend in thousands to get their children through PSC! In reality it is not their fault. We have still not overcome the colonial mentality of 'Ma-Bab' Sarkar.

In recent times the government in Maharashtra does not think it necessary to consult teachers and educationists on the subject. The government will come out, I am sure with some 'Sarkari' intellectuals in support of their scheme. But in reality, if the government persists with the scheme, it will only bring ruin, academically and psychologically, to career of a generation of Indian citizens. Government should wake up and scrap the scheme immediately.

Chapter - 53

How to Achieve the Purpose without Board Examination?

(The Free Press Journal, 25 September 2002)

"Indian education is afflicted by the fact: not only every government but every politician, when he becomes minister for education wants to change system of education......."

I had written in these columns against the proposed public examination for Primary students of IV standard (Primary Certificate Examination scheme can only bring ruin, August, 10/02). Now the Maharashtra government has reversed their decision partially. The students of unaided schools are exempted from it, while students from aided schools will have to give the examinations. But the latter have been given a bonus: they will not be forced to give another examination at the school level but would be promoted on the strength of their performance at the unit tests and mid-term examination.

Let me say at the outset that this classification of students for applications of compulsion to appear for examination on the grounds of their being in aided schools is totally unjustifiable and judicially not maintainable. To elaborate the point further: Is the Board examination in the interest of a student?

If yes, what is the rationality in excluding my child from it, just because he goes to an unaided school? Is the examination, an unnecessary compulsion imposed by the government? If yes, why only children going to aided schools be subjected to it? Either way, if the case goes before the court, I am sure judges are bound to strike it down!

Now in essence, when you analyse various explanations issued by the government authorities so far, the underlying purpose behind the government insistence in holding the examination boils down to their assertion that the examination result will testify whether teachers have done their duty as teachers. This is particularly emphasised in reference to rural schools. Thus, the aim is not to directly benefit students, but indirectly i.e. to benefit students, only if as a result of examination, the teachers were to take their jobs seriously and begin to teach effectively!

Then certain questions need to be raised and answered: First, government officials feel that aided government schools under Zilla Parishads (ZP) and Municipal bodies normally do not do their teaching for the good of children. If so, why tag along with them teachers who teach in private aided schools?

Second, assuming that teachers in aided primary schools run by public bodies, do not teach-an assumption itself open to question, at least in Mumbai city, as recently when I addressed a gathering of nearly two hundred primary teachers of the BMC.

I found them very enthusiastic of their new assignment of teaching English in Municipal aided schools. But, it is possible that in some municipal and ZP schools teachers may not be performing teaching as their primary responsibility. Why this situation exists? It is largely because, ZP politicians use such teachers to perform their errands; hence, they feel protected.

Third, if teachers are not performing their primary responsibilities government at large are also responsible for that. Often looking at the government circulars asking teachers to be spared for non-teaching tasks, such as duties in conduct of elections, census, Shikshan Abhiyan, propagation of family planning etc. in addition to attending of meetings and setting of papers for various public examinations' teachers are left with limited hours of work during working sessions! Added to it, now government even desires teachers to collect rice from the ration shops, bring it to schools and cook and serve the children mid-day meal!

Fourth, added to the above in recent past of motivation to perform well. This is because they are paid paltry sum of ₹ 3000 per month as Shikshan Sewaks for three years that too without vacation pay or any increments! When some one else is performing the same job but paid almost double that and when even a peon is paid double of his salary, why single out new teachers to be Sewaks?

At the cost of little deviation, I strongly feel that our politicians and IAS officials should lay an example before our teachers by accepting only a nominal pay. Maharashtra Pradesh Congress Committee President, Govindrao Adik has made a suggestion that Ministers should accept only a one rupee salary per month.

Really laudable proposal they should do it for at least for a period of three years! But equally important is that IAS officers too make a sacrifice looking at the precarious financial position of the government. Even otherwise, we need to implement the Prashasan Sewak concept. After three years of half wages they any way have the cream in governance!

Be that as it may, fifth, what are the education inspectors doing to see that teachers do their job well? Interacting with some of these inspectors during the last forty years, I have a feeling that the quality of inspectorate has deteriorated beyond comparison! Often instead of appointing highly motivated teachers as inspectors, men from administrative cadre, often without any teaching background are appointed as inspectors. Even these officials lack academic zeal as their background is developed only in administrative skills.

Hence the government can achieve their purpose of making teachers in rural schools managed by ZPs work and produce good results, relatively, without imposing a public examination on children at a tender age of 9 plus.

What need to be done is to limit teachers only to teach and not use them for any activities unrelated to teaching and at the cost of teaching days. Second, the government need to create an inspectorate consisting of academics of high calibre to inspect public and private schools.

The inspectors are brought into the inspectorate on loan for a fixed period of four to five years after which they go back to their parent department of institution. The inspectorate should be freed from administrative responsibilities.

To create the inspectorate the government need not recruit new manpower at all. The last thirty years have seen education expenditure increasing on bureaucracy than on grants-in-aid to schools. In any bureaucracy, there is always a small percentage of personnel which is highly committed to their work.

Educational bureaucracy cannot be an exception. From within the existing education bureaucracy government can create an inspectorate with single purpose of seeing that teachers perform their tasks as well paid shikshan sewaks.

Chapter - 54

American Studies Losing Importance in Mumbai University

(The Free Press Journal, 15 October 2002)

"....US being in forefront of globalisation, all those who deal with international issues need to know about the US."

The United States (US) is commonly referred today as the only super power in international affairs. This places a responsibility on the Indian society to encourage a body of scholars who are conversant with the American history, politics, society, administration, culture and civilisation-what is generally called as American Studies so that they can explain the developments in the US accurately to the Indians and to the Indian government to act in the interest of Indian nation.

With globalisation of economy other human activities too inevitably are drawn into global vortex. Thus, not only economy is global but how you treat your economically deprived people is also a matter of global concern. Thus, on the one extreme, national security concerns are becoming global on another extreme even issues of local governance has become global. Thus, US being in forefront of globalisation, all those who deal with international issues need to know about the US.

This makes it incumbent upon Government of India and its educational administrators to make adequate provision for the study of the subject. However, since independence the University Grants Commission (UGC) has given step motherly treatment to the study of US. One of several reasons then advanced was that the initiative has been taken by the US government in funding teaching of American studies in India.

Hence, India need not spend its scarce resource on teaching of America. The US government funded some of these activities by using PL 480 rupee funds that was available for their use. These were funds generated by the US sale of food grains to India in the 1950s and the 1960s for which India had paid in rupees. The rupee funding that was available with the US government in India ended in 1998. By then Cold War was also over. The US no longer thought it worthwhile to spend their hard currency in enabling Indians to learn about the US.

It is also unwise for a society to depend upon a foreign government for the study of that society and its politics. But government has always taken an illogical view that to encourage study of a region or a country that ought have the need for study their language. Since US is a country that can be studied with English language unlike the study of Russia, which cannot be done without knowledge of Russian no concerted and widespread efforts were made to teach the American studies.

As a result, every year some ministers, bureaucrats, journalists and teachers among others visited the US for short periods and on their return turned instant specialists on the US. In reality their knowledge of the US is so superficial that it can be made out by numerous encounters with these visitors. Ten years ago, Doordarshan English news at 9.30 pm on October 28, 1992 informed listeners that the election to Electoral College to elect the American President is on the basis of "proportional representation."

In fact it is a unique system called "winner take all" system whereby a presidential candidate winning a plurality of popular votes in a state wins all the votes of electoral college from that state! I am sure the news editor must have visited the US on a short-term programme!

If the above discussion shows a need for a serious study of the American society and politics, the next question is: what is then the state of affairs in the Mumbai University today? The Mumbai University, incidentally, was the only university besides JNU in New Delhi that provided an opportunity to study America in depth. The

University in 1960 with the initial assistance from the US government was able to establish a position of Reader in American Government and Politics for the purpose.

Ever since the 1960s there have been on an average seven to ten students offering the subject for their specialisation. What is interesting is the fact that even after the Indo-US relations touched its nadir during the Bangladesh War in 1971 there were five to six students enrolling in the University to study the subject. This number had been steady till 1994 when then head of the Department retired.

Unfortunately since then those heading the department in Kalina were not interested in the promotion of American studies as an area of study. Their attitude has been one of hostility. The academic leadership at the higher levels in the university has, it appears, no vision beyond the immediate exercise of power and retention of their positions.

As a result, on record there are no students since 1994 offering the subject. In fact, the students were discouraged by asking them to choose a different area of study. What is damaging the long-term interest of the university and students is the fact that the position of Reader in American Government and Politics is reserved for the ST (scheduled tribes). Without sounding any disrespect, it is difficult or impossible to get an expert to fill the position from amongst ST to teach American studies.

My understanding is that an isolated post like the Reader in American Government and Politics-since it is only one of its kind cannot and need not be covered under the reservation policy. This seems to be a deliberate action on the part of the person or persons charged with decision-making in the University.

It is deliberate, because for the last almost eight years the subject has not been offered in the university. A cash starved government that is too keen to use education as the first item on the agenda to reduce the budgetary allocations can make an effective argument that the position need not be filled, as there is no demand for the subject. Then the American studies would wither away in the Mumbai University without the state having a Marxist or left front-led government.

Chapter - 55

Case for Rotation of Department Headship in Mumbai University

(The Free Press Journal, 3 December 2003)

"Rotation (of headship) can work for the good of the department if the Head knows that he or she can provide lasting leadership only by consulting the colleagues and taking them alongwith him or her."

Telgi scandal for weeks now has completely clouded other developments affecting our society. One such development is of challenge to a routine administrative decision of Mumbai University appointing Dr Surendra Jondhale as the head of department of Civics and Politics by incumbent head, Dr (Mrs) Nawaz Mody. Since the matter is in the High Court it is improper for me to comment on the merits of the case.

But issues involved in general, deserve public discussion. Mumbai University appoints heads of departments by rotation. The University Grants Commission (UGC) had asked universities in 1983 to introduce the principle of rotation in the appointment of heads of departments. The University of Mumbai is generally slow in implementing any educational reforms. Being an ancient institution, there is lethargy in every field and the confidence that its antiquity is a safety cover that could see university through a crisis. But under the pressure of teachers' association, the Mumbai University in 1993 introduced the rotation system in principle. But when anything is done with a view to help persons problems occur.

And problems began with the first resolution on rotation of headship approved in 1993 under the tenure of the then Vice Chancellor (VC), Dr S.D. Karnik. In Civics and Politics Department two professors were selected on the same day. On the retirement of the then Head, Dr Ramesh Babu in August 1994, Dr Karnik appointed Dr (Mrs) Nawaz Mody as the head. By seniority in the cadre of Readers and seniority in terms of age and experience, Dr (Mrs) Mody was the junior most but was selected to be the professor along with Dr (Mrs) Marina Pinto. Even between the two newly selected professors, Dr Pinto ought to have been appointed as the head in terms of seniority and age.

But Dr Karnik had handpicked Dr Mody to be installed as Sir Pherozeshah Mehta Professor of Civics and Politics by setting aside all norms of academic performance, seniority, fair play and justice. A glance through the minutes of academic council of the time would confirm how qualification for the post of Sir Pherozeshah Mehta Professor were manipulated. The tip of the manipulative iceberg is revealed in the judgement delivered by honourable judge of City Civil Court. Shri Hemant Deshpande dismissing the suit filed by Dr Karnik against the then editor of Lok Satta, Dr Aroon Tikekar.

The presiding judge narrating how a VC as the head of the university and the chairman of the selection committee could influence the selection, said the following; "It is also admitted by the plaintiff (Dr Karnik) in his explanation that he had personally helped Dr Mody. There are other instances of some indirect favours to Dr Mody and in explanation the plaintiff has admitted that his decision to take Dr Mody on the management Council was wrong. This itself is sufficient to show that professor Mody had good relation with the plaintif..." Dr Karnik. Throughout the process of advertising of the post to prescribing qualifications etc. Dr Mody was a member of the University's highest decision-making body Executive Council.

Having selected her as a Professor by ignoring the UGC norm that at the time of selection a professorial candidate should have experience of successfully guiding Ph.D. research and claims of other senior readers in the department, Dr Karnik could not have ignored the ambition of Dr Mody to head of the department. Hence, the resolution passed under his dispensation said that the headship "cannot be claimed as a matter of right...but that it shall be a privilege conferred by the Executive Council..." Thus a university supposed to be run democratically invented the science of "privilege" to justify granting headship to Dr Mody.

In American universities chairmanship of a department is a position held by an associate professor (Reader) aspiring to a tenured professorship. Professors do not demean themselves by indulging in housekeeping activities. Professorship is a time to excel in research by producing good research work. But in Indian universities half-baked scholars clamour for headship as a licence not to do any academic work; after all they carry the burden of running the department! Then privileges begin to look as though conferred by the almighty on immortals if not a hereditary grants!

The result is that some professors invent alibis to stick to the position of head. They come to acquire such self-esteem that they feel that working in the department with some one else as the head is psychologically damaging to their personality. Then they rush to High Court (HC) to challenge the rotation per se or after they are dethroned after the end of their term though they would have been the beneficiaries of the rotation scheme to begin with. Some others begin to think that the department or even the university will begin to sink if they do not occupy the headship!

In the meanwhile the criteria for the headship also began to rotate with every change of VC! Beginning from "privilege" in 1993, it had come to rely on "seniority-cum-merit" in 1999; then came to rest on "seniority" as the sole criterion by November 2000. Under rules or bending of rules, Dr Mody has enjoyed the status of the head for nine years with a break of one month. After her two consecutive terms of three years each, in October 2000. Dr Lionel Fernandes was the head, but he retired at the end of October 2000. She again enjoyed the office for three years.

These development actually should force the University authorities from the VC and down the line to devise rules, which have durability beyond the tenure of a VC. In other words, the practice of every VC trying to change the rules should stop. If the VCs are unable to see that rules are long lasting, the Chancellor should step in to see that VCs do not bend rules to accommodate their favoured ones.

Second, by no means a person should get two consecutive terms under the pretext of some one is on probation or is only a lecturer or has not served for minimum five years and so on. If a newly appointed VC can be trusted to exercise powers wisely and run a university, a lecturer or a reader or a professor can perform duties of a head equally well.

Third, a strict academic audit of performance of the teachers should be undertaken to see that professors produce eminent Ph.D. scholars, bring out socially useful or even pure research, which enriches knowledge. It is highly regrettable that teachers who claim to be great academics follow fraudulent practices of showing collection of lecture summaries of a seminar or collection of faculty addresses as a personal and or departmental research work!

Academic audit of the heads of departments ought to be very rigorous. Those who are invited to head the audit panel must be outsiders with high reputation. Otherwise having done such morally unpardonable acts of academic frauds, such professors fear a change of headship under rotation system and try to avoid it by hook or crook.

Rotation can work for the good of the department if the Head knows that he or she can provide lasting leadership only by consulting the colleagues and taking them along with him or her. In such situations, new heads will not undo the good changes introduced by a head. The present case in the Civics and Politics Department indicates that one can climb in the university hierarchy by bandwagon effect but cannot stay there forever!

Chapter - 56

Inter University Centre for Astronomy and Astrophysics

(One India One People, May 2004)

"IUCAA can boast of fully computerised library on the subject of astronomy and astrophysics.....equipped with an instrumentation laboratory [with] do it yourself culture.....and mini super computer centre [with] worldwide connectivity...."

Inter University Centre for Astronomy and Astrophysics (IUCAA) was set up by the University Grants Commission (UGC) as an autonomous institution in December 1988 on outskirts of Pune University. The concept of Inter University Centre (IUC) developed because study of certain subjects required enormous funds and in-depth focus for a longer period. These are also subjects, which every university may not be in a position to offer, as it requires huge investment on infrastructure.

Then there is always the question of accountability of teachers in the eyes of state governments in terms of lectures taken and minimum number of students in a class. The state governments are not concerned with research or spending resources on it. It is inevitable as government represents voice of the majority and as Narayana Murthy put it in his 14th Foundation Day Lecture of IUCAA, "majority is average and mediocre..."

IUCAA can boast of fully computerised library on the subject of astronomy and astrophysics containing over 20,000 books and 100 journals. It is equipped with an Instrumentation Laboratory where do-it-yourself culture is encouraged. Equally important is the Computer Centre that with 30-networked mini super-computers provides worldwide connectivity to users easy access to astronomical data.

Ancient India was known for scientific study of the universe , the sun, the moon, stars and their influence on human beings. That feeling one gets while entering the IUCAA campus even as a stranger to astronomy. The scientists' residential complex is called Akashaganga-the Milky Way Galaxy. The main complex housing institutional buildings is called Devayani-stands for great galaxy Andromeda. The main office block is called Aryabhattaafter the fifth century astronomer. The library and the computer centre are located in the block named after sixth century astronomer-Varahamihira, while Instrumentation Laboratory reminds you of eighth century astronomer Brahmagupta. Lecture halls are located in the block named after the 12th century astronomer, Bhaskara. Quadrangle is a place where you can sit at the feet of statues of Galileo Galilei, Isaac Newton, Albert Einstein, and Aryabhatta.

Who are the modern users of this first class facility? First, any teacher of Astronomy or Astrophysics from anywhere in India or even abroad can take a short-term or long-term project on his special field of research and for a specific period as per his need to visit the IUCAA for in-depth study and laboratory work. For Indian teachers of the subjects, there is the UGC funded Associateship programme. In 2001-02, there were 88 Associates working, on different topics. Some of these as listed in the annual report 2001-02 include a wide variety from classical gravity, gravitational waves, alternate theories of gravity, sun and solar system, theoretical physics to atomic physics.

Second, this is the ideal place for students interested in pursuing their studies in Astronomy and Astrophysics for M Sc or Ph D. Every year the Centre provides fellowships to interested students to do doctoral and postdoctoral work in the field. These fellowships are nationally advertised so that anyone interested in the subject can compete and carry on with his research work in the idyllic beauty of Pune suburb, which looks like a village with urban facilities. The selection is done on the basis of a Joint Entrance Screening Test which is held by 14 IUCs in the country. The research candidates have to be on a full-time basis to carry on research in the IUC and are given stipends and also contingency grants.

To carry out the above activities, one Centre is well supported by its core faculty of nearly 48 professors and Associate professors who in addition to carrying out their own independent research also help visiting scholars. The annual outlay of the IUCAA is about ' 6 crores. I was interested in finding out obviously the contribution of the Centre to the society. In the last 14 years, I am told that it has produced 18 PhDs. As it happens with other institutions of higher learning like the institutes of technologies, here too, many have gone abroad after their PhD - 13 of the 18 - though some have come back to join the Centre as its core faculty members.

However, Dr Jayant Narlikar its former director stated in the report 2001-02 that though IUCAA had "probably the best performance in the number of PhDs produced per faculty member for astronomy institutions in India" he is worried over difficulties in attracting "good talent to astronomy."

Hence, the Centre is also involved in programmes for popularization of science. Last year an exhibition on 100 years of Noble Prize was held with the active involvement of school students IUCAA has plans for a 2 metre new technology telescope for observation research. Particle Physics and Astronomy Research Council of the government in United Kingdom are building the telescope. It is going to be located on a hill near Giravali about two-and-half hours drive from IUCAA.

The Centre also has an outreach programme to create interest amongst the school students. One specific programme that should be of interest to our readers is the School Students' Summer Programme. Similarly, another programme is that of Vacation Students Programme where in MSc students from all over India from the fields of physics and engineering can participate.

Pune is an educational city with many deemed universities and institutes. IUCAA is one such centre of which every Indian should be proud. I hope it will produce astronomers who would win Noble prize in the near future.

Chapter - 57

Let Every School Decide which History Textbook to Follow

(The Free Press Journal, 20 August 2004)

"...education be developed 'on the foundations of professional excellence and intellectual integrity' without making it a prisoner of political ideology."

No nation witnesses in the world such a fight over History books as we see in India between Arjun Singh of Congress and the Bharatiya Janata Party (BJP). Arjun Singh from the day one of his assuming the office of Union Minister for Human Resources wanted to scrap all history books published by the National Council for Educational Research and Teaching (NCERT), a central government body as the previous government led by the Bharatiya Janata Party brought them out. He alleges that the former Human Resources Minister, Murli Manohar Joshi had brought a change of history books used by the central schools. His rationale, if any, is that these books promote communalism while he and the Congress party to which he belongs are the votaries of secularism.

But secularism or communalism is not the central theme of this article. But the concern is: in his pursuit of his brand of secularism, he is causing confusion amongst students in regard to Indian history. They would have read one set of books earlier prescribed as prepared by the NCERT. Now, even before the exams are over, they are being asked to read another set of books as prescribed texts on history.

At another plane, he is denying the children benefit of knowing different interpretations of history. He is trying to project his party point of view, rather his own point of view, as the history in India. This is a point of view, which is influenced or rather shaped by the Marxist historians in India. These historians characteristics are many. One is enough to know where they stood and why were they discredited. For them globally, world war began only when Hitler attacked the Soviet Union in 1941, not in 1939. And because Britain became an ally in the war against Hitler, Marxists supported British rulers in India in their suppression of freedom movement.

But even in Arjun's pursuit of what left leaning journalists call detoxification of history books, people are attributing motives to Arjun Singh. In other words they do not accept his rationale as the real explanation for his actions. There are two motives attributed to Arjun Singh. First, it is said that he is positioning himself as an undiluted secularist so that he can claim the Prime Minister's position. Though, at present the seat is not vacant and there is no possibility of Sonia Gandhi aiming to replace Manmohan Singh with him, in case there is a compulsion to change because of coalition politics, he can project him as the right person. Second, he is carving out a niche for himself within the Left lobby. You have to recall, how having said that foreign direct investment is welcome in the field of education, he closed the door under the pressure of Left. He also admitted, that his change of mind was prompted by the Left.

A related issue is that if his party can have a point of view on history, other party mainly the BJP also could have its own viewpoint. Then the opposition party also should have right to project its own point of view. We Indians seem to me as the only national community, which do not have a national spirit. Where also do you find historians, and their political cronies or in other way-politicians and their cronies, try to glorify achievements of invaders, and undermine strength of natives, except in India?

In the process, Arjun Singh is causing tremendous harm to Indian educational system, culture and national spirit. In the field of education even students have expressed their concern at frequent changing of history books on political grounds. The students ask to be left alone to read history books and make up their own minds on the history of India. Why can't we permit the schools to prescribe their won books out of multiple books written as textbooks for a particular standard as per the government prescribed syllabus.

I remember even during the British rule in India, there were no government sponsored or commissioned textbooks. The books were commissioned by different private publishers and submitted them to the government for its approval as a textbook. It is only the politics of socialism that brought in the government production and control of the school textbooks. This way, the government acquired control over book production so that one more lever was added in the licence-permit-quota-Raj during the heydays of the Congress rule in the 1970s.

This enabled as a next step for the government in power to acquire a control over the thought process of students studying in schools by providing a uniform presentation of history with a single interpretation. It is thus the Congress government and not the BJP or Shiv Sena in Maharashtra, for instance, which produced textbook on Shivaji for IV standard making it a monotonous reading. Why can't the government withdraw completely from the business of textbook production and distribution? It should merely lay down the syllabus from time to time leaving the production of textbooks to the publishers. This will bring more than one textbook on any subject and in particular history so that every student and teacher can read more than one textbook on the subject.

In this particular instance of controversy of history books Arjun Singh is getting rid of books produced by the NCERT under the BJP led NDA government. This way he is also causing a huge loss to the government funded NCERT. In other words, Arjun Singh is wasting government resources to pursue his political ideology granting that it was something done by the previous government.

Hence, it is time for the UPA government to stop repeating the mistake committed by the previous NDA government. The Prime Minister has done well in stating that education be developed "On the foundations of professional excellence and intellectual integrity" without making it a prisoner of political ideology. Since governments are likely to be coalition ones in future and they might change every four or five years, governments better leave it to every school to decide which of many textbooks to prescribe for history as long as it is Indian history.

Chapter - 58

Is Money Meant for Education Rightly Spent?

(The Free Press Journal, 26 October 2006)

"The government collects education cess from several sources. Has any MP or MLA ever tried to ask a question as to whether money meant for education is spent always for education?"

Sarva Shikshan Abhiyan (SSA) is a federal programme. Recently I read in the newspapers that SSA organised a ten-day training programme for primary teachers from private-aided schools in Mumbai. A less important aim of the SSA is to sensitise primary teachers to gender equality. It is also reported that teachers feel that the entire programme is an insult to the teachers as they are already sensitive to gender equality. That is also borne out by the fact that in most of the school leaving examinations girls top the rank holders. The SSA actually has laid a greater emphasis on the goal of achieving the goals of universal primary education by 2007 and elementary education by 2010. The idea, as I can understand was to see that those who never were enrolled in schools to be enrolled or to bring back to school system those who dropped out or to retain those who are likely to drop out from the school system. What is the record of the programme in achieving these two goals?

Federal funds are passed on to the states and states pass on funds to municipal corporations to implement the federal scheme. But how far has the state of Maharashtra been successful in really bringing into school system those kids who otherwise would not have been able to see the steps of a school building?

From the limited experience I have of managing one educational trust, which runs a Kannada medium school from Balwadi to the secondary classes, I have my doubts as to whether the state government has taken the goals of universalisation of primary and elementary education very seriously. The state government has used in the city of Mumbai, SSA resources as a supplement to its resources, in reducing its inability to provide regular maintenance grant to schools. The process of globalisation and Maharashtra government going bankrupt began, more or less the same time in the 1990s, thus, the government having no funds to provide to schools even 6 per cent of maintenance, which it had reduced from earlier 12 per cent. But now while providing money under SSA to schools, the heads are asked to buy chalks or dusters of a particular size and in a particular manner as though the head even need that to be told! Brihan Mumbai Municipal Corporation (BMC), which has budget larger than poorer states like Orissa, also does not appear to be spending money to bring children under school education or retain them within the primary educational system. Instead, funds are utilised for providing money to teachers for projects to prepare teaching aids or holding seminars etc. but I am yet to come across any mention of funds being made available for the basic purpose of universalisation of primary education!

A lot of activities can be undertaken even in a metropolis like Mumbai to see that extremely poor in urban slums are brought into the school education system. No doubt the girls are provided books and all children are provided with mid-day meals. But urban poverty, which as a major disincentive to parents in sending children to school as much as in rural areas, cannot be removed just by providing mid day meals and books.

We, on the other hand every year go out to encourage parents to send their wards to schools. Whenever, teachers from our school have gone out to campaign with the probable parents in slum areas in Mulund, Mulund-Thane border areas, Kalwa and other nearby areas, children are invariably found to be naked or semi-clothed as they cannot afford to buy sets of clothes even to school going children. We promise them uniforms. If the school has provided them with a set of uniform, they would like to wear it while going to school. But at home the child often will go semi-naked.

The enrollment in vernacular medium schools is dwindling. It is a common problem faced by all vernacular medium schools in Mumbai. Those children from well-to-do families go to English medium schools. But only those who cannot afford to pay high fees in English medium schools send their children to vernacular medium schools. The BMC seems to think that they can meet this challenge by converting a large number of present primary schools into English medium schools so that BMC schools can have enough strength. But if the BMC educationists have faith in the principle that children ought to study at least at the primary level in their mother tongue then it need to be more innovative in attracting students to primary schools and also to retain them there.

First thing it needs to do is to do away with fees. The BMC insists that private aided schools charge the children, even girls-may be ₹ 20 to ₹ 25 per month for studying in these schools. The BMC does not charge such fees in the schools directly run by them. Teachers in aided privately managed schools strongly believe that the BMC does it because they would like to discourage children going to private aided schools, but come to BMC-run schools. But parents prefer to send their children to such privately managed aided primary schools rather than the BMC managed as the former have a better standard of teaching.

This problem becomes acute to minority language schools like Kannada where such private schools may be far away from the child's place of residence. In such situations, a child may be required to pay fees of ₹ 20 per month, if it goes to a nearby BMC school, it need not spend money on fees. Additionally it has to spend another ₹ 300 per month on bus. Such expenses are beyond reach of the parents when mother may be working as a housemaid and father may be day labourer. Apart from this kind of corruption, there is a larger issue of accountability. Is there any one in this country who is ever concerned as to how the programme is implemented? The government collects education cess from several sources. Has any MP or MLA ever tried to ask a question as to whether money meant for education is spent always for education? At least SSA funds are not!

Chapter - 59

Mumbai University Restoring the Lost Glory

(One India One People, October 2006)

"The author reminisces glorious past of the Mumbai University, ... laments its decline and suggests measures to restore its lost status"

Mumbai University, in its earlier incarnation, Bombay University, is one of the three oldest universities in India, founder in 1957-the other two being Calcutta and Madras. Setting up of three universities was the direct outcome of British Parliament taking over the power of governing British Indian provinces from the East India Company. On July 18 this year Mumbai University began its sequicentennial celebrations in the presence of a galaxy of politically influential people. The presence of politicians incidentally shows changing emphasis within the university system.

Aroon Tikekar, the then Editor, Lokmat in his biography of the University of Bombay, *The Cloister's Pale* recall students doing *Shramdan* during the development of University's new campus at Kalina in 1969. Teachers along with students also joined out of love for the University. I was one of several teachers who participated in Shramdan. Politicians present in large numbers at the function to celebrate 150th year of the university had not participated in Shramdan. If I sound critical, let me state at the outset that I am proud of being an alumnus as well as a teacher for 25 years in the University Department of Civics and Politics.

Sometimes people eminent and not so eminent, get awards and social praise merely because of having lived a long life! Mumbai University, having existed for 150 years, undoubtedly has many achievements, but it also has many shortcomings. I would like to draw here a broad sketch of its salient achievements in pre-independence period, main limitations since independence and direction it can take in the next two decades-or to use the President's favourite phrase, by 2020.

A glorious past

What is the uniqueness of Mumbai University? What are its achievement? The first thing that strikes is its architectural grandeur which has earned it the status of a heritage building. I am still nostalgic about its library where I could read even in hot summer without a fan. It's so cool inside!

One of its great contributions is that it functioned as a source of liberal education when British were consolidating their hold over the country. As an affiliating university, it had its jurisdiction spread from Karachi to Karwar for a long time. And times were such that one had to struggle to get education only a few highly motivated, highly gifted ones and those who had financial backing could get into the university system. No wonder, Bombay University provided a liberal venue. It gave the nation early nationalist leaders like Mahadev Govind Ranade, Bal Gangadhar Tilak and several others. R. G. Bhandarkar, an eminent Indologist was also one of its first graduates.

The President of India in his speech on the occasion of 150 years celebrations of the University said it could claim as its alumni men like Mahatma Gandhi, former Prime Minister of India, P.V. Narasimha Rao, eminent Jurist, Nani Palkhiwala and scores of others. However, there is a lurking doubt: What is the extent of contribution of the University in shaping the lives of these men? Isn't it the environment of freedom movement that shaped their outlook rather than their university degree?

However, can Mumbai University claim great heights of achievements so as to stand tall, just like its Rajabai Tower after independence? Can it claim to have something unique unlike many other universities in independent India? After independence, it started well as the City University. Former Vice Chancellor, Dr M. S. Gore says in his foreword to *The Cloister's Pale* "the most distinguished fact about the inception, evolution, growth and development of the University of Bombay has been its close link with the development of the city of Bombay". However, in 1974, government expanded its geographical sweep. Its jurisdiction since then extends to megapolis of Mumbai and rural areas of Thane, Raigad and Ratnagiri. With this the university began to lose its uniqueness as an old university with a long history. Today it is just a state university.

The decline

Three main causes can be highlighted for the decline of Mumbai University. First, there is all pervading political influence, direct and indirect, in day-to-day functioning of the University. Till 1974, Mumbai University used to have an eminent public figure as its Vice-Chancellor last one was retired Chief Justice of the Supreme Court, P. B. Gajendragadkar. Since then the state government has introduced a system of appointing a fulltime paid Vice Chancellor. With it, politics has crept into all bodies of the University and the outcome is erosion of university autonomy.

The fault lies with the system of appointment of Vice Chancellor. Though the Chancellor is supposed to appoint the Vice Chancellor on the recommendation of a duly constituted search committee, in fact he who has the maximum political pull gets nominated. Since 1974, with sterling exceptions, it would not be an exaggeration, if I say that the political weight of an aspirant for the prestigious post of Vice Chancellor has been in direct proportion to his ability for political sycophancy! The nadir was reached in 1990s when a Vice Chancellor would come and tell teachers that though he is the head of the university, he had to serve his political masters! Yes! Mumbai University had the unique status in having a former Vice Chancellor going to prison on charges of corruption!

Such political appointees would only see how they could make their positions as a stepping stone for much higher politically disbursed offices! May be a chairmanship of the Public Service Commission or chairmanship of the University Grants Commission or other positions, which provide them with commissions! Unfortunately, because of such appointments, academic excellence has been a major casualty.

During his recent visit to Mumbai University, President Abdul Kalam observed, "Political parties should be 30 per cent political and 70 per cent developmental. But in our country, it is just the opposite. "Since our politicians indulge in politics most of the time, for mediocre Vice Chancellors, it has been hundred per cent politics! Late Professor Ram Joshi, who was the Vice Chancellor in the late 1970s once told me that VCs run to the government for consultation, on everything even where under the 1974 Act, they are not even remotely required to do so.

However, 20 years later Maharashtra Universities Act of 1994 has ensured it absolutely necessary for the Vice Chancellor to run to the government in all decision-making. Today in effect, the University, has turned into a bureau of the government department of Higher Education where it cannot appoint even a sweeper without the government permission!

This happens more obviously in Mumbai University, as it is just across Oval Maidan from the Mantralaya. And majority of our ministers come from rural Maharashtra to draw their pound of flesh from the riches of Mumbai while in power, without contributing anything to it. They enjoy highly educated vice-chancellors hovering around them!

Second, which follows from the first, in a big way, is over centralisation of powers by the government over the working of the University. Centralisation is all pervasive. The best illustration is power to sanction new colleges. Mumbai University has been since inception primarily an affiliation and not a teaching university. It's only since independence that the University had set up post graduate teaching departments in a big way. Today, the University can only give a proposal to start a new college but it is only the government, which can grant permission to start it. The power to decide opening of new colleges, affiliated to Mumbai University has become the politician's fallback cushion whenever they are out of power. This has become a major source of political patronage and corruption in the field of higher education. Gone are the days when public-minded charitable trusts were encouraged to start a college. As an affiliating university, its status is directly affected by the quality of its colleges.

Third, a significant problem with the Mumbai University is its culture of sharing of responsibility for inaction. Everyone should see what everyone else does. It is a cover for bureaucratic inaction emerging from its own ignorance. In the process, nothing gets done. Ignorance of what University means, is enormous within the university staff. For them it is just an employment. In 1989, I saw a report prepared by the Mumbai University. I was shocked. Barring the Registrar and a Deputy Registrar, a large number of Assistant Registrars did not hold any degree. The state government has seen the universities, as an employment provider to those with minimum qualifications.

In the background of everyone insisting to see what everyone else does, let me give on illustration. I worked for 13 months as Director, College Development Council in 1989-90. While the University Grants Commission provided that the Director would be directly reporting to the Vice Chancellor, the Pro-Vice Chancellor and Registrar wanted me to report to Vice Chancellor through them which I refused to accept. By directly interacting with the Vice Chancellor, I was able to get grants of several colleges and individual scholars cleared by the UGC (University Grants Commission). If I had indulged in the bureaucratic game of pushing papers and make them disappear, I would not have been able to get done one-tenth of what I achieved in 13 months.

What is tragic is that Mumbai University has Public Administration as a subject in MA. But it has not been able to think of reforming its own administrative system for speedy decision making. But who cares? After all, the post as I said, is only a stepping stone for something more lucrative to come. It won't come if you try to be innovative, on the other hand, flowing with the tide, can take you to the greener pastures!

Thus, what the Acts of 1974 and 1994 did was to give a severe blow to Bombay University's uniqueness by standardizing it along with other universities in the state. Simultaneously, it also removed its unique relationship with Mumbai city by adding colleges from adjoining districts to reap the benefits of the name of Bombay

University. The result is that Bombay University has become Mumbai University and has been reduced to the status of a semi-urban university.

Bring in autonomy

What needs to be done to restore Mumbai University's status as a unique university? First, make it a city university once again as a teaching and affiliating university with its jurisdiction limited to Mumbai city. Second, restore its autonomy in normal functioning. Let me add that in a democracy like ours, university cannot be immune to politics.

But what ought to be done, at the least, as in the American state universities, is let the state legislature discuss once a year, performance of the university while approving its budget. Then leave it alone without interfering in university decision making. Today, that is a tall order. University autonomy has become an unknown concept.

However, restoring autonomy is only possible by making it a central university, to give it a national outlook and also have sufficient funding to maintain excellence in education. Allahabad University in Uttar Pradesh has become a central university and there is, I understand, great improvement in its functioning. So far governments in Maharashtra had tried to provide stamp of greatness to rural colleges by their affiliation to Mumbai University. But this has not raised the standard of higher education provided by these colleges. On the other hand, Mumbai University has lost its status as a national institution.

Professors in other universities of Maharashtra who teach in Marathi medium tell me that the government has made haste in switching to Marathi medium, without adequate planning and provision of facilities like text books on latest developments in any area. Hence, instead of reduction everyone to a lower standard, the best and the brightest ones in the rural areas can be provided scholarships to study in Mumbai University after making it a 'national university.'

Finally, after limiting the jurisdiction of Mumbai University to Mumbai city, there is a need for creating two more universities. One for the districts of Konkan to manage colleges now affiliated with Mumbai University like Thane, Raigad and Ratnagiri call in Konkan

University. Another for the city of Navi Mumbai. Other cities in India like Delhi or Hyderabad, for instance, have more than one university. Delhi has Delhi University, Jawaharlal Nehru University, and Jamia Milia, not to mention scores of deemed universities. Hyderabad has Osmania University, Jawaharlal Nehru Technological University, and Hyderabad University (central university), in addition to many deemed universities. The state government must reduce Mumbai University's responsibilities by establishing a university in Konkan and another in Navi Mumbai to re-establishing university in Konkan and another in Navi Mumbai to Mumbai University exclusively as the city university.

Chapter - 60

The World is Our Lecture Room

(The Hindustan Times, 26 January 2007)

"The time is ripe for India to set up more quality-conscious international universities"

Sam Pitroda, Chairman of the National Knowledge Commission (NKC), in a teleconference address to vice chancellors of Indian universities in Mumbai advocated setting up more universities to meet growing demand. He pointed out that as against the need for at least 1,500 universities there are only 363.

This is a very sensible suggestion, from a person who was responsible for the telecommunication revolution in India in the Eighties and Nineties. Hopefully, it should lead to a revolution in higher education and at the same time improve the quality of educational institutions. There is no doubt about the need for more universities. Only 11 per cent of our youth in the 17-23 age group go for higher education.

However, the question is who will set up these new universities? Central and state governments have no money for higher education. Since the Sixties, everyone involved in educational policy-making have advocated allocation of at least 6 per cent of GDP for education, but the figure has, in practice, not crossed 3 per cent. Hence, the new universities should operate with government recognition but without grants-in-aid. Based on my experience in managing an unaided college in Mumbai, I can say that even unaided colleges would be in demand, provided they offer good infrastructure and quality education. High fees would not deter those seeking better educational opportunities.

A novel concept to consider while setting up new universities either by the state or private foundations is to set up international universities, for instance, the international University of Mumbai or the International University of Delhi. Other major cities could set up similar universities.

Though the concept of international universities is new in India, it is common in the United States. Following the American model, other countries such as Egypt and Kenya have set up international universities. I have had experience teaching at the Florida International University, Miami, and it is worth emulating. International universities must give the highest importance to maintaining standards towards that goal, they need to attract the best teachers, if necessary from abroad. A mixture of foreign and Indian professors would be a gain on practical grounds. It would justify the 'international' component in the name.

International universities would cater to two types of students. First, they ought to aim to attract 50 per cent of their student population from abroad or from countries in the neighbourhood. Many foreign nationals would like to study in India, not necessarily for subjects that are unique to Indian civilisation and culture (dance, music, yoga philosophy, Ayurveda, etc.) but for conventional subject like engineering, medicine, chemistry and physics. Students from developed countries like the US, where the cost of education is rising rapidly, could opt to study in India. Non Resident Indians would find it an important service provided to them by the country of their origin.

International universities would also serve as instruments to cement the bond of friendship among South Asian countries. Thus, for instance, as international university in Chennai could attract students from Sri Lanka or Maldives while one in Kolkata could cater to students from South East Asia. They would also draw students from developing countries who may find the cost of education in the US or Britain too steep.

The other segment of students in international universities would be Indian. This will help them in various ways. First, even 60 years of Independence, Indians have not overcome their colonial mindset. They continue to suffer from the 'foreign' syndrome whereby all that is foreign in seen, as being good. Also, those who cannot afford to get a foreign degree can at least have the satisfaction of being exposed to foreign teachers along with foreign students.

An important point to note is that India is a signatory to the General Agreement of Trade in Services (GATS) as envisaged by the World Trade Organisation (WTO). By the end of this year, foreign universities would be legally entitled to have a commercial presence in India and offer degrees without collaborating with an Indian university. Those looking for a foreign degree could head for these universities as study in India would make it cheaper.

The presence of major foreign universities such as Johns Hopkins, Harvard or Yale or the London School of Economics would be a threat to Indian universities. Establishing international universities would certainly help the Indian university system to meet the challenge at least halfway.

Chapter - 61

Keep the Channels Open

(The Hindustan Times, 23 March 2007)

"It's time India become more liberal towards Fulbright scholars coming to the country"

Much has been reported on the Indian government asking US scholars planning to visit India on a Fulbright programme to change their research topics or on the inordinate delay in granting them a visas. One fallout of the controversy on Fulbright scholars is that people want to know more about the Fulbright fellowships.

Fulbright fellowships were initiated by the US after it emerged as a superpower post WW-II. It was introduced in India in 1950. Since then more than 7,500 scholars-Indians and Americans-have availed of the fellowship to study in each other's country.

But one may ask: What purpose does an exchange of scholars serve? It is all too evident that in a globalised world it is important to know more about the countries one is dealing with. In such a world, India needs experts who are knowledgeable about the US and vice versa. As a secondary player in a world dominated by the US, India's need is more urgent than that of the US.

However, in the case of Indians going to the US, there have been two lacunae. First, every Indian who has travelled to the US even for a week imagines he is an expert on that country, particularly of its systems of government, society and history. Doordarshan, for instance, once described that the electors to the Electoral College, who elect the US president, are elected on the basis of "Proportional representation." In reality they are elected by a unique system of "winner take all."

Second, because of American interest in funding study of America globally, Indian policymakers took the stance that since Americans are spending on promoting understanding of America, India need not promote the study of America!

Yet, in the past, particularly during the peak of the Cold War, the government of India looked at visiting Americans with suspicion. A liberal American professor, a friend of India who initially came as a Fulbright Scholar, was driven away in the 1980s despite his good work. During the Emergency, Ms Indira Gandhi was looking for ways to limit the number of Americans visiting India as Fulbright scholars. One false yardstick she proposed was that India would give as many visas to visiting Americans as the US gave to Indians visiting the US on exchange programmes.

On the face of it, India's stand seems valid. But though the programme is bilateral, India's financial contribution to the exchange was next to nothing. Since the US foots the entire bill, it couldn't be blamed for the uneven traffic.

It cannot be denied that the Fulbright programme had Cold War aims such as winning friends to its point of view. In one of my interviews with the founder of the exchange programme, Senator J. William Fulbright, I had asked why more Fulbright grants went to small East European countries like Hungary or Poland as compared to India. He admitted that this was because of Cold War compulsions.

Even during the Cold War years, American government agencies implementing the exchange programme did not question the subjects for research submitted by Indians. I studied the controversial role of National Security Advisers in policy-making by taking cases like the Bay of Pigs Crisis, the Vietnam War and the Iran Contra scandal. Not only was my motive in researching such a sensitive topic, in 1976 and again in 1982, not questioned but I was extended all help in acquiring classified papers from the Presidential Libraries. As for the visa, I got it in just days.

However, in those Cold War years, there were instances of public hostility to my study. After I had delivered a radio talk in Illinois, on the working of the American National Security Council, for instance, a caller asked whether I planned to provide American information to the Soviet Union.

But after Bill Clinton's visit to India in March 2000, to begin with, and since the July 2005 civil nuclear deal and George Bush's visit to India in March 2006, American public perceptions too have radically changed. When such is the changed American outlook on India, it is unfortunate that we should continue with the Cold War mindset and regard with suspicion the topic selected by their Fulbright scholars intending to visit India. If they wish to study Hindu-Muslim migration patterns, Left politics in Kerala or right politics in Chhattisgarh, they should be allowed to do so without hindrance. There have been excellent studies by American scholars on Muslims, Shiv Sena, RSS, Congress and other political parties. It is high time that our policy-makers change their Cold War mindset and open themselves to developing a new India-US equation in a globalised economy and international politics.

Chapter - 62

Schools: The Way Forward

(Hindustan Times, Mumbai, 30 April 2007)

"It is time Mumbai University organised its subjects under schools and allows for studies across departments. That is only way ahead for the university to restore a vibrant academic life".

When for the first time I went to the US as a Fulbright research fellow, I was affiliated to the School of Advance International Studies, Johns Hopkins University, Washington, DC.

When I returned, a question that often came up was: how is it that I went to a School, that too after teaching in Bombay University's Postgraduate Department of Civics and Politics for over six years? The question then, as now, shows lack of familiarity in India with the system of schools in Universities.

What the School system does is to place all interrelated subjects under a broad discipline. For instance, all social science subjects such as anthropology, economics, politics and sociology could be placed under School of Social Sciences. Similarly, there could be a School of Life Sciences or School of International Relations (IR) or Languages.

While newer universities in India, particularly Central Universities, have followed the school system, Maharashtra is yet to adopt it. Mumbai University as one of the three oldest universities in India, has the system of Departments organised around subject. For instance, Sanskrit, Economics, Chemistry, Mathematics and Civics and Politics. A Director or a Head leads each Department.

The present system of subject centric departments has obvious advantages. First, it enables teaching of a subject in depth, thereby contributing to its vigorous growth. Also, it is a system that has stood the test of time, being in practice for about 150. Secondly, it enables members in the department to specialise in different sub-disciplines within a department. Finally, subject-wise organised departments are small in size and, as such, easier to manage.

However, departments have proved themselves unable to face the challenges of the knowledge explosion and the demand for interdisciplinary studies. In the 1950s, someone teaching international politics was deemed an expert in all that pertained to the external relations of a nation-state. It is no longer so today. There is national security, foreign policies of different nations, international economic relations and international organisations among others. But even these sub-disciplines are out dated. Very often a new subject crops up calling for immediate attention and specialisation.

Further, these subjects crisscross the boundaries of the traditional departments. Thus for instance, where do you place a subject like Climate Change? More than one department could legitimately make a claim for it-Geography, International Relations, Law. Or it often happens that a department dodges its responsibility to add a on a subject. This is the case with a vital subject like Intellectual Property Rights.

However, with the knowledge explosion, subjects starting off as a topic in a subject could later turn into an important subject by itself. This showed up the limitations of department system. It is difficult to develop interdisciplinary teaching or research studies in the present system. In the 1980s, the politics department developed a course on Political Sociology. Around the same time The Sociology Department also went for a course on Sociology Politics. But there was no coordination whatsoever on either developing course content or teaching of the course.

The situation on the research front is worse. In more than one case, students who had done their M.Sc in defence studies were denied admission to do research for their Ph.D in Political Science on the specious ground of incompatibility of subjects, though the topics related to national security. If it were a school system, the School of Social Sciences would have enabled the student to work on it as defence studies and politics are subjects under social science. On the other hand, during my visit to Cambridge University, I found that the Department of International Relations Social Science reaching out to welcome students with a physics-pure science background to enroll for a degree in international relations.

Hence, it is encouraging to know that Mumbai University is planning to introduce the concept of broad-based schools in place of the present system of subject oriented departments mainly it will help break barriers created by departments organised discipline-wise and enable interdisciplinary studies. Hitherto self-contained departments would become units of a school, forcing them to enlarge their vision to become flexible in their teaching and research. The School system within a University will place sultanates of the present Departments under a dean. Since many social sciences departments would be under one dean, policymaking on teaching, introduction of new courses guiding of research would become easier, providing flexibility. However, Deans should be well qualified persons with doctoral degree and research experience. The present pattern of college teachers without a Ph.D. or guiding experience sitting in judgment on research would no longer be acceptable.

The School system cannot, however, be introduced in isolation from other related reforms. It will demand logical extension of flexibility in allowing students to choose the course they wish to study on the basis of the credit system. In the present department system, students need to take courses from within departments. In the 1950s it was still possible for a student to take four out of eight papers from another department. But in the 1980s, in the name of economy, this was scrapped. However, there are departments such as African Studies or Central Eurasian Studies that are permitted to offer a group of four papers. Since students do not want to study four papers in an uncertain job market, these departments could get some takers if they allowed one papers to be picked.

The broad-based schools system would work well if students are offered courses from any department or any school, the only condition being that to claim specialisation in one discipline, a student needs to obtain the requisite minimum credits in it. In other words a student should be able to take a course in English language, another course in physics, a third in statistics, yet get a degree with specialisation in, say, economics or international relations.

However, unfortunately governments have always been pushed into accepting innovation only when there is a dire need to trim costs. It would be disastrous for higher education if the government tries to push the school system in universities only as an economy measure and expect professors within a school to teach any subject, from agricultural economics to monetary economics, irrespective of specialisation. This kind of thinking has been built into the minds of decision-makers since an IAS officer heading the agriculture department for three years moves with ease to Finance or Education.

Chapter - 63

Need to Strengthen Research in Universities

(One India One People, April 2007)

"To strengthen universities as integral units of social life offering both research and higher education, we need to provide more universities offering quality education to larger number of student population"

National Knowledge Commission (NKC) Note on Higher Education (November 29, 2006) speaks of "a quiet crisis in higher education". One of the several symptoms of it, as identified by the NKC, is the fact that even after 60 years of independence, there is not even one university in India, which is "the best" in "the top fifty, in the world". Another report recently said that for every one patent held by an Indian, overseas Indians hold 30,000 patents.

One conclusion that could easily be drawn from the above statements is that those Indians who are in the field of higher education and involved in research are, by and large, very competent but do not perform well in India; but once they go abroad they do extremely well. This is also a statement, which I have come across during my work for the last 47 years in the field of higher education.

How does one explain this state of affairs? What remedial measures can be taken? Is there any hope for better performance by the future generation which is studying in schools and colleges now and intend to make a career in the field of higher education and research?

Causes for mediocrity

Why is the picture of higher education and research in India so dismal? Some protagonists of Hindi even today blame all ills in the field of higher education to our continued use of English language. After sixty years of independence, however, there is no scope for blaming the British for the current state of affairs in the field of higher education. They established universities on their model to create a backup staff for their officers who could speak their language (English) and share their ideals. Even after they have withdrawn, we have not been able to replace their language and ideals with our language and ideals for generating our creative patents and products, if the foreign language is the cause.

There is however, one problem with blaming English-a foreign language in which much of our higher education and research is conducted today. In support of blame-game on the language of research as a cause for lack of substantial output in the fields of research, we can advance the case of Japan where much of higher education is provided in Japanese and Japanese have been able to achieve excellence in academic and innovative research. Eminent journalist M.V. Kamath in his article 'What is wrong with our higher education?' We lack world class! says, Japan has 11 amongst world's top 200 universities while India has only three.

At the same time two instances can be cited against the argument of language as the cause of poor performance by Indian universities. First, many universities in India use regional languages as the medium of instruction but there aren't many cases of any original research being produced. Second, number of Americans who were able to conduct innovative research that won them patents or awards had come from other countries. The best illustration is that of the many who participated in the US Atom Bomb project, were mostly immigrants from Germany. Many Indians who get their patents registered abroad were also not necessarily from English medium schools.

Thus, the main cause for the lack of commendable research work in India is the lack of infrastructural facilities and funding. As a result, there is a lack of commitment on the part of faculty members, to research as an integral part of higher education. The government, which provides much of the funding for the higher education, is also not interested in demanding research output as a part of accountability of the teachers. M.V. Kamath mentions the fact that Mumbai University does not figure anywhere in the list of top 200 universities in the world. During my stint as a professor in Mumbai University, there was never a concept of insisting on research or appreciation or research done. If you do it, you do it for your own satisfaction. Government Babus who come to determine allocation of funds ask one question. "How many hours of teaching work do you do?" Research activities are not quantifiable!

In case one succeeds in getting some funding by one's own initiative, others see to it that obstacles are created in using such funds as it imposes uncalled for responsibilities for research on others in the department who wish to remain unaccountable by limiting their activities to quantifiable lectures. I was instrumental in getting a Ford Foundation grant to Mumbai University to promote research in International Relations. Alas! I became a mute witness to the return of the grant by the university to the Ford Foundation because of manipulation of a colleague to which Vice Chancellors easily succumb!

But the scarcity of resources is only a limited factor responsible for the current dismal status. The primary fact is a blow given to research in the universities by the first Prime Minister of India Pandit Nehru. Instead of strengthening universities in the area of research by fortifying their laboratories, he set up university independent laboratories called regional laboratories in the country. As and when new subject came up demanding teaching and research like biotechnolgy or cellular biology, new labs under the control of federal government were set up. The trend has not only continued but has been extended to ridiculous extent of setting up of independent universities offering one discipline like medicine or law.

The governments have found this device easier to accommodate their cronies in key positions, without much opposition. But it has only weakened the universities in their primary task of teaching and research in the field of higher education, since it has also led to thin out and evaporate scarce resources by spreading it into many centres of research rather than in few universities.

This also brings out the desire of politicians to control centres of research through intervention and sheer contempt they have for university autonomy. This itself is related to, generally their own low standing in the political equations, particularly in states of Indian Union. Ministers of Education have been political lightweights. Often education has been a slot reserved to accommodate a minority community member. Sometimes educationists are brought in but changed when political necessary. Triguna Sen, an educationist, was appointed by Mrs. Gandhi, for instance, as an education minister but when he was shifted to Chemicals, he reportedly protested stating "he knew something of education but of chemicals, he knew next to nothing". He was told to inform the Prime Minister his final decisions, by the next day. He informed her that that he would keep chemicals, after all!

Sheer contempt to education and research activities also come from semi-educated politicians who would say that despite having studied only up to IV standard and they could become the CM. Politicians would also cite Bill Gates as a computer genius but academically a high school drop out. This approach today is seen widely in the educational institutions run by the politicians. The fallacy is every politician thinks that he is a carbon copy of Bill Gates-just because he is a school drop out.

Urgent remedies

It is necessary to strengthen universities in the field of research. It is heartening to note that NKC has said that not withstanding the presence of Institutes of Technologies as "islands of excellence", "universities are the life blood of higher education."

To strengthen universities as integral units of social life offering both research and higher education, we need to provide more universities offering quality education to larger number of student population than mere seven per cent in the age group of 18 and 24 as we do today. These universities could be differentiated on the basis of kind of their intake: for instance Open University for distance education or National University for an all India intake. To meet the challenges emerging from the presence of foreign universities in India we should also come forward to promote International Universities where Indians can study side by side the students from abroad. Such an International University must also have the best faculty drawn from an international pool. This could help check Indians going abroad for study by providing them opportunities to interact on a constant basis with foreign students and teachers.

Chapter - 64

Government should not Harass Private School Managements

(The Free Press Journal, 30 May 2007)

"if the government grants are reduced or not given at all, the government loses its moral and even legal right to tell the school management that they would not collect donations"

Since 1991 the government of Maharashtra has embraced the policy of denying financial aid to private aided schools in the State. Reducing grant given for general maintenance of the school is the means towards this goal. In achieving this goal various means are adopted. In the recent years the simplest thing is to check whether the school management has taken quotations, before making any purchases, if not, items are simply held not eligible for aid irrespective of whether the item is reasonably priced or physically available for verification on the site or the reasons for not inviting quotations are recorded etc.

Second, insist that electricity bill be in the name of the Head of the School. Now, the building is owned by the trust and trustees would have applied for power whenever building was constructed. However, the government has begun to hold power bill as a non-grantable item if the bill is not in the name of the head of the school. It is the same story with water and the telephone bills. Government clerks could go to the ridiculous extent. They have now begun to insist that grant amount be spent through accounts where one signatory is the head of the school!

Third, as though the government owns the school building just because it gives an annual rent, the small minds in the educational bureaucracy ask schools to inform them if classrooms are let out to meetings etc to outsiders and whether the school collects any amount for the same! On the other hand, what government gives as rent, and if it gives, the so-called rent is not even sufficient to maintain one toilet in the school!

Fourth, there is the yardstick of number of students in a class. The government says there should be an average attendance of 40 in a class. To get it, you need at least a strength of 45 in a class. It is not very difficult for an English medium school. But it is a well-known fact in Mumbai at least that regional language schools, including Marathi schools are finding it difficult to maintain that number. Should fluctuating number be the criterion to reduce grant? Should therefore, they be denied their grant?

Fifth, grants have also been denied on flimsy grounds, like the qualifications of the teachers. I find it most unreasonable for the Maharashtra government to insist that the training qualification, for instance, B. Ed, be one that is obtained from within Maharashtra! There are linguistic minority schools in Mumbai who may not get teachers trained in Maharashtra to teach in minority language schools. What is wrong if a Kannada School in Mumbai gets someone with a training qualification obtained from Karnataka?

If a clerk is able to deny aid in a year altogether to a school or pay a small amount compared to the school's claims of say, ₹ 3 to 4 lakhs he would be considered as an efficient person. But he would be willing to forget his efficiency yardstick if you grease his palm with few thousands! The managements which run schools meant for poorer sections of the community would not be able to withstand arm-twisting tactics of the corrupt clerk for long!

All these changes have come about after the federal government embraced liberalisation, privatisation and globalisation (LPG) as a policy framework. But the government has not spelt out its policy approach to education since the LPG. The government appears to be a confused lot, as it seems to be always the case with them. If the government is really short of funds, it should clearly come out with a policy statement on private funding of school education. The original goal of government under Pandit Nehru was to spend six per cent of the GNP on education.

The present Maharashtra government had come to office by pledging to spend seven per cent on education. It has never been reached; we are not even any way near it. A report says that the Maharashtra government spends only two to three rupees out of rupees one hundred it collects, on schools education. Since in a country where more than 40 per cent of the population still lives below the poverty line, there cannot be reduction of government allocation to school education.

If the money is a problem the government need to classify schools on the basis of clientele served by the schools and the nature of location of a school. On the face of it, it can divide the schools in three categories, schools in areas of slums, middle class areas and schools in areas where well-to-do people live. This cannot be the only criterion to classify schools, as I do know that areas where well-to-do people live, could also have poor and schools catering to their needs. Hence, combining both these criteria schools can be graded.

The schools catering to the needs to poorer sections could get full financial assistance, the schools providing education to middle class children could get 75 per cent grants, while no aid need to be given to schools serving the well-to-do classes. The government has as it is come out with the concept of permanently unaided schools. But such schools should be provided where clientele is well-to-do people. Such schools should not be allowed in the poorer areas of the state.

But unfortunately the government has either reduced the grants-in-aid to established unaided schools indiscriminately without any objective norms. But one thing is clear: Whether aided or unaided, government control over the educational institutions has only increased.

Hence, before the government implements the above scheme, it should do away with irritants of unnecessary and unacademic controls by government. The government meaning its Babus should be trained to adopt a liberal approach. During the time when grant-in-aid used to be given, the government had a right to insist that capitation fees are not collected by schools. But if the government grants are reduced or not given at all, the government loses its moral and even legal right to tell the school management that they would not collect donations. On the other hand, the charity commissioners/tax authorities ought to see that donations collected are ploughed back into the school/educational development.

Chapter - 65

Bidding for an M.Phil

(Hindustan Times, 11 June 2007)

"There is money in higher education. Hence the government is keen to sanction authority for colleges seeking permission to offer Ph.D and M.Phil degrees".

The Maharashtra government seems bent upon making universities the pocket boroughs of politicians in power. The latest move is to make colleges seek government permission if they seek to offer facilities leading to research degrees like M.Phil. or Ph.D. This is in addition to the permission from the affiliated university.

Research is a serious academic activity. In some universities like JNU and other central universities an M.Phil is a prerequisite qualification for a Ph.D. In some universities like Mumbai, an M.Phil is an independent degree between the post graduate degree and Ph.D. These are high level degrees that many seek to get but only a few attain.

Then, is the government, made up of a bunch of politicians who do not need any qualifications whatsoever to become ministers, and their babus going to decide whether a college is suitably equipped to guide students and award Ph.D degrees? The experience with the government's handling of education so far does not inspire confidence. It is highly unlikely that the government will use its power to ensure quality in education in college and centres. On the contrary, the government's move is prescription for disaster in higher education.

Even now, the government is the nodal authority for granting permission to educational trusts to start a college under the Maharashtra

Universities Act, 1994. Earlier, the power was vested with the universities under the Act of 1974. True, trusts are expected to submit their application for a new college to the university, but the latter can only recommended their case to the government.

Hence, it is really the government that is empowered to grant permissions. And the government enjoys enormous powers in this respect. What is more intriguing is that the ministers do not share this power they hold over colleges even with their bureaucrats. In the usual course, ministers act on the advice of bureaucrats who process the university's recommendations. The Committee of Ministers headed by the Chief Minister decides on the number of approvals to be given during a year and, accordingly a list is prepared not necessarily based on the recommendations of the university, but as political patronage. Thus, if the government wants to give, say, 100 approvals in a year; the Congress will decide on 50 and the Nationalist Congress Party on the other 50. The outcome is always controversial: a trust with a building already in place might apply for permission three or more times while another influential trust politically well connected or promoted by politicians can start a college even in a coaching class or a shed on the promise they would be constructing a building once it gets the approval.

What is more, even if an existing college wants to introduce a course that the university shows in its curriculum, such as B.Sc (IT), a professional course in the faculty of science, one cannot introduce it without the government's approval!

The government, going by news reports, is said to be concerned that quality would be compromised if more centres were to offer an M.Phil degree. This is in the context of the University Grants Commission (UGC) making M.Phil and Ph.D qualification mandatory to enter the teaching profession as a substitute for passing the National Eligibility Test (NET) or the State Eligibility Test (SET).

But the government's concern regarding quality is not genuine-it is mainly concerned about the financial implications. There are a large number of new teachers in colleges in the state who have not been confirmed in their jobs because they are yet to clear NET or SET. Once they obtain an M.Phil or Ph.D, the government would have to confirm them and give them long term benefits.

The state government's fear partly stems from the UGC's intellectual poverty and its incompetence in deciding once for all whether a new entrant to teaching in higher educational institutions ought clear an eligibility test in the subject matter or quality in research techniques or acquire a qualification in pedagogical methods.

To improve the standards for Ph.Ds awarded by a university, certain practical steps could be taken at no extra cost to the government or the university. Such measures must begin at the top. It would serve as proof of commitment on the part of the authorities.

To begin with, ministers, civil servants and all those in the highest level of university administration, must be barred from registering for the Ph.D degree in any university in whose administration they are even remotely connected. During my 35 years of direct association with universities in India, I have noticed that serving IAS and IPS officers have come with proposals for enrolling for Ph.D largely based on the material they or their subordinates have collected in the discharge of their duties in the departments headed by them. A Secretary of Revenue wanted a Ph.D to be conferred on him on the basis of a study of drought conditions in Maharashtra! It is unethical for these officers to use such material to get a degree for themselves and to pressure universities into registering them as Ph.D students. The ban should be extended at least for five years after their retirement as well. In the US there are instances when Under Secretaries have been sacked for using office facilities to write books.

The government's insistence that colleges intending to introduce M.Phil and Ph.D obtain its prior permission is a direct assault on university autonomy. The claim that its purpose is to maintain the standards of education is a mere excuse to centralise powers and sell favours. In the process, the government is destroying concept of university autonomy.

If the trend continues, the day may not be too far off when the minister of higher too far off when the minister of higher education will run the universities from Mantralaya. It is a great irony that in the age of economic liberalisation, the government is pursuing academic centralisation.

Chapter - 66

The Plight of Schools Told to Close Down

(The Free Press Journal, 25 June 2007)

"starting a school or a college is not an easy task-unless a business house, a well-connected politician or a non-resident Indian as a commercial venture establishes it...."

A report on unauthorised schools (not in the Free Press Journal) numbering 29, and another 15 colleges in Thane District goes on the present official version on these so called unauthorised educational institutions. Correspondents generally do not make, it seems, any effort to contact management of some of these schools or colleges to find out reasons as to why they are running these unauthorised schools. Yet, those interested in sensationalising reports call those who are running these so called unauthorised schools as "unscrupulous elements."

Undoubtedly there could and there are such elements in the society. But invariably such elements are well connected with politicians in power. Hence, they know it well that they would suffer no harm because of it.

On the other hand, often the government is, equally or more responsible in creating such situations where management is forced to run a school technically without government permission. Thus, for instance, during the academic year 2006-07 the Government of Maharashtra gave permission to according to one report, nearly 1495 schools to commence permanently on unaided basis. The government has money for erecting statues of leaders here and there but no money to perform primary social functions of educating the common people. It is worth nothing in this connection that a recent global report states that corrupt officials in some countries siphon off 80 per cent of funds earmarked for education. Rajiv Gandhi stated this long back in the 1980s, when he said only 22 paise from a rupee allocated for a social purpose actually reaches them.

Today, in one sense we have become a developed nation where nothing goes without a legal challenge, as in the west. A body of Managements in the Nagpur bench of Bombay High Court challenged these permissions given by the government. From the press reports I can gather that the well established schools in different areas feared that new schools coming up would eat up their admissions. This would not have been the case, however, as these permissions were on permanently unaided basis. The Nagpur bench, however, set aside the permission granted by the government. However, these schools, in the meanwhile after getting the permission had enrolled students. The very fact that these schools could attract students though they were started on permanently unaided basis shows an acute need for them in those areas where they were started. It also seems that there was some political rivalry between two groups that really led to the legal challenge to humiliate the minister of education.

Starting a school or a college is not an easy task unless a business house, a well-connected politician or a non-resident Indian as a commercial venture establishes the trust start such as institution. But for any other social service organisation, it is a huge task of raising funds to construct a building to house the school and also bear initial deficit on salaries and provision of infrastructure.

In this kind of class action involving a large number of schools permitted on permanently unaided basis, could lead to good, bad and ugly being treated alike and all asked to be closed. Should the government grant permission for a school started in a developing township like Navi Mumbai and another in rural area on the same basis of permanently unaided? What about parents ability to pay?

All these schools, which initially received their permission to start, however, were asked to close down by the government in response to the judgement of Bombay High Court's Nagpur bench. The government itself should have moved the Supreme Court to see that the stay given by the Nagpur bench of Bombay High Court is vacated in the larger interest of the public since it had given the permission on the basis of a study of need for schools in the areas where these were started in first instance. The evidence does not show that government has taken such an initiative nor the government has been very active to see that Court's objections are met.

It shows that government's commitment to provide education to all is only a sloganeering without deep commitment. However, once the schools were asked to close, Zilla Parishads and Municipal Corporations were prompt in trying to close down the Schools irrespective of consequences of such actions. In such case officials are keen to demonstrate that they always act to enforce the law! For the lower level official, it is another golden opportunity for corruption to make quick bucks by exploiting fears of the schools management. Very strangely government officials who never acknowledge letters, are quick even to make site visits to threaten legal action against the schools refusing to close down.

In my opinion, sometimes judiciary does not try to distinguish good, from bad and ugly and treat all of them as a class under the cover of its judgment. Under these circumstances some private managements, which were affected by the judgment of the Nagpur Bench of Bombay High Court, have moved the Supreme Court by coming together under the banner of Forum of Permanently Unaided Schools. Should government official refer to these schools as illegal or Unauthorised or started by unscrupulous elements.

No doubt, it is the right of government to keep such unscrupulous elements out from the field of education. But those who have become victims of the government's bad administration cannot be blamed for keeping their schools open until the SC decision is delivered.

Chapter - 67

Admission Chaos: Govt must allow more School, College Divisions

(The Free Press Journal, 17 July 2007)

"Under these circumstances, what necessary is: the government should immediately sanction additional division in all city colleges and high schools. These divisions ought to be on aided basis. Any sanction of additional division on unaided basis would be tantamount to forcing students with lower percentages to opt for paying higher fees"

The Maharashtra government has a polity of providing free education to all girls up to HSC. Boys also get free education till standard X. The only condition is that the student ought not to fail in the middle of his/her career. But at 15 plus age, boys are not in a position to decided on their career goals as such they too look for further education by continuing to queue up for XI standard admissions.

This policy has become a problematic one to many educational institutions this year. The reason: SSC Board's competitive populism led to every one getting 30 marks bonus in their maths papers as a policy. This fits, into untold story of the SSC Board's unspelt policy desire to be considered as progressive as the Delhi's CBSE which awards marks very liberally. This in turn, help CBSE students to better perform in term of securing admissions into good colleges.

The liberal policy was seen by public, as it ought to be. Some of the headlines speak for the public approach to the issue. One newspaper said: "By grace of maths: 30 mark largesse helps SSC students fare better" another paper said "30+ marks give state 8 per cent jump." Addition of marks had the state a bumper crop of 75.0 per cent results this year while it was only 66 percent last year.

But the impact of the SSC board's liberal marking policy on the admissions to Higher Secondary sections as a policy was never anticipated. Those newspapers had anticipated the rush for admissions. The state authorities were mum on the matter hopelessly thinking that 'we will cross the bridge when we near it'.

Now that the fourth list is out and admissions are all over, it is widely reported that there are still several thousand students waiting to get admissions into higher secondary sections.

The government will come out with its usual statements: No one will remain without admission; every one seeking admission will get into the higher studies etc. Politicians are also doing their own bit in the matter to help students. They go to different higher secondary schools; claim how they helped the trust to set up a degree college or Jr. College. But speaking as far as Mumbai city is concerned one can see clear trends amongst students. The obvious one is: students no longer want to travel long distance to attend a college of his choice; he would rather choose to study in a neighbourhood college.

What could solve the problem? It will not help by government opening guidance centres in different areas of the city. This used to be a practice in the 1990s. But these were dispensed with because they became centres of corruption: students were favoured with admission support in favoured Jr. Colleges, for a consideration!

Under these circumstances, what is necessary is: the government should immediately sanction additional divisions in all City Colleges and High Schools. These divisions ought to be on aided basis. Any sanction of additional divisions on unaided basis would be tantamount to forcing students with lower percentages to opt for paying higher fees. In some schools as I know of them, they have their own large number of in-house students yet to be admitted. These are often students who have studied in Marathi or Kannada or Hindi medium and as such they would prefer to have one subject in their mother tongue. Hence, such students cannot be simply asked to choose another Jr. College where seats might be available without the language option. The government has the other option of opening of new Jr. Colleges in the areas where there is currently felt need for them. Such colleges at this moment may be difficult to be opened at short notice, as it requires lot of infrastructure to being an educational institution. Yet if the government is well disposed to think of sanctioning new institutions, it could do so. But care should be taken to see that aided institutions are permitted in areas where local population deserves an aided institution and not because the local corporator or MLA is influential! It is not an imaginary observation. It has happened in case of starting a degree college. As an applicant to start a degree college to cater to Kannada linguistic minority in Mumbai, who mostly study in Kannada medium because they are the first generation of school goers, I was given permission by the Maharashtra government to start a college after a wait of three years "on permanently unaided basis." When I asked the basis of this decision the then registrar introduced me to a politician hailing from Chief Minister's district, who got the permission to start a College on an aided basis! Obviously what matters are political connections and not the need of the society! What can happen to a Degree College can happen to a school as well!

Hence, a mix of opening extra divisions and new colleges can meet the immediate challenge of meeting admission needs of those who have passed their X std this year. It is heart-breaking situation to see parents pleading for admissions in the existing institutions. The government must come out and help to provide education to all.

Chapter - 68

Let's Say *Bus* to This Nasty Problem

(Hindustan Times, 12 February 2008)

"BEST's unhelpful attitude is one of the obstacles to providing safe transport to school children"

On January 28, there was an LPG cylinder blast in a Maruti van carrying 12 school children back home, which killed three of them. That brought another series of sermonizing and breast-beating among officials and school authorities. School Education Minister Vasant Purke had promised to act last year. Deputy Chief Minister R.R. Patil is reported to have promised stern action against those responsible for the tragedy and a change in policy.

Hindustan Times correspondents, talking to representatives of a few elite schools in South Mumbai, have broached the idea of a "model bus system" involving schools hiring contract buses to pick up and drop children from common points. Is it a novel and workable solution? While many schools with students from middle class families have had such a scheme for long, it is unlikely to work in a school catering to poor minorities, like the one in Jogeshwari where the LPG cylinder accident happened.

I say that with experience, as a trustee of a Kannada linguistic minority school in Mulund, where children come from faraway places, as such schools are very few in the city, I find that it is beyond the means of parents to pay ₹ 300 or more per month as bus fees while paying only ₹ 15 as school fees. In such situations, parents rely on unauthorised services of private rickshaws or private vans in which children are packed like sardines.

What can be done in a situation like this? I approached the General Managers of BEST and Thane Municipal Transport Corporation (TMT), with a proposal to introduce a bus to pick up children from key points, which spilled over to some parts in Thane. Though TMT authorities were willing to introduce a bus service if the BEST gave a No Objection Certificate (NOC), BEST remained unmoved at least for three years so far. On the other hand, one officer advised me to get a private bus service introduced despite my telling him why that's not possible in the style on Queen Antoinette who had said if the poor do not get bread, let them eat cake. Yet, I am still hopeful of the proposal eventually materializing, because its time has come.

An alternate solution to such problems in catering to the needs of transporting children of poor parents, is for the state to introduce special buses during school hours to collect children and drop them at their respective schools within a neighbourhood. Alternatively, the government ought to provide school serving poorer sections of the people with buses under the Sarva Shiksha Abhiyan (SSA). If SSA is really to succeed in bringing all children under educational system, it is not enough that children are provided with books, uniforms, mid-day meal and milk. It must also enable them to reach the school of their choice by providing them free transport. Only then one can hope that every child gets compulsory primary education.

Unfortunately, these schemes fail to be implemented or even considered, until calamities happen and there is a public outcry.

Chapter - 69

Avoid tragedies: Provide School bussing for Kids

(The Free Press Journal, 16 February 2008)

"Children be enabled to reach the School of their choice by providing them free transport; so that every child gets compulsory primary education in the country".

In our ancient Indian myths and folklores, we have numerous stories of human sacrifices to appease one or the other gods. For instance, very common is rain god, asking him to show his shower power! I remember a Kannada folklore where a husband, returning home after his work asks his mother the whereabouts of his wife. His wife had sacrificed her life to placate rain God so that barren land could be cultivated again!

Even in modern Indian democracy it seems as thought nothing happens without a large number of poor being killed before popular government decides to act on a policy. Nothing happens unless all-powerful ministers take a decision to adopt a policy, normally under public pressure. This is illustrated by the LPG cylinder blast in a Maruti van carrying 12 school children back home, which killed three of them on 28th January this year.

That brought another series of sermonizing and breast-beating at the high levels of policy making. School Education Minister, Mr Vasant Purke said: 'I said so' last year and he promised to act this year! A wise man after the tragedy! Deputy Chief Minister, R R Patil is reported to have promised stern action against those responsible for the tragedy and a change in policy.

Suddently, newspapers also spoke of "Model bus system" involving schools hiring contract buses "to pick and drop children from common points." Is it a novel and workable solution? While many schools with elite and higher middle class student-clientele have such a scheme for long, I have implemented it since 1985, in Mulund, it is unlikely to work in a school catering to poor children from slums or one like that from Jogeshwari catering to Muslim minorities.

I say that with experience. As a trustee of a Kannada linguistic minority school in Mulund, where children come from far away places, since Kannada schools are very few in the city of Mumbai; parents find it beyond their means to pay Rs 300 or more per month as bus fees while paying only Rs 5 or 15 as schoold fees! In such situations, parents rely on unauthorised services of private rickshawas or private vans in which children are filled as sardines in a tin! Otherwise, they give up their choice of mother tongue for primary education but go to any other nearby school.

What can be done in a situation like this? I approached General Managers of the BEST and Thane Municipal Transport Corporation (TMT), with a proposal to introduce a bus to serve our catchment areas which spilled over to some parts in Thane. Though TMT authorities were willing to introduce a bus service if the BEST gave a No Objection Certificate (NOC), Best remained unmoved at least for three years so far. On the other hand, one officer advised me to get a private bus service introduced, despite my telling him why that is not possible- in the style of queen Antoinette who had said if poor do not get bread, let them eat cake! The BEST is more worried about their jurisdictional turf than serving public! Yet, I am still hopeful of eventually the proposal materializing.

Another alternate solution to such problmes in catering to the needs of transporting children of poor parents, is for the state to introduce bussing to run special school buses during shcool hours to collect children and drop them in respective schools within a neighborhood. It is unfortunate that our socialistic, democratic and pupulist governments at the Centre and in states never so far thought of introducing, what is a common practice in the United States, called 'bussing' in which school children from a neighborhood are collected and dropped at schools. A public authority servicing the cause of education invariably does this.

How is it that the Indian federal government, which has come out with Sarva Shikshan Abhiyan (SSA) to bring every child under the primary education, has never thought of providing school bussing? If SSA is really to succeed in bringing all children under educational system, it is not enough that children are provided with books, uniforms, mid day meal and milk, but also enable them to reach the school of their choice by providing them free transport. Then and only then one can hope that every child gets compulsory primary education in the country.

However, if the government does not wish to provide such service immediately, the government ought to provide to trusts/schools serving the cause of education of such poorer sections of community with buses under the SSA. However, to implement above schemes, our great leaders, need not wait till more human sacrifices are offered to make them open their eyes. Or do our Ministers refuse to come out of their mythological world!

Chapter - 70

BMC Needs to Learn a Thing or Two

(Hindustan Times, 4 April 2008)

"Private schools bear the burden of school education, yet they get only a trickle of government aid"

What is the state of affairs in primary education in Mumbai? Nothing to cheer about.

Basically, there are two kinds of institutions which share this responsibility on behalf of the state. First, the Brihanmumbai Muncipal Corporation (BMC), which directly runs primary schools. Second, there are primary schools run by private trusts. These are recognised by the BMC, run with or without aid from it.

The trusts provide primary education as a social responsibility. In that they carry a great burden in helping the BMC to bring quality education to the masses.

The Constitution mandates under Article 45 of Directive Principles that the state provide free and compulsory education to all children below the age of 14 within ten years. Though 58 years have passed since the Constitution was adopted, the directive principle remains unimplemented. The Government of India has come out with the Sarva Shiksha Abhiyan (SSA) to implement the Directive Principle in question. Yet success is nowhere in sight. This only emphasises the continued significance of private trusts in providing access to education to the young.

But, going by the attitude of the bureaucracy, it would seem that the BMC regards private trusts as intruding on its turf. Its acts of commission and omission have hindered the working of private trusts in the field of primary education. The BMC practices blatant discrimination against private primary schools.

The first and the most glaring discrimination is in the matter of fees in aided private primary schools. These school are forced to collect fees because they get insufficient aid. This is in violation of the Constitutional directive of "free and compulsory education for all children until they complete the age of fourteen years."

There is absolutely no doubt that parents, if they can afford it, would send their children to private aided schools. It is simply because private aided and unaided schools are better managed than BMC-run schools.

To attract children to municipal schools, the BMC offers children free milk in tetra packs. But its inability to manage the programme is borne out by the recent incident of children being hospitalised after drinking free milk. Again, free milk is not extended to children attending aided private primary schools. In private schools teachers normally follow the rule of tasting the food before it is served to children.

Second, teachers in aided private primary schools are not paid on par with teachers in BMC schools, even if their salary is paid directly by the BMC. The scales of teachers in BMC schools were revised in 2000 and again in 2005. Private primary school teachers scales were revised in 2000 but implemented only in 2005. And there are no signs of their being given the arrears by the BMC. As a result, teachers in aided schools are a dissatisfied lot; they perform better than BMC teachers but take home a much smaller salary.

Teachers and the management of private schools become, financially speaking, losers in another sense too. The BMC wants private schools to reimburse to the BMC account one-twelfth of the total fees collectable irrespective of whether the fees are actually paid by the students. Since all students in these schools are not necessarily able to pay the fees at all or pay on time, the management is forced to pay from its resources the difference.

Third, the management of aided private primary schools, are not paid rent. Generally, management would use the rent received from the BMC to attend to urgent repairs and maintenance of the school building. But if the educational trust manages a secondary section in the school building, the state government would take vicarious pleasure in denying the rent to classroom used by the primary classes on the assumption that the BMC would have given the rent.

Fourth, the BMC does not give private aided schools any maintenance grant. Since to give the salary of teachers, BMC officials perhaps think that they have done their bit. Management is told in as many words "Giving salaries to teachers in a big deal, manage the rest!"

All these are clear indications that BMC does not appreciate the role played by private managements in running schools. In the absence of these schools, the public would have been left to the not too tender mercies of the municipal schools. It does seem like the government wants to shut them down.

All this despite the fact that the BMC and the state collect grants from the Central Government, recently, the Centre has released Rs 9,359 crore under Sarva Shiksha Abhiyan.

But the state seems to be using the grant to replace its own contribution. In other words, the very purpose for which the fund was created is defeated. I hope MLAs should raise the issue of discrimination in the use of SSA money by the state and the BMC in relation to aided primary schools.

Chapter - 71

Some Pitfalls in Implementation of Right to Education

(The Free Press Journal, 30 June 2010)

"The fact that RTE was implemented hastily by the UPA II is evident from several inherent fault lines like 'no fail' policy in Primary Schools (Std I to VIII)"

Prime Minister on behalf of the UPA II released recently its one year's progress report to public. Naturally, I am sure UPA II would look forward for the public response to it. I would like to comment on one item from it as an educationist and educational administrator. The report card claims credit for the government's successful implementation of Right to Education Act, which was passed by the Union Parliament in August 2009 and implemented by it on all fools day April 1, 2010. The report card claims it as a significant social legislation that is going to benefit *aam aadmi.*

No doubt it is an extremely important social legislation if implemented, to support its underlying spirit. But as of today more appropriately as per its date of implementation, it seems to fool the *aam aadmi.* My journalist friend tells me that I should first state my main conclusions and then advance the reason for the same. On that line, I would say that in a rather hasty implementation of RTE, the government has been very generous in conferring certain absolute rights, where it is the 'others' who have to implement them. In many cases, the burden seems to be on the private schools' management. It is not even a case of robbing Peter to pay Paul! Here Peter and Paul both are bankrupt! But government is watching the fun!

What does it mean? Take for instance, RTE implementation in Mumbai! Almost all primary schools, aided, partially aided or unaided and permanently unaided, minority-run or non-minority run temporarily permitted or a century old, were at the receiving end. At the clerical level, they were given in the month of April 2010 questionnaire type forms with an authoritative statement to bring it filled within a week's time.

Not one was briefed or given a circular sent as to the purpose for which information was sought! Whole exercise smacked of the approach: "I tell you, get it done. Don't ask questions." It is only when on May 25 a newspaper carried a write up, that some managers of private primary schools realised the survey was related to the implementation of the RTE! But strangely the press report states that all those who do not fill the form will lose their registration. There is, of course, no consultation or taking private management into confidence.

Take another circular issued by the Maharashtra government. It specifically asks the schools not to 'fail' a child till VIII standard because the RTE considers this as primary education. But the BMC and the Maharashtra government for all practical purposes considers, in effect, only up to standard V as the primary section. But what will happen to a child who has gone into the VIII standard? Throughout the years the child has not appeared in any examination. Should the school declare that such a child has passed the VIII standard? Suppose you hold a special examination after the child is tutored and still fails! What happens then? As a dropout from VIII standard, when the young boy or girl enters the job market, should employer treat him as VIII pass or failed? Will the government propose to conduct an examination at the end of the academic year and conduct an examination to certify the child as primary qualified person? Nothing, absolutely nothing is clear! Does the RTE believe in equality of treatment not only for children receiving education, but also the educators of these primary school children? I hope it does, if not it ought to. If educators are satisfied and happy only then can they provide good education to the children under their care.

Then take the example of BMC, the so-called richest municipal corporation in India. It gave its teachers fifth and sixth pay commission scales, but refuses to give sixth pay commission's scales to teachers in BMC aided private primary schools. The children are discriminated against in more than one way. While the children in BMC primary schools do not pay any fees-RTE insists on free and compulsory primary education to all-but children in private aided schools are made to pay ₹ 20 to ₹ 25 as monthly fees! Not only are those children in BMC run primary schools given uniforms, mid-day meals, etc.

On the other hand, as a manager of a private primary school. I know it well that when our teachers go from door to door in hutments to promote education in private primary school, parents ask them: "What do you give our children, if they come to you?"

If we say that we will give uniforms, books (by taking help from donors) and BMC gives you a hot mid-day meal, the parents say, we get all that in BMC schools and much more, like nutritious milk, biscuits, and a variety of other items and cash as well!"

Why does the BMC do it? This is so as it would like to discourage all children from going to private aided or unaided school. They suffer from the disturbing fact: Despite making provisions for so many goodies for children, why do the parents still prefer to go to private primary schools?

To add insult to injury, in front of a private aided primary school and another unaided private primary English School, BMC starts an English medium school within a distance of 100 feet! When the school management points out to the rule that no school can be permitted within a distance of one kilometer, the BMC, tongue in cheek, writes to inform them that the rule is not binding on them.

But the state government, while giving permission to private aided or unaided primary schools asks the management to see that it does not affect any existing school! Isn't this a step to force the private management to close down their schools so that the public is left with no choice other than to go to BMC run primary schools?

Chapter - 72

Eradicate Fundamental Causes Behind Rising Fees

(The Free Press Journal, 12 July 2010)

"Parents and do-good-lobbies ought to know that source of fundamental problems in rising fees or collecting some donations from parents now and then unrelated to admissions, lies in government not spending enough on education and its incompetence or unwillingness to eradicate corruption in the field of education."

All around there is a rising trend in prices, practically of all commodities and services. Middle class parents are affected most. But who is contributing most to the rise in prices? Undoubtedly it is the central, state and local government bodies! Central government's increase of diesel, petrol, CNG and PNG prices recently had cascading effect, because all goods need to be transported; hence contributing to the price rise. The State contributed to the trend by increasing process of milk as a matter of fact in the last three months milk prices has gone up by six rupees per litre. As a result, when the fees in schools and colleges go up, parents blame it on management. If their children go to unaided institutions, their woes are further compounded!

Naturally, when parents are affected, 'do good lobbies' come up to fight on their behalf taking a few rupees from already harassed parents. These neither have any experience of problems faced by the management in running educational trusts, nor do they have any in-depth knowledge of the governing process. They would not have contributed even for buying a chalk piece! Neither politician who use them is a community leader even after he becomes minister of education-despite most of them having family trusts managing education, mostly as a commercial enterprise! They begin to play politics with educational institutions projecting them as source of all evil, to cover the failures of the government! The Prime Minister recently said there should not be too much populism! There should to be no populism at all in providing education to community. He should direct at least Congress ruled states to stop populism!

Then what are the fundamental causes for the current problems? First, is the drastic reduction of government spending on education, since 1991 liberalisation, privatisation and globalisation. In 1994, Maharashtra government reduced maintenance grant given to aided institutions from 12 per cent to 6 per cent of the total expenditure. Worst still, government has not been able to provide even at the reduced rate maintenance to aided schools for the last six years! Government gives peanuts as rent for the building. In this respect, government is worst than moneylenders who squeeze their victims! If you are running primary classes, government reduces rent for the classrooms used for primary classes, but BMC follows state leadership in not giving rent or maintenance for decades!

Then, Maharashtra government began giving permission to open school and college on unaided and permanently unaided basis first only English medium school on the slogan, if parents want English education they ought to pay for it. Now, there are locations in the city, where within a radius of one kilometer, there would be an aided English medium School because it was started before 80s and another school started after 1984 or so on unaided basis. Obviously parents would like to admit their children in aided English medium school than unaided one creating problems for both! Later even regional media schools like Marathi, Kannada or Gujarati were also permitted to be opened on permanently unaided basis. Several existing regional media schools are facing the threat of course, yet Maharashtra government in 2006 gave permission to nearly three thousand permanently unaided schools, including many Marathi schools. An interesting fact is that there is absolutely no perspective planning done to determine number of schools required in a locality. A funny instance I know is: A case where CIDCO a government agency-gives land to a trust on the condition to start a Marathi school but government gives it permanently unaided status! How many Marathi parents would like to send their children to unaided meaning high fee Marathi schools, when for the same fees they can get admission in English medium? The result: While existing aided Marathi schools do not get enough students, newly started unaided Marathi schools, though permitted to charge high fees, do not get enough students! Hence, both struggle financially to survive!

Under these circumstances, aided schools need additional resources to maintain their building and infrastructure facilities, as they have not received their maintenance grant for six or more years! If you open one toilet block for repairs you need over a lakh of rupees. If you don't provided clean toilets, good drinking water and ceiling fans at the time of examinations, parents complain, then government issues the decree because it is worried about high court strictures! But if you charge some extra money for repairs, parents grumble and politician, to get some cheap publicity, comes with a few goons to ask you to stop charging extra to parents! There is a water scarcity, school spends for a bore well, may be three lakhs that you spend, but BMC, would continue to charge arbitrarily for water consumption! Schools are now made to pay power bills not as per the tariff charged for residential buildings but at commercial rates!

Second, there is growing cancer of corruption! In the 1970s inspectors who came to inspect your schools were happy if you entertained them with chicken curry meal! Today, he and even she too-I say this to inform those who think that women are less corrupt-ask shamelessly for money. If you need a certificate from BMC that you provide clean drinking water, with influence you have to pay fifteen thousands as bribe! If you have newly constructed school building, getting water connection, power connection, occupation certificate, or building completion certificate or getting NOC from fire Department etc., would involve lakhs of rupees in bribes to be paid to municipal and other authorities!

If aided school do not get their legitimate grants from the government, and if unaided schools do not get permission to charge sufficient fees to maintain building and pay salaries, where do you get money? Hence, parents and do good lobbies ought to know the source of fundamental problems in rising fees or collection some donations from parents now and then unrelated to admissions, lies in government not spending enough on education and its incompetence or unwillingness to eradicate corruption in the field of education. Correct these two fundamentals and fees will come down!

Chapter - 73

Populism in Education Augurs ill for Quality

(The Free Press Journal, 10 August 2010)

"Former PM, Manmohan Singh rightly advised politicians that populism in education augurs ill for quality; hence author recommends populist measures in RTE like parents managing schools etc be done away with"

Prime Minister Manmohan Singh recently and rightly, advised politicians to avoid populism. Of course, that applies equally or more seriously to governing parties than the Opposition. While the ruling party flaunts the Right to Education (RTE) as a major achievement of UPA-II, I would like to submit that populism in democracy is an evil, it has dangerous fallout in education. Two cases of populist provisions in the RTE illustrate this.

First, a most ridiculous provision in the RTE that expects all private aided schools other than those run by the State directly or by local authorities to each have a School Management Committee (SMC). What is highly objectionable is the provision that three-fourth of these SMCs shall comprise parents. It's obvious the government intends to hand over the control over these schools to parents. Is it tenable?

Private aided schools are run by the public charitable trusts, according to their own constitution approved by the charity commissioner. How can RTE compel existing privately managed schools to hand over the running a schools to a majority of parents? Most such trust were established with some vision, while parents as clients or service recipients cannot be expected to share the school's goal. Managing a school even if it is aided involves the huge responsibility of fund raising. During my role as someone who associated with the managing an educational trust for the last 40 years, I have witnessed that parents are extremely reluctant to participate in any fund raiding activities. In these 40 years, I have come across only one parent who voluntarily walked up to me to give a handsome donation! What most parents want is good education at the lowest cost!

This idea of entrusting school management committee to parents even in state or local body managed schools, will prove ruinous for a good quality education. Parents, per se, do not possess abilities to manage schools, while SMCs are expected to plan development, spending of grants and supervision of the school activities. How many parents would be able to spare time for such activities? Of course, alternative of handing over the SMCs to bureaucrats of the state/local bodies would also be worst than the parents-dominated SMCs. What needs to be done is to provide SMCs with an admixture of public spirited educationists, parents and officials to manage the state local bodies-run schools.

Another problem is the RTE's prescribing of a heavy penalty for running an uncertified school. I no way suggest that the government permit them, but it's more than often that it is the government policies that can categorise a genuine school into an unauthorised school due to technical reasons. Further, the RTE rightly states that as far as possible elementary education ought to be in mother tongue. But to take an instance of Maharashtra state it seems to have no policy on Marathi medium schools.

In 2006, then education minister Purke had extended permission to start 1495 schools most using Marathi as medium on permanently unaided basis. But, soon these became victims of a public interest litigation that finally ended in the Supreme Court, permitting all these schools to continue in January 2008. Even as these schools grew by natural growth into secondary sections, the government has no policy that will authorise them.

If you ask officials they will coldly say after Standard VII, send them to some other schools. but school children are not like our modern democratic politicians.

Politicians just have no problem at all to hop skip, jump and change parties as long as it suits their interest. However, most children are found to be attached to their school and its teachers that they mostly do not want to leave after spending seven to nine years there, and join another school.

Situations like these make the system prone to corrupt officials looking to make a quick buck by threatening to use RTE provision of Rs one lakh fine and if continued despite fine, daily impose ₹ 10,000 as additional fine. The Centre, therefore, should suspend the RTE provisions that ask states to ensure regularisation of all schools apart from levying fines. The essence of RTE is to see that every child under 14 gets education and not collect fines under various pretexts from schools that want to share the dream of the founders of Constitution to ensure quality education for every child.

Chapter - 74

Can We Chop off a Hand for Making a Mistake?

(The Free Press Journal, 8 September 2010)

Author asks: "when criminal are law makers, and neither the judiciary, nor the election commissions nor the political parties are in a position to set things right, how can one expect teachers alone to be demigods cent percent?"

I happen to read an article by a Delhi-based journalist arguing for abolition of Teachers' Day because in the name of second President of India, S. Radhakrishnan, according to him teachers are equated to Goddess Saraswati. I have been a teachers since 1960 and taught at school, college and highest level of University for all these years. No one has treated me as a God, though I have received maximum respect from my students! But journalist makes his case, particularly because of some of Principals and teachers in a few schools in India, in the recent past were accused of being responsible for deaths of school children under their care.

I do not support children being caned for irresponsible behaviour on the part of educators at any level. I also wish that educators be a role model to their students and in society at large. However, because of democracy and the concept of mass education, not only those who are moved by idealism of being a teacher but because he or she could not get any other job in accordance with his or her qualifications particularly as a result of government policy of reservation, some not so good persons get into the profession. But they are there in every profession be it journalism or politics which is the dominant profession and in which every average good for nothing person wants to get into!

Anyway if one is to argue, because of a few bad apples, throw all, we need to do away with all awards and all honours. For instance, a few Indian cricketers in the past were involved in match fixing allegations that have damaged the credibility of cricket as a game. (Of course, they could be accommodated as MPs.) The journalists do get many awards, but do they really deserve them? During the last elections in Maharashtra, allegations of paid news were widely made against several journalists. On the other hand, paid news might have received publicity now, but it is widely prevalent in the past in Mumbai and prevails even today as well.

However, politics is one profession, wherein any one can be absolved of all crimes, if you have muscle or money power or both. A politician, for instance, goes to attack a principal of a college or school such attacks have become too many, he takes with him, a battery of journalists-print and electronic-to cover and immortalize his achievement, irrespective of whether prima facie, his grievances were legitimate or not. Many politicians do it just to get themselves notoriety and recognition as a politician. But if a principal protests, journalist does not publicise it.

During the mid-1990s when Mumbai University was cursed with a politicking and corrupt vice-chancellor with the blessings of politicians then in power, certain unfounded allegations were made by journalists of a prominent and highest selling newspaper against me and my colleague in Mumbai University at the behest of the vice-chancellor who later had the unique distinction of being imprisoned on the charges of corruption. But when I sent a letter rebutting the charges, it was not published despite my repeated requests. The journalist in question now is an anchor of TV news channel! I am sure he will get one day an award as the best TV journalist! Without any fear of contradiction, I can say that news coverage given to the small events in the life of aspiring artiste or politician is largely by giving gifts to the journalists. We are in this state of affairs currently in our social and political life because a majority of so-called leaders of the society hold their positions through corruption or favouritism.

When criminals are law-makers, and neither the judiciary, nor the Election Commission nor the political parties are in a position to set things right, how can one expect teachers alone to be demigods cent per cent? As a result, even the teachers' day awards are subject to politicking and corruption, and rarely given on the basis of merit alone! Hence, let us remember the saying Yatha Raja Tatha Praja (as the King-ruler; does, so do the people). Let us improve at the highest level of governance to improve the society, so as to get the ideal teachers. Till then let critics know that more than one public opinion polls, have shown that ordinary people trust a teacher more than his elected politician or neighbourhood journalist.

Chapter - 75

Regional Media Schools in Mumbai as well as in the Nation do not have Good Time

(Mulund Meet, 6-12 August 201[illegible])

"Lack of demand proved disastrous for these vernacular medium schools and this inadvertently led to the closing of most of them"

Mulund is an utterly cosmopolitan suburb. Though Gujaratis and Kutchis form the base of the pyramid one would not be surprised to find North Indians, South Indians, Maharastrians, Bengalis, Sindhis and Punjabs (with a mini area of their own), Christians, Muslims and Parsis form the upper cone of the pyramid.

As it was the launch of our first issue, we wanted to bring together 'thinkers' from different part of our suburb irrespective of their cast, religion or culture. At Mulund Express, we aim to weave a social fabric of communal peace and harmony. in accordance, our first visit was to meet Dr. P.M. Kamath.

"He is one of the most reputed educationists in Mulund. Go and seek his blessings", my Editor Dr. Manish Kothari advised me. I prepared myself through the usual drill of an interview process. With a questionnaire ready in hand, I rang the bell to Dr. Kamath's house.

A sprightly young man of 72 opened the door for me. It was THE Dr. P.M. Kamath, An aura of wisdom, warmth and astuteness hung around him. He cordially showed me my seat, a deep maroon velvety couch, as he took a similar seat adjacent to mine.

Kannada Sangha Mulund-Thane started Kannada Primary School in 1957. It is the first institution managed by Vidya Prasarak Mandal, Mulund (E) when it was founded on 26th March 1960.

Hon. Secretary of Vidya Prasark Mandal, Mulund, Dr. Kamath spoke at length about the Mandal's objectives and its journey till now. Their main objective has been to provide opportunities in education where the students are exposed to the best curriculum and reach out to students in the weaker sections of the community. VPM has successfully managed to not only provide the best education but also have raised the bar for other organisation to emulate.

Established in 1960, VPM's first venture was to take over the management of Kannada Primary School, the only Kannada school this side of the suburb. Today, this school has been renamed as Smt. Sundaribai Manjunath Kamath Kannada Primary School on 12th February 2011 in honour of Dr. Kamath's late mother.

Dr. Kamath reminiscences about how the noble trustees of Moti Pachan allowed one classroom to be used as a school for the benefit of Kannada medium students, way back on 1957. Entire Mumbai had only second Kannada School—at SMPR. Wow, isn't it amazing? SMPR is also the first school to be set up in Mulund. SMPR is truly a historical structure in Mulund. The Kannada school was conducted in SMPR. 'School' is not a precise term as the school meant just one classroom.

Dr. Kamath's evey shine with compassion and fond memories of gratitude as he speaks about the inter-community love, bonding and enthusiasm shared by affluent Gujarati and Kutchhi families with the Kannada community in that period. At a later date, the trustees of Moti Pachan School also allowed the Kannada School to progress and start a secondary school in the same premises. It was run there until 1972.

Due to paucity of infrastructure, it was decided that the Kannada school be held from 7 am to 12.30 pm, post which it was time for the Gujarati medium school to begin. Due to the generous nature of a few philanthropists like Shri. R Z Shah, Late Shri, Karia and Late Shri, Maniklal Gandhi the school was fortunate enough to see better days.

Today, with around 11 instituttions under their able patronage VPM not only provide education to students from affluent families in English medium but also to underprivileged children residing in slums in Kannada school.

Dr Kamath larnents the decling of students opting for vernacular medium in recent years. He point out the beginning from early 90's parents would want their children to be educated only in English medium schools. Thus all vernacular medium schools had to suffer as the number of applicants dropped drastically. According to Dr Kamath, though Kannada Primary Schools everywhere in Mumbai face decline in enrolment, VPM has maintained a steady strength over a decade. Though under RTE 2009, government is supposed to provide free education; BMC insists collection of tuition fees of ₹ 15 to Std I & II and ₹ 20 to std III and IV per month. And parents are in no position to provide even this measly amount. The costs are borne by VPM.

These days, most of the students who study in their vernacular medium schools are from homes that are economically poor and those who do not have even 15 rupees to pay if required. Today, Dr. Kamath elucidates that, teachers from the Kannada schools visit every slum area around the month of February, in Mulund, Thane, Airoli and Kalwa and entice students and parents alike to send the children to school. "What are the perks?" asks the parents. Perks are uniform, shoes, books, computer classes and not to forget a full meal.

Lack of demand proved disastrous for these vernacular medium schools and this inadvertently led to the closing of most of them. VPM found an opportunity in the calamity and slowly but gradually started their English medium schools. Today they boast of 11 institutions with schools is CBSE, ICSE and Centre for International Studies with two newly set up schools in Airoli.

Apart from education, VPM is actively involved in disbursing old clothes in good useable condition among other activities. Readers who wish to donate can get in touch with Ms. Anita Gujran on 022-25639195 to know more about the procedures involved. Volunteers to help out on the distribution day will be highly appreciated. Keep watching this space, as we bring to you eminent personalities of Mulund on a weekly basis. You are also welcome to suggest people whom you thing have contributed immensely to the society in whole.

Chapter - 76

Service in Education is my Payback to Society

(Speakout, 9-15 December 2012)

'Speak Out 'introduces 'Mulundkars' the distinguished citizens of Mulund, who are silently serving the society since decades. To highlight these. dignitaries each week we will carry a brief interview with these luminaries. This week Speak Out' Editor Uttam kumar Pipada and Sub-Editor, Mansoor Khan spoke to Mulund's well-known educationist Dr. P.M. Kamath, former Professor of Politics, Mumbai University, currently Hon. Secretary, Vidya Prasarak Mandal, Mulund; Hon. Director, VPM's Centre for International Studies (Regd.) and Hon. Convener, VPM's Institute of Professional Studies. He has dedicated his life to education and terms his service to education as his payback to society.

Cornerstone in education, Dr. P.M. Kamath, is a name that is revered for his illustrious and selfless service of over six decades in education. In a freewheeling interview to 'Speak Out' Dr. Kamath says, "I am the only person in my family to have studied above class VII". He adds, "Due to family's financial condition I was also likely to wrap up studies early but thanks to my maternal uncle who helped me study further and later thanks to my intelligence I was able to complete my MA in Political Science with Scholarships. I vividly remember I stood Second in University of Bombay in 1964."

Hailing from Mulki, a district in Mangalore. after completing his education, Dr. Kamath was flooded with lucrative offers in Banks and other government concerns but Dr. Kamath was keen in paying back to the society that he owed from the society . He says,

"My education has been a result of my uncle's and the society's obligation towards me, hence I decided to take a career in education and educate many more deserving children like me who despite aptitude are denied education due to financial crunch."

Hence Dr. Kamath took up teaching at Dr. Babasaheb Ambedkar College of Arts, Commerce and Science, Mahad, Raigad in 1964. Later Dr. Kamath joined the prestigious SIES College in 1967 and continued till 1972. After this from 1972 till 1997 he joined as Professor of Politics, Mumbai University and taught Post Graduate students.

Dr. Kamath's association with VPM dates back to 1962. Recollecting his early days he reminisces, "I got associated to VPM as an honorary member out of enthusiasm to guide the upcoming institution. It was in the year 1962, that I joined the institution when the secondary section of Kannada medium was taking shape. Since then by the grace of God the institution has achieved many milestones and is going strong"

Speaking about the many achievements he says, "I am happy to announce that after a humble beginning in 1957, since then today VPM has around 5000 students and has expanded its wings to Airoli where VPM has initiated an International School." He adds, "I am proud to say that VPM is today is imparting education in all the major boards of education. For example our Jr. College is affiliated to Maharashtra State Board , the English medium is affiliated to C.B.S.E. and our VPM's National Integration School is attached to I.C.S.E. Board."

Elaborating about the Airoli's VPM's National Integration School Dr. Kamath informs, "National Integration Schools with Kannada and Marathi as medium of instruction began in June 2005. VPM's international School (ICSE), established in the year 2007, has been constantly on the road to success transforming young children into model citizens of the country. Last year our fist batch of Grade X passed out with flying colours and the school registered cent percentage result."

Today at the age of 75, Dr. Kamath is still active and aspires to have and Engineering College. He says, "During my visit with

Maharashtra Chief Minister, Prithviraj Chauhan. I have put forward the proposal and also expressed my desire to dedicate VPM to the State of Maharashtra as part of the State's Golden Jubliee Celebration. The honorable C.M. has assured me and agreed to take positive steps to fulfill my dream." Dr. Kamath has visited the US on various fellowships-Fulbright American Council of learned Societies Ford Foundation, German Educational Foundation, the Truman Foundation and the USIS-for study, research and teaching and attended numerous National and International conferences and seminars in the area of specialization. He taught a course on National Security Policy in the Florida International University Miami. He has published Fifteen books on International Relations, Foreign Policy and American studies.

Academic Honours: Olive I. Reddick Award for the Best Paper in Social Science category from the Indian Association for American Studies (1981); 'Presided over annual conference of Indian Association for American studies in 1993 (Goa University) and 1994 (Lucknow University). Presided over International relations section of XVII Indian Social Science Congress, held in Bangalore in 1993 and delivered key note address to the plenary session on development of India as a modern democratic secular and Egalitarian Nation During 50 years of freedom of India at XX Indian Social Science Congress, Visva Bharati Shanti Niketan in 1996; delivered key note address again at XXII Social Science Congress, at Gandhi Gram in March 1999; won then 1st prize for the essay on "Should India Switch Over To Presidential System of Government?" from the Indian Institute of Public Administration (Maharashtra Branch) in July 1998.

He is a man of many portfolios a member of Rotary Club of Mulund Hills (2001-2007) and also Executive Trustee, Indian Association for American Studies Trust. Hon. Secretary Vidya Prasarak Mandal (Regd.) President, Fullbright Alumini Association, Mumbai Chapter.

He works tirelessly towards bringing about a balance in society in terms of equal opportunities and rightful benefits. His ceaseless encouragement and support has played a major role in the growth and expansion of the VPM's groups of schools and colleges.

Chapter - 77

Globalisation and International Schools

(Teacher, 2013)

"Why do international schools exist, and what are they exactly?"

India in the two decades since 1991 has seen a huge increase in the number of international schools from Kanyakumari to Kashmir and Kandla to Kohima, Liberalisation, privatisation and globalisation has increased private participation in managing schools by industrial magnates and politicians through various kinds of trusts.

Education is not the only sector affected by liberalisation, privatisation and globalisarion, Cricket and the film industry have also been affected.

While the development of international schools is an effect of liberalisation, privatisation and globalisation, it is also in turn a cause, sinceint ernatio nal schools introduce internationalism to a growing number of people, both expatriates and locals who until now have largely remained in their country of birth.

That is changing, since economic liberalisation has encouraged the movement of people from one country to another. Again, schools international schools encourage this by enabling more mobile people to find an acceptable education for their children. Simply stated, those who are mobile prefer to send their children to international schools.

What makes a school an international school?

International schools are subject to the relevant legislation and regulation in the state in which they operate, but there are otherwise no specific rules pertaining to an international school. In effect, any school may describe itself as an international school or indeed use the words 'international school' in its name.

Even so, there are a number of general features that typically are present in international schools, although all of these may not be present in every international school.

Most international schools are led by a highly competent and capable principal, often from an educationally advanced country and with a reputation as an educator in his or her country of origin. It has to be said, of course, that local candidates would make equally competent and capable principals of international schools and that the country of origin of principals of international schools may in fact be irrelevant.

Most international schools offer a range of subjects that expose students to an international environment, particularly in terms of second languages but also subjects like history or economics, components of which can expose students to an international context.

Related to this, most international schools recruit native speakers to teach in their second language program.

Most international schools operate language and literary clubs that expose students to second languages and the culture of countries that speak those languages.

Most international schools offer exchange programs with other international schools, enabling visits between 'sister' schools. It will also help young Indian students to be open to dialogue with foreign culture and civilisations. In India, many international schools work closely with binational boards like the United States-India Educational Foundation or British Council to facilitate such exchange.

Most international schools offer music and dance, particularly to expose students to other cultures.

Most international schools offer an international curriculum such as the International Baccalaureate or Cambridge International

Examinations or the curriculum of a country other than the country in which the school is located. Many international schools focus on application-oriented and project-based approaches to teaching and learning to deliver the curriculum.

Most international schools offer co-curricular programs with an international flavour, such as the Model United Nations program.

It may be the case that some international schools have facilities like indoor swimming pools, a sports pavilion and manicured playing fields, but such facilities are by no means the rule for international schools and do not in themselves necessarily increase the internationalism of an international school.

Students graduating from international schools typically have acquired an international perspective. Those international schools with an applicationoriented and project-based approach to teaching and learning could be expected to graduate students who are well adapted to higher education. Students graduating from international schools are also well placed to gain admission to universities in countries other than the country in which their school was located.

Chapter - 78

A Report Card of the Modi Government

(One India One People, August 2015)

"It's been a mixed bag from the current Modi government, where education reforms are concerned. The controversy over the Human Resources minister's educational qualifications aside, there are some good proposals in the pipeline. There are certain welcome steps which are being debated. The best one is the proposal to increase the age of school admission from present five to six; even seven should be considered, as toddlers should be allowed to enjoy their free years. During the British rule, school admission was at seven.

The BJP led NDA II (National Democratic Alliance II) government under Narendra Modi has established itself as a harbinger of much needed changes, since it came to power in May 2014. There is an excellent list of achievements directly under the Prime Minister (PM) in the area of foreign affairs, national security and defence. He has coined several attractive phrases in English as well as in Hindi to make certain that Indian voters are impressed by them. There is thus, 'Make in India' or idea of 'Red Carpet' welcome to investors instead of subjecting them to Indian bureaucracy's 'Red Tape,' and many others.

Educational arena

In the field of education, the PM has chosen Smriti Irani, as the Minister of Human Resources Development (HRD). She is the youngest person in the cabinet; she too is fond of developing several catchy phrases in Hindi/Sanskrit like 'Beti Bachao Beti Padhao',

'Padhe Bharat Badhe Bharat' etc. But early in her innings, she created avoidable controversies about her educational qualifications. She took certain hasty steps in her over enthusiasm to implement certain, in my opinion, nationally good programmes, like introduction of Sanskrit in KendriyaVidyalayas, on which she had to beat an early retreat. But the media and opposition parties like the Congress have been mocking her mainly because of her lack of higher educational degrees.

But record of even highly-qualified HRD ministers like Dr Murli Manohar Joshi during the NDA I or during eminent lawyer, Kapil Sibal's tenure under UPA II has been mixed. Sibal for instance, is a very smart and quick learner; that I learnt from a personal encounter with him. I was facing a problem with the CBSE (Central Board of Secondary Education) in Delhi, which was objecting to giving their affiliation to our English High School because the building in which we housed it, also accommodated a Kannada medium school affiliated to the Maharashtra State Board.

I posed him in Mumbai a question: If your objective under the Right to Education (RTE) is to universalise education, why should the CBSE object if a school building being used by the CBSE is also used by a State Board school? Within 10 days, a new rule was made to accommodate use of the school building by any other institution as long as it is not put to 'commercial use', and we got the permission! But Sibal was not necessarily good when it came to other school issues, which will be discussed here below. Point is, as long as you have your ear close to the ground reality, not having a degree should not matter!

Higher education

What have been the achievements of the HRD ministry? Though 13 months are a short period to make an impassioned assessment, there has been the creation of new IITs (Indian Institute of Technology) and IIMs (Indian Institute of Management); while the move is good, the effort has to be to create world class infrastructure. The creation of the National Digital Library is another good move. Similarly, a new scheme of 'Global Initiative for Academic Network' has been launched to bring to India, globally best known educators. There are many other initiatives, but space is a constraint!

School education

In the field of school education, Smriti Irani has done well in trying to introduce Sanskrit; but her hasty move turned out to be her undoing. It is a tragedy of Indian education that during the British times Sanskrit was taught widely in schools and colleges. However, it was gradually withdrawn from schools and colleges. There are great advantages for all Indian languages in studying Sanskrit, as these are rooted in that language. Today, the younger generation is unaware of it. When I say in the Hindi heartland *Jalapatra* the audience says, "Oh, you know Hindi". When I have used that word in Gujarat, students have expressed surprise, that I speak Gujarati!

Necessary changes

More urgent changes are required in school education – Primary, Secondary and Higher Secondary; some to be changes in the so called reforms of former HRD Minister, Kapil Sibal and a few pro-actively by the present Minister. Certain disastrous changes introduced by Mr.Sibal should go. For example: 1. If an over-age student, who has not had any education – formal or informal, seeks admission, he should be admitted to a class according to his age and not according to his level of academic achievement. 2. Age for admission not to be insisted; schools are expected to admit on the basis of estimated age.

The previous government's order not to fail any student on whatsoever ground/s till Class VIII is not a good decision and needs to be changed. Primary school children do not commit suicide because of failure in a class. RTE is fundamental, but there is no fundamental right to pass! Dr Pallam Raju, successor to Mr.Sibal had favourably spoken about changing these atrocious prescriptions, but went out of office without achieving his aim. A student enrolled in a school has a right to know the level of education achieved by him or her. How can children learn that there is a grading system in the society? It is inevitable in all walks of life!

However, it is also necessary for the minister to proactively take certain steps such as, nationally implement uniformity in the number of classes covered by a specific section like Primary, Upper Primary, Secondary and Higher Secondary. As of today, while CBSE and ICSE

(Indian Certificate of Secondary Education) consider up to Std. V as Primary, within Maharashtra, there are different patterns like some considering up to Std IV as Primary, while some are calling up to VII as Primary!

The worst feature of the RTE as envisaged by the previous government and unfortunately also embraced by the present at the federal level is an overwhelming emphasis on universalisation, without any concern for quality of education; main concern is to make every child enter a formal educational institution. The emphasis on quality of education is completely missing. This will ruin a generation before the government realises its folly and agrees to change.

There are certain welcome steps which are being debated. The best one is the proposal to increase the age of school admission from present five to six; even seven should be considered, as toddlers should be allowed to enjoy their free years. During the British rule, school admission was at seven.

Conclusion

Comparatively, in my opinion, higher education in India is better than school education. It has become a standard expression that even after 68 years of Independence, we have not been able to produce a world class university that can be counted in the world's top 200! But, our higher education has created a sense of urgency to reform education in the United States as evident from Obama's frequent references to the fact that Indians are capturing American jobs!

However, the problem of qualitative universal literacy is gigantic. Last year, the UNESCO published their Annual Education for All Global Monitoring Report, which stated that India alone has 1.38 million children in the age group of 6-11, who have not seen the doors of a school. India is the fourth top illiterate country. India needs to double the allocation for education. In 1999, it was 4.34 % of the GDP and it came down to 3.35% in 2012, according to a World Bank report.

Even if the government wants to achieve a semblance of universal education, it needs to construct 100 thousand primary schools with eight rooms and every room accommodating 30 students. The task is not impossible but the government needs to take a bold decision to double allocation in the budget for education. Instead of doing that, the governments under the UPA II and the NDA II have been following the same policy—since it is decided by the same bureaucrats. Thus, there is the pressure on privately managed schools to admit 25 per cent of the children under RTE. The Supreme Court had exempted minority run schools from the RTE reservation. But the bureaucrats are busy finding out where and how the pressure can be mounted on minority run schools to accommodate students under RTE quota!

Chapter - 79

Is there a Fundamental Right to Pass?

(October 2015)

"Equal opportunity for education is a fundamental right of any child, but they do not have a fundamental right to pass," says the author

Right to Education Act, 2009 provides that a child in primary section be not tested in the traditional sense of examinations and annual policy of promotion to higher class. A new policy replaced it with a Continuous Comprehensive Assessment. But heart of the policy is not to fail a child. Irrespective of inherent IQ difference of the child, onus for its getting educated and promoted was put on the teacher! This dictum is fine for the first four classes-I to IV or even up to V.

But child ought to know there is an intellectual gradation of the humans in the society some performing better than the other. Hence, under the present rules, if a teacher in school is motivated and committed to educational development; it is a torturous test for a teacher! Teacher has to struggle till her conscience permits her to declare that child deserves the promotion to a higher class!

The result in effect is that child does not know that it is an average one; or below average; a parent always thinks his child is a genius- another APJ Kalam! But Parents have to know in the early stage of education that Right to Education is a Fundamental Right. But there is no Fundamental Right to Pass!

The UPA II government created a mess of promotion policy; instead of clearing it, the present government has tried to introduce a system of examination from the backdoor to test the acquired knowledge of the pupils in most regressive bureaucratic procedure of Competency Test. Some Babus have devised the exact test to be administered from class II to VIII, without leaving any discretion to the teacher or the head of the school.

A careful study of the test booklet reminds me a circular sent by Inspector of Education, prescribing the size of chalk that could be purchased under monetary peanuts given to the schools as aid under *Sarva Shikshan Abhiyan* (as the government has stopped giving any non salary grant to schools), as though schools do not have any idea of administration! Exactly in that way, in the administration of the Competency Test, the government does not give any freedom to the head or the teachers of a Primary School; obviously it does not trust the schools.

Hence, booklets prepared by the government prescribe every step to be taken by the schools. As an exception to the rule, it has given one freedom to the teacher; testing material can be taken to the class either in a -bag or in a basket! If these tests are continuously administered and examined at the government level, whole lot of primary teachers in the State would not know how to formulate a question, administer it and examine the answer scripts!

Next step is for the government to take over the conduct of remaining examinations. Now what remains in the school education with the school is to conduct of examinations for IX and XI because X and XII examinations are already conducted by the government. The current trend shows that it will not be too far away from the reality! Ground is already laid; government has centralised all data under its control under a great misnomer, called SARAL. That is not really *saral.*

> Government is mesmerized by the computer technology that has enabled them to centralize the entire task of School Education! It is now driven by the single factor of saving money spent on education! It increases the cost of educational bureaucracy-that doesn't matter, probably!

Written in October 2015. Two paragraphs were used as part of interview by Ms. E. Vijayalakshmmi Rajan, Assistant Editor, OIOP in her article, "Pappu eighth class pass hai!" in November 2015 issue.

Index

A

Abdul Kalam, 274
Academic achievement, 143
Academic interest, 132
Academic job, 16
Academic military interactions, 142
Accident, 313
Administrative officer, 82, 118
Administrator-turned historian, 69
Adult education, 45
Affiliating University, 33, 272, 303
Africa, 50, 109
African Studies, 289
Airoli, 341
Albert Einstein, 260
All Global Monitoring Report, 354
All India Federation of University and College, 165
All India Medical Council, 212
All round development of child, 217, 225
Allahabad, 96
Allahabad University, 276
America, 252
American Government, 253
American government agencies, 284
American Government and Politics, 253
American model, 280
American National Security Council, 285
American President, 252
American scholars, 285
American studies, 251, 252, 345
American studies in India, 31, 252
American universities chairmanship, 257
Ancient India, 260
Ancient India, 14, 32, 260
Ancient Indian Education, 41
Ancient Indian history, 16, 69, 73.
Ancient institution, 255
Ancient religion of India, 70, 74
Ancient University, 31
Ancient-Indian history, 16
Andhra Pradesh, 115
Anita Gujran, 11, 341
Annual Education, 354
Annual increments, 138
Annual maintenance grant, 161
Anti-Capitation Act, 23, 163
Anti-defection act, 238
Anti-interview lobby, 152
APJ Kalam, 357
Arabic, 86
Ardhamagadhi, 86

Arjun Singh, 263, 264
Armed teenager-militants, 209
Aroon Tikekar, 256, 271
Aryabhatta, 260
Aryan and Dravidian races, 74
Aryan-Dravidian hypothesis, 74, 75
Aryans, 69, 71, 74, 75
Aryans and Dravidians, 16
Aryans invading North, 74
Aryans were invaders, 75
Aryans were the original inhabitants of India, 75
Asia, 75, 109, 114
Assistant Registrars, 275
Associate Professors, 31
Astronomy and Astrophysics for M Sc or Ph D, 260
Astronomy Research, 261
Attractive pay packet, 134
Audit squads, 161
Australia, 239
Authentic Indian source, 71
Avenue for corruption, 66, 224
Ayaz Memon, 11

B

B R Tol English High School, 200
G.K. Gokhale, 33
Bal Apte, 175
Bal Gangadhar Tilak, 38, 272
Bal Shikshan Parishad, 147
Balwadis, 223
Bangalore, 345
Bangladesh War in 1971, 253
Bar Associations, 26, 212
Bar associations, 197
Barrister Antulay, 221
Basmati, 228
Bay of Pigs Crisis, 284
Benares Hindu University, 129
Bharatiya Janata Party, 263
Bharatiya Janata Party Government, 73
Bihar, 77, 95, 137
Bill Clinton, 210, 285
Bill Gates, 294
Black African students, 19, 109
Board of Examinations, 173
Bombay, 85, 90, 103
Bombay High Court, 27, 173, 306
Bombay High Court decision, 28
Bombay Municipal Corporation, 126
Bombay Police Act, 127
Bombay University, 9, 271
Boycott of Iraqi goods, 210
Brihanmumbai Muncipal Corporation, 319
Britain, 264
British administration, 223
British Council, 348
British Imperial designs, 70, 74
British Indian provinces, 271
British Parliament, 271
British rule, 14, 354
British rule in India, 75, 265
British rulers, 95
British Secretary of State for India, 70, 74
British times, 353
Bureaucratic perks, 56

C

Cambridge International Examinations, 348-49
Cambridge University, 289
Central Asia, 70, 74

Central Board of Secondary Education, 352
Central Eurasian Studies, 289
Central Government, 161
Central Government's policy, 161
Central Institute of English and Foreign Languages, 115
Central pay scales, 167
Central Universities, 287, 301
Centre for International Studies, 341
Centres of Higher Learning, 35
Chatrapati Shivaji Chair, 141
Chemistry, 288
Chennai, 280
Chhattisgarh, 285
Chief Justice of the Supreme Court, 273
Children in Armed conflict, 209
Children's Exploitations in hazardous industries, 27
China, 141
Chinese territory, 115
Church-run schools, 223
City Civil Court, 256
Civics and Politics Department, 256
Civil nuclear deal, 285
Climate Change, 288
Clinton administration, 209
Co-operation in fighting terrorism, 209
Coaching classes, 211
Cold War, 252, 284
Cold War periods, 33
Cold War years, 284, 285
College building fund, 219
College Development Council, 275
Colleges or Universities, 19
Commercial Capital, 19
Commercial Capital of India, 19
Commercial presence, 240
Communal colour, 71
Competency Test, 358
Concept of perks, 167
Continuous Comprehensive Assessment, 357
Control over fee structure, 15
Corporate Social Responsibility, 28
Corrupt Campuses, 16
Cost of education, 225
Crash programmes to award M Phil degrees, 138
Critical remarks, 78
Cross-border supply, 240
Cultural and educational activities, 188
Cultural and religious hegemony, 70

D

Damodar R. Gudi, 13
Dearness Allowances to teachers, 26
Death-rate of under-five, 209
Deemed universities, 277
Defence security studies, 141
Defence Studies, 18, 21
Delhi, 277
Delhi International University, 33
Delhi University, 119, 277
Democratic Front government, 215
Dens of corruption, 118
Department of International Relations, 289
Deputy director of education, 199
Developing countries of Asia and Africa, 109
Development Administration, 158
Development Fund, 17
Director of Hospitals, 19
Directors for School, 237

Documentary evidence, 16
Doordarshan, 127, 283
Doordarshan English news, 252
Dr (Mrs) Nawaz Mody, 255, 256
Dr G Ram Reddy, 109
Dr Jayant Narlikar, 261
Dr Lionel Fernandes, 257
Dr M. S. Gore, 273
Dr Murli Manohar Joshi, 352
Dr Nawaz Mody, 175
Dr Ramesh Babu, 256
Dr S D Kulkarni, 69, 74
Dr S.D. Karnik, 256
Dr Surendra Jondhale, 255
Dr Babasaheb Ambedkar College of Arts, 344
Dr Manish Kothari, 339
Dr Pallam Raju, 353
Drivers, 236
Dying children in Iraq, 209

E

E Vijaylakshmi Rajan, 39
East European countries, 284
East India Company, 271
Economic and political power, 100
Economic mess, 61
Economic power, 127
Economic sanctions, 209
Economic sanctions in Iraq, 210
Economic sanctions on Iraq, 209
Economics, 241, 287
Education Commission, 16, 64
Educational administration, 61
Educational administration in the state, 212
Educational administrator, 212
Educational bureaucracy, 250
Educational institutions, 118
Educational Trusts, 17, 27, 200, 221, 229
Egypt, 280
Election Commission, 280, 337
Electoral College, 252, 283
Electoral politics, 75
Engineering College, 344
English High School, 352
English medium, 154
English Medium School, 15, 17, 35, 60, 85, 102, 151, 177, 228, 269, 292, 325, 341
English newspapers, 69, 73
Enterprising students, 182
Entrance Screening Test, 261
Entrance tests, 143
Eradication of spitting, 20
Esplanade Court, 195
Executive Council, 256
Executive Trustee, 345
Existing pay scales, 129

F

Faculty of medicine, 174
Fate of a child, 148
Federal Bureau of Investigation, 220
Federal Government, 20
Federal level, 32
Federal Services, 24
Fee Structure of Unaided Schools, 225
Field of textbook manufacturing, 62
Fifth Pay Commission, 165, 167, 177, 188, 201, 205
Fifth Pay Commission scales, 188, 201, 205, 215, 231
Financial activity, 115
Financial bankruptcy, 205
Financial burden, 201, 206

First army chief, 141
First Five Year Plan, 81
Florida International University, 280
Florida International University Miami, 345
Ford Foundation, 345
Foreign degree, 240
Foreign nationals on Indian soil, 114
Foreign Policy, 345
Foreign student advisor, 113
Foreign Students, 19, 114, 240
Foreign Universities, 30, 239, 281
Formal education, 10
Foundation Day Lecture, 259
Free and compulsory education, 18
Free milk, 320
Free Press Journal, 305
Freedom movement, 32
French, 86
Fulbright American Council, 345
Fulbright grants, 284
Fulbright pre-doctoral research fellowship, 137
Fulbright Programme, 33, 34, 283
Fulbright Scholars, 33, 283
Fullbright Alumini Association, 345
Fundamental Right, 357

G

Galileo Galilei, 260
Ganapatiphule, 208
Gandhi Gram, 345
General Agreement of Trade in Services, 30, 239, 281
General B. C. Joshi, 21
General Science, 243
General Shankar Roy Choudhary, 142
George Bush, 285
German, 86
German Educational Foundation, 345
Ghatkopar, 13
Ghatkopar committed suicide, 169
Global Initiative for Academic Network, 352
Goa University, 345
Goddess Saraswati, 335
Golden Jubliee Celebration, 345
Good hygienic habits, 126
Gopalkrishna Gokhale, 38
Government and municipal schools, 28
Government audit squads, 82
Government babus, 16
Government bureaucracy, 58, 132
Government hospitals, 19, 117
Government of Maharashtra, 153, 231
Governor of Maharashtra, 175
Govindrao Adik, 249
Grace marks case, 175
Grant-in-aid to junior colleges, 65
Great galaxy Andromeda, 260
Gross National Product, 17
Gujarat, 17, 86, 127, 328
Gujarathi, 86
Gujarati, 328
Gujarati medium school, 340
Gurunath D. Joshi, 13

H

Harvard, 281
Hazardous labour, 207
Head Departments of Education, 24
Hemant Deshpande, 256
High quality of education, 22
Higher Education, 291

Higher educational administration, 77, 130
Higher educational institutions, 131
Higher educational qualifications, 130
Higher Secondary Certificate, 99
Highest donations, 148
Hikes of marks, 77
Himalayas, 69, 73
Hindi, 17
Hindi Bhavan School, 215
Hindi literature, 78
Hindi medium, 310
Hindustan Times correspondents, 313
History of Civilisation of Ancient India, 75
Hitler, 32, 264
Hong Kong, 115
Hotel management, 239
Housing facilities, 129
Human Resources Development, 39, 166, 351
Hungary, 284
Hyderabad, 115, 277
Hyderabad University, 277

I

I K Gujral, 165
IAS Association, 130
IAS cadre, 130, 237
Imperial Rule of India, 73
Income Tax authorities, 224
Indian Administrative Service, 166
Indian armed forces, 92, 142, 209
Indian Association for American Studies, 345
Indian bureaucracy, 34
Indian Certificate of Secondary Education, 354
Indian civilisation and culture, 280
Indian Council of Social Science Research, 50
Indian cultural heritage, 114
Indian glory, 43
Indian history, 69, 73
Indian History and Culture, 70, 74
Indian Institute of Management, 352
Indian Institute of Technology, 352
Indian national disease, 126
Indian National Freedom Movement, 32
Indian origin in various countries, 114
Indian Scholars, 34
Indian Social Science Congress, 345
Indian students, 19
Indian universities, 47, 279, 292
Indira Gandhi, 284
Individual teachers, 16
Indo-US relations, 253
Indus Valley Civilisation, 70, 74
Inspector of Education, 358
Institutional support of democracy, 197
Instrumentation Laboratory, 259
Inter University Centre for Astronomy, 32, 259
Inter-state movement, 18
Internalise Post Graduate Examination System, 24
International affairs, 251
International Baccalaureate, 348
International economy, 115
International exchange of students, 109
International investment, 30
International Law, 158, 182
International Monetary Fund, 61
International Politics, 181, 182

International Relations, 34, 111, 293, 345
International schools, 347
International Students' Hostel, 111
International University, 19, 33, 113
International University at Chennai, 33
International varsities, 114
Iran, 27
Iran-Contra Scandal, 34
Iraq, 27
Iraqi children, 210
Iraqi president, 210
Isaac Newton, 260

J

Jackson Heights, 126
Jadavpur, 96
Jagdish Nanavati, 227
Jamia Milia, 277
Japanese, 292
Jawaharlal Nehru, 15
Jawaharlal Nehru Technological University, 277
Jawaharlal Nehru to Rajiv Gandhi, 15
Jawaharlal Nehru University, 277
Jawaharlal Technological University, 115
Johns Hopkins, 281
Johns Hopkins School of Advanced International Study, 139
Johns Hopkins University, 287
Joint secretary, 131
Jr. College, 35, 227, 310, 344
Judicial magistrate, 196
Junior colleges, 57, 191, 213
Junjunwala College, 13
Justice Deshpande, 175
Justice Shah, 211
Justices Agarwal and Deshmukh, 173

K

K. J. Somaiya College, 13
Kalwa, 268, 341
Kamalesh Sharma, 209
Kannada folklore, 315
Kandla, 347
Kannada, 86, 90, 213, 268
Kannada community, 340
Kannada High School, 13, 213
Kannada linguistic minority in Mumbai, 311
Kannada linguistic minority school, 313
Kannada linguistic minority, 316
Kannada Primary School, 340, 341
Kannada Sangha Mulund, 340
Kannada school, 340
Kannada School in Mumbai, 298
Kannada teacher, 13
Kanyakumari, 347
Kapil Sibal, 352, 353
Karachi to Karwar, 33, 272
Karnataka, 148
Kashmir, 209, 347
KendriyaVidyalayas, 352
Kenya, 280
Kerala, 148, 285
KG classes, 147
Kindergarten schools, 223, 244
Kohima, 347
Kolhapur, 13
Kolkata, 280
Kona Prabhakar Rao, 174
Konkan, 276
Kurla Court, 196
Kutchhi families, 340

L

Lack of financial resources, 48
Lalit Narayan Mithila University, 137
Lashkar-e-Ansar, 209
Latin America, 50
Law Department, 196
Law-makers and bureaucrats, 64
Leave travel concessions, 123
Liberalisation, privatisation and globalisation, 298
Liberation Tigers of Tamil Eelam, 208
Linguistic Minorities, 17, 106
Linguistic schools, 36
Loksatta, 175
London, 70
London School of Economics, 281
Lord Macaulay, 14
Lotus, 125
LPG cylinder, 313
LPG cylinder blast, 313
Lucknow University, 345

M

M S Kambli, 65
M.V. Kamath, 65, 292, 293
Madarasas in Pakistan, 209
Madhukarao Chowdhary, 10
Madhya Pradesh, 77
Madras, 96
Mahad, 344
Mahadev Govind Ranade, 38, 272
Mahadev Ranade, 33
Maharashtra, 16, 53, 78, 96, 161, 174, 215
Maharashtra Bal Shikshan Parishad, 147
Maharashtra Chief Minister, 174, 345
Maharashtra Educational Institutions Prohibition Act, 223
Maharashtra Government, 19
Maharashtra Pradesh Congress Committee, 249
Maharashtra State Board, 344, 352
Maharashtra State Examination Board, 245
Maharashtra University, 115
Mahatma Gandhi, 33, 272
Malayalam, 17
Maldives, 33, 280
Malpractices, 137
Management Council, 176
Manager-client relationship, 178
Mangalore, 343
Mango, 125
Maniklal Gandhi, 340
Manmohan Singh, 32, 37, 264
Manohar Joshi, 176
Marathi, 85, 152, 328, 344
Marathi daily, 175
Marathi medium, 276
Marathi medium school, 87, 152, 332
Marathi schools, 90, 298, 328
Marathi-medium schools, 152
Marathi-speaking people, 87
Marine Lines, 215
Marxist or left front-led government, 253
Marxist Political Thought, 158
Marxists, 264
Marxists supported British rulers, 32
Massacre of children, 210
Mathematics, 288
Max Mueller, 70, 74
Mayor of Mumbai, 219
Medical colleges, 100

Medical education, 237
Medical expenses, 117
Medical expenses to teachers, 119
Medical facilities, 117
Medical faculty, 174
Medical treatment for teachers, 117
Miami, 280
Mid-day meals, 268
Middle class parents, 327
Military Barracks, 13
Military-industrial-academic cooperation, 142
Milky Way Galaxy, 260
Minimum qualifications of teachers, 122
Minister Mulayam Singh Yadav, 85
Ministerial sycophants, 77
Minority linguistic, 162
Model United Nations program, 349
Mohammad Bin Tughluq, 199
Mother Theresa charities, 220
Mother tongue, 17, 38, 85, 269
Moti Pachan School, 340
Ms Tendulkar, 228, 229
Mulayam Singh Yadav, 85
Mulki, 343
Mulund, 13, 38, 152, 201, 213, 327, 368
Mulund Express, 339
Mulund schools, 204
Mulund-Thane border areas, 268
Mumbai city, 35, 153, 248
Mumbai International University, 33
Mumbai University, 24, 30, 31, 34, 161, 196, 241, 251, 271, 273, 274, 276, 277, 287, 293, 336, 344
Municipal aided schools, 248
Municipal authorities, 233
Municipal bodies, 248
Municipal Corporations, 36, 134, 267, 307
Municipal schools, 228
Murli Manohar Joshi, 263
Muslims, 285

N

Nagpur bench, 306, 307
Nanavati Studio, 227
Nani Palkhiwala, 272
Narendra Modi, 351
National and International conferences, 345
National and Regional languages, 17
National bird, 125
National Cadet Corps, 91
National Council for Educational Research and Training, 263
National Day celebrations, 110
National defence force, 92
National Democratic Alliance, 351
National Digital Library, 352
National disease, 125
National Educational Test, 166
National Eligibility Test, 21, 302
National Entrance Test, 135, 142
National flower, 125
National fruit, 125
National integration, 18, 44, 105
National Kannada Education Society, 13
National Knowledge Commission, 33, 34, 279, 291
National Integration School, 344
National Network, 127
National Parliament, 26
National Security Advisers, 284
National Security Policy, 345

National University, 294
Nationalist Congress Party, 302
Naval Chief in Bombay, 142
Navi Mumbai, 19, 277, 306
NDA government, 265
Negative image of Indians, 110
New Delhi, 141
New Educational Policy of the Rajiv government, 62
New fee structure, 235
New fees-structure, 231
New text-book, 73
Nikhil Laxman, 10
Ninth Five Year Plan, 17
No Objection Certificate, 314, 316
Noble Prize, 261, 262
Nominal rent by the government, 162
Non Resident Indians, 280
Non-government employees, 118
Non-resident Indians, 114
Non-salary expenditure, 233
Non-salary grant, 228
Non-teaching employees, 118
Northern universities, 77, 78, 137

O

Open University, 294
Orissa, 268
Osmania University, 115, 277
Outside invaders, 70
Oval Maidan, 274

P

P C Alexander, 175
P. B. Gajendragadkar, 273
P.V. Narasimha Rao, 15, 17, 61, 272
Paan chewing, 126
Padhe Bharat Badhe Bharat, 352
Pakistani Inter-Services Intelligence, 210
Pali, 86
Panchasheel and global diplomacy, 141
Pandit Nehru, 141, 293, 299
Paper setter, 23
Parent Teacher Associations, 67, 225
Parent-management relationship, 25
Parent-Teacher Associations, 25
Parents and Teachers' Association, 177
Particle Physics, 261
Patna University, 78
Payment of higher salaries, 44
Peacock, 125
Pension and gratuity, 135
Permanently Unaided, 35, 299
Persian, 86
Personal contacts, 148
Petty shopkeepers, 236
Pherozeshah Mehta, 256
Physical Education, 13
Poland, 284
Political rivalry, 306
Political Science, 289
Political Sociology, 288
Politician-run professional colleges, 200, 204
Poona, 90
Poona University, 21, 96
Post graduate degree, 132, 301
Post Graduate students, 344
Post-retirement benefits, 135
Post-World War II Period, 31
Postgraduate Department of Civics and Politics, 287
Postgraduate examinations, 25
Postgraduate institutions, 57

Poverty-stricken families, 207
Prashasan Sewak concept, 249
Pre-independence period, 272
Pre-Primary classes, 153
Pre-primary education, 223
Pre-Primary Schools, 153
Presidential Libraries, 284
Presidential System of Government, 345
Preventive Social Medicine, 173
Primary Certificate Examination Scheme, 30, 247
Primary or Secondary schools, 152, 155
Primary School Certificate, 30, 243
Primary school teachers, 126
Prime Minister Narasimha, 141
Prithviraj Chauhan, 345
Private coaching classes, 45
Private educational trusts, 15
Privately managed aided primary schools, 269
Privately managed schools, 269
Privatisation and Globalisation, 18
Priya Tendulkar, 29, 227
Pro-Vice Chancellor, 275
Prof Ram Joshi, 151
Professional Colleges, 18, 102
Professor Ram Joshi, 147, 153, 274
Professors of public administration, 132
Psycho analytical study, 169
Public Administration, 275
Public prosecutor, 227
Public Service Commission, 273
Public-minded charitable trusts, 274
Punjab University, 169
Purchase by payments, 137

Q

Qualification of PhD, 138
Queen Antoinette, 314

R

R (Mrs) Marina Pinto, 256
R C Dutt, 75
R P Rastogi, 129
R Z Shah, 340
R. G. Bhandarkar, 272
R. R. Patil, 313
Raigad, 273, 276, 344
Railway stations, 126
Rajabai Tower, 272
Rajasthan, 77
Rajiv Gandhi, 15, 51, 306
Ram Joshi, 244, 274
Ram Joshi Committee report, 244
Rash driving, 127
Rastogi Committee, 23, 165, 166
Ration rice, 228
Ratnagiri, 273, 276
Red Carpet, 351
Red Tape, 351
Reddick Award, 345
Regional media schools, 35
Religious communities, 162
Reputed English-medium schools, 151
Rickshaw, 236
Rickshaw drivers, 60, 86, 151, 154
Right to Education, 18, 37, 208, 331, 352
Right to Education Act, 323, 357
Romantic nostalgia of India, 114
Rotary Club, 78
Rotary Club of Mulund Hills, 345
Royal Asiatic Society, 70, 75

RSS, 285
Rulers, 264
Rural areas of Thane, 273
Rural schools, 248
Russia, 252
Russian, 86

S

S. Radhakrishnan, 121, 335
Saddam Hussain, 210
Sai Suresh, 11
Sale and purchase of the Ph. Ds, 21
Sam Pitroda, 33, 279
Sanskrit, 87, 288, 351, 353
Sanskrit or Hindi, 87
Sanskrit Scholar, 74
Sanskrit scholar turned historian, 74
Sarva Shiksha Abhiyan, 36, 314, 319, 321
Savitri Rao, 11
Savitribai Phule fellowships, 220
Scheduled tribes, 253
School education Minister, 313
School Education Minister Vasant Purke, 313
School Education Secretary, 228
School Management Committee, 331
School of Advance International Studies, 287
School of International Relations, 287
School of Life Sciences, 34, 287
School of Natural Sciences, 34
School of Social Sciences, 287, 289
School Students, 261
School trusts, 23, 163
School's development fund, 162
School's Management Committees, 37
Scientific study of the universe, 260
Secondary School Certificates, 66
Secretaries and additional secretaries, 131
Seed of schism, 75
Selection grade, 166
Seniority-cum-merit, 257
Serious research, 48, 143
Shankar Dayal Sharma, 121
Sharad Pawar, 115, 127
Shikshan Abhiyan, 248
Shikshan Maharshis, 163
Shiv Sena, 206, 223, 244, 265, 285
Shiv Sena-BJP, 223, 244
Shiv Sena-BJP alliance, 223
Shivaji University, 13
Shopkeepers, 154
Singapore, 126, 239
Sixth pay commission's scales, 325
Social workers, 36
Sociology Department, 288
South Asia, 96
South Asian countries, 33, 280
South Bombay, 117
South East Asia, 280
South Mumbai, 313
Southern University, 137
Soviet Union, 32, 220, 264, 285
Soviet Union's intelligence agency, 220
Sri Lanka, 27, 33, 208, 280
Standard of education, 45
Starting salary, 134
State Assemblies, 26
State Board school, 352
State Educational Test, 166
State Eligibility Test, 302
State Entrance Test, 131, 139

Student-teacher ratio, 26
Sudama V. Shastri, 13
Sudanese student, 110
Sudhir Joshi, 152
Sukhdev, 169
Summer Programme, 261
Sundaribai Manjunath Kamath Kannada Primary School, 340
Super Powers, 31
Supreme Court, 178, 187, 273, 307
Supreme Court of India, 9
Surat, 127
Swami Vivekananda, 16, 71, 75

T

Tamil, 17
Tamilians of the South, 70, 75
Tata Institute of Social Science, 115
Teachers and management, 206, 220
Teachers benefits of LTC, 19
Teachers' Day, 121
Teachers' health, 19
Teaching community, 24
Teaching profession, 43
Teaching-machine, 57
Telgi scandal, 255
Ten-day training programme, 267
Terrorist organisation, 209
Textbook manufacturing, 62
Thane, 276, 341
Thane District, 305
Thane Municipal Transport Corporation, 314, 316
Traditional sense of examinations, 357
Translations of the Vedas, 70
Truman Foundation, 345
Trump Presidency, 39
Twelfth standard examination, 170

U

UGC funded Associateship programme, 260
UN Security Council, 209
Unaided degree colleges, 179
Unaided educational institutions, 23
Unaided English Medium Schools, 22, 35, 199
Unaided English Schools, 27, 215
Unaided primary schools, 325
Unaided professional colleges, 179
Unaided school, 14, 29, 59, 162, 215
Unaided Schools Forum, 227
Uncertified school, 332
Under Secretary, 56, 57
Undergraduate classes, 57
Undergraduate College, 25
Undergraduate degree, 24
Undergraduate salary levels, 216
Uniform language education pattern, 17
Union government, 95
Union Minister for Human Resources, 263
Uniqueness of Mumbai University, 272
United Kingdom, 261
United States, 10, 113, 126, 251, 280
United States or Europe, 113
United States-India Educational Foundation, 348
Universities Act, 274, 302
Universities Committee, 43
Universities in Maharashtra, 82
University affairs, 175
University at Kolkata, 33
University authorities, 182
University campuses, 16, 110, 144

University Department of Civics and Politics, 271
University examination system, 23
University Grants Commission, 21, 129, 138, 165, 251, 255, 259, 275, 302
University of Bombay, 271
University of Delhi, 280
University of Hyderabad, 115
University of Mumbai, 173, 227, 255, 280
University of Poona, 141
University teachers, 53, 54
Unqualified Babus, 15
Untold hardship, 117
Untouchables, 127
Upper castes, 127
Urban poor, 208
Urban poverty, 268
Urdu, 86
Urdu medium, 17
Urdu medium schools, 17
US Atom Bomb project, 292
US federal structure, 109
US government, 252
US president, 284
US president Bill Clinton, 210
US Society and politics, 31
US Universities, 34
US Universities Heads of Academic Departments, 31
Uttar Pradesh, 73, 85, 276
Uttar Pradesh Government, 73

V

V V John, 122
V. A. Kulkarni, 13
V. P. Singh, 15, 62
V. P. Singh government, 62
Various aspects of the field of education, 10
Vasant Purke, 313
Vasantdada Patil, 14
Vast economic potential, 100
Vedas, 70, 74
Vedas and Puranas, 41
Vedic times, 69, 73
Vernacular medium schools, 269, 341
Vernacular schools, 206
Vice Chancellor, 24, 38, 48, 78, 111, 129, 144, 173, 256, 273, 293, 336
Vidya Prasarak Mandal, 9, 13, 213, 340, 345
Vietnam War, 34, 284
Vigyan Bhawan, 141
Vile Parle, 227
Vishweshwar Theertha Swami, 13
Visva Bharati Shanti Niketan, 345
Vithalrao Anantrao Kulkarni, 13
Vocational courses, 170
Vocational institutions, 170
Voluntary donation, 28
Voluntary donations, 220

W

Wadala, 13
Waiting rooms, 126
Washington, 287
Washington DC, 139
Watchmen, 154
West Bengal, 148
Western education, 71
Western region, 115
Western scholars, 75
Western style, 71
Western translation, 75
Western World, 33

Western writings, 75
Withdraw economic sanctions against Iraq, 210
Work Experience, 126
World Bank, 61, 354
World Bank report, 354
World Trade Organisation, 30, 239, 281
World War II, 31

Y

Yale, 281
Yamunabai Laxman Salvi, 169
Yashpal Committee, 147
Yatha Raja Tatha Praja, 337

Z

Zilla Parishads, 248, 307
Zimmedar Kaun, 227